Praise for *Effective Management in Practice*

"In this book Robin Wensley applies his extensive experience and wisdom in mapping four key strands of the managerial process – an interrogative approach of asking key questions, being critical in thinking about our thinking, learning how to organise for both central command and local agility, and appreciating evidence-based management in context specific situations. Through these four strands Wensley provides a treasury of 'practical wisdom' that adds to 'common sense' in important and insightful ways."

Professor Andrew H. Van de Ven, Vernon H. Heath Professor of Organizational Innovation and Change, Carlson School of Management, University of Minnesota

"Robin Wensley's new book, *Effective Management in Practice: Analytical Insights and Critical Questions*, should be in the bookshelf (or eReader) of every manager, policy-maker, and academic who is interested in understanding and advancing our thinking about management. Wensley's viewpoint emphasises the clash of interests and perspectives that is central to real organisations. He puts the fact of 'multiple truths' on centre stage and describes how judgement and action evolve out of questioning, the skilful use of evidence, and 'practical wisdom.' If you are looking for easy tricks guaranteeing success in management, pass on by. However, if you are intrigued, or even fascinated, by how talented people wring insight and action out of difficult situations, get Robin Wensley's book now."

Richard Rumelt, Harry and Elsa Kunin Professor of Business & Society, UCLA Anderson

"Robin Wensley is one of the most thoughtful management writers around. In this book he avoids advocating simple solutions to managerial problems; there aren't any! However he does provide valuable insights which managers then need to apply to the everyday complex organisational situations that they face."

Geoff Easton, Professor of Marketing (Emeritus), Department of Marketing, Lancaster University Management School, Lancaster University

"Managers typically use few analytic tools for decision making. Yet we know how susceptible they are to bias and error. Here Robin Wensley brings welcome conceptual clarity and a good deal of common sense to provide real insights and to show how managers can overcome such bias. It is a lively read which managers and academics alike will find useful and illuminating."

Gerry Johnson, Emeritus Professor of Strategic Management, Lancaster University Management School, co-author of *Exploring Strategy*, FT/Prentice Hall

"Written in expressive language and founded on evidence and experience, this treatise offers both academics and practitioners a fresh insight into their learning journeys. Bridging the gap between the two camps needs a continuous dialogue of understanding and foresight. This book provides the essential linkage and so commands respect."

Professor Peter McKiernan, Dean, School of Management and Governance, Murdoch University, Perth WA

"In this book, Robin Wensley has deeply probed and neatly dissected the soft underbelly of academic and practical efforts to build a firm intellectual basis to guide managerial action. Relying on his vast experience, encyclopaedic knowledge, and sharp mind, he puts to flight both the pretensions of academic social science and the casual confidence of not very reflective practitioners in favour of a method that keeps asking questions of particular situations in search of a plausibly effective line of action. If the most common form of managerial error is not the absence of certain knowledge, but the lack of a will and capacity to inquire into particulars, then this book will set both academics and practitioners on a far better course than many are now pursuing."

Professor Mark Moore, Kennedy School of Government, Harvard University

EFFECTIVE MANAGEMENT in PRACTICE

SAGE has been part of the global academic community since 1965, supporting high quality research and learning that transforms society and our understanding of individuals, groups and cultures. SAGE is the independent, innovative, natural home for authors, editors and societies who share our commitment and passion for the social sciences.

Find out more at: **www.sagepublications.com**

Robin Wensley

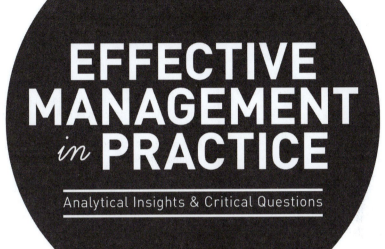

EFFECTIVE
MANAGEMENT
in PRACTICE

Analytical Insights & Critical Questions

Los Angeles | London | New Delhi
Singapore | Washington DC

Los Angeles | London | New Delhi
Singapore | Washington DC

SAGE Publications Ltd
1 Oliver's Yard
55 City Road
London EC1Y 1SP

SAGE Publications Inc.
2455 Teller Road
Thousand Oaks, California 91320

SAGE Publications India Pvt Ltd
B 1/I 1 Mohan Cooperative Industrial Area
Mathura Road
New Delhi 110 044

SAGE Publications Asia-Pacific Pte Ltd
3 Church Street
#10-04 Samsung Hub
Singapore 049483

Editor: Kirsty Smy
Editorial assistant: Nina Smith
Production editor: Sarah Cooke
Copyeditor: Neil Dowden
Proofreader: Derek Markham
Indexer: Judith Lavender
Marketing manager: Alison Borg
Cover design: Francis Kenney
Typeset by: C&M Digitals (P) Ltd, Chennai, India
Printed in India at Replika Press Pvt Ltd

© Robin Wensley 2013
First edition published 2013

Library of Congress Control Number: 2013931853

British Library Cataloguing in Publication data

A catalogue record for this book is available from
the British Library

ISBN 978-1-4462-7260-2
ISBN 978-1-4462-7261-9 (pbk)

For Sue, who is often on my shoulder and
always asks the right question,

and to Helen, Ruth and Ben who have been
both insightful and patient

Contents

Preface   xiv
About the Author   xvi

INTRODUCTION   1

The Four Starting Issues   1
   Issues of Audience and Translation   2
   Coping with Multiple Truths and Some Untruths   3
   Impact and Horse Kicks   4
   On the Shoulders of Others   6
The Four Strands   6
   The Importance of Questions   6
   Being Critical   8
   Learning from Military Practice   8
   Insights from Research   9
The Chapter Sequence   9

CHAPTER 1   EXTENDING ANALYSIS IN EFFECTIVE
MANAGEMENT   15

The Legacy of the Sixties   15
Extended Analysis: Both Analysis and Synthesis   17
   Meta-Analysis and Systematic Review   17
   Beyond Naive Realism   20
   The Relationship between Analysis and Process   21
The Interrogative Mood   23
Issues of Representation   24
   Lists and Columns   24
   The Two-by-Two Box   25
Introducing Time and Movement   29
Choices, Decisions and Action   31
Rationality in Practice: Simplification Approaches   33
Conclusion: Coping with Complex Rationality   35

CHAPTER 2   NEVER STOP LEARNING   36

Some Basic Ideas   36
    Surprises, Conjectures and Refutations   36
    Double-Loop Learning   38
    Boxes, Boundaries and Questions   40
The Reflective Practitioner   40
Sources of Learning beyond One's Own Practice   41
    What about "Organisational Learning"?   44
    Using Internal Data in a Systematic and Challenging Manner   48
Conclusion: Reprise on the Reflective Practitioner   50

CHAPTER 3   EVIDENCE AND ENGAGEMENT   52

Evidence-Based Management   52
Risk, Uncertainty and Profit   53
    Risk and Uncertainty   54
The Wisdom of Crowds (Sometimes)   55
Isomorphism and Lemmings   56
Unexpected Events and Isolating Mechanisms   57
Dialectic, Rhetoric and Consensus   58
    Formalising the Dialectic Approach   59
    The Nature of Consensus   59
    Traditions for Sustainable Transformation   60
Engagement and Management: Scientific Knowledge and
    Folk Wisdom   61
    Street Mathematics and the Issue of Wider Context   61
    Folk Wisdom and Common Sense   63
The Nature of Academic Practice: Statistical Analysis
    and Evidential Claims   64
Learning from the Clinical Medical Experience of Evidence-Based
    Practice   66
    From Medical to Social Science   68
Return to Managerial Relevance and the Issue of Timeliness   69
Conclusion: Getting the Best out of Engagement   70

CHAPTER 4   TOOLS FOR THINKING   72

Introduction: Comparing Perspectives in 1975 and 2009   72
Complexity and Chaos   74

The Structure of Systems: The Ubiquitous Tree   75
   Cluster Analysis Trees   77
   Analytical Hierarchy Process (AHP)   78
   Decision Trees   79
   Influence Diagram   83
Open and Closed Systems   84
   Growth   85
   Feedback   87
Modularisation and Loose–Tight Linkages   88
   Dynamic Systems and Emergence   89
   Networks   90
Basic Game Theory   92
   Principles: Normal Form Games   93
   Multi-Period and Multi-Player Games   94
   Simulation   94
Insights from Simple Experimental Games   96
   Prisoner's Dilemma   97
   Win–Win?   98
   Ultimatum Game   99
   Penalty Game   100
Conclusion: Bounded but not Restricted   103

CHAPTER 5   MAKING SENSE OF THE NUMBERS   105

Concentration and Dispersion of Variables   105
   The Problems of Averages   105
Forms of Representation: Frequency Plots and Box Diagrams   107
   Frequency Plots: Normal and Fat-Tail Distributions   107
   Box Plots   109
   Advantages of Box Plots   110
Understanding Outliers   111
Significance, Correlation and Causality: What's Significance
   Got to Do with It?   113
Type I and Type II Errors   116
Type III Error: Answering the Wrong Question   118
Type IV Error: Asking the Wrong Question   119
The Rule of 10 Per Cent   119
Mediators and Moderators   121
Time Series Datasets: Lead and Lag Structures   126
Casual Causality   127

Conclusion: Half a Statistical Loaf may Be Better
    than the Whole   129

CHAPTER 6   RETURNING TO PRACTICAL WISDOM: THE
    FRAMEWORKS FOR ANALYSIS   131

Practical Wisdom: Reasoned Analysis and Deliberate Action   131
Watching Out for Boxes, Linear Diagrams and Other
    Simplifying Tools   133
    The Dimensionality of the Problem Space   134
    The Orthogonality of the Categorising Variables or Factors   135
    Revisiting the Two-by-Two Box   136
Introducing Dynamics into a Static Representation   138
Dr Who and the Time Dimension   140
Specific Representations and Implicit Assumptions   142
Contradictory Common Sense   142
Conclusion: Common and Uncommon Sense   144

CHAPTER 7   THE CENTRAL ROLE OF STORIES   145

Organisational Success and Failure: The Perils of "Learning
    from the Past"   147
    The Shell Study   149
    The Success or Failure of Mergers   149
    The Honda Case: Interpreting Success   151
Fads and Fashions   153
Revisiting the Onus of Proof Issue   156
When and How Does the Decision Get Made?   157
    Insights from Stories   159
    Numbers as Stories   160
The Narrative Approach   162
Conclusion: An Effective Role for Analysis
    in Management Practice   164

CHAPTER 8   LINKING THE CLASSROOM
    TO THE WORKPLACE   165

Learning from Case Studies   165
    What Are Case Studies For?   167
    Differences between Case Study Learners: Novices and Experts   169
The Challenge of Simulating and Learning from
    Management Practice   170

Video Material   171
Experiential Exercises: Simulations and Projects   174
Conclusion: Learning through Questioning   176

CHAPTER 9   AN ONGOING DECISION PROCESS
       OF QUESTIONING AND DISSONANCE   178

Thinking, Seeing and Doing   178
The Case for Slow Thinking and Procrastination   182
Thinking Fast, Thinking Slow   183
In Praise of Dissonance   185
Debates, Dialectics and Dissonance   187
Making Some Sense of Innovation   188
Questions and Answers: the Central Role of "Interrogation"   190
    Prepare well   191
    Promote a path of least effort   191
    Be methodical   191
    Be patient   191

CHAPTER 10   PUTTING THE MASTERS BACK INTO
       MANAGEMENT EDUCATION AND DEVELOPMENT   193

Administration, Management and Leadership   194
Stress Testing the Analysis   196
Innovation as Hard Work: The 3M Post-it Story   197
Innovation and Entrepreneurship   199
Understanding Strategic Leadership   200
    The Power of Small Leadership   201
    Leaders and Followers   202
    An Alternative View on Strategic Leadership   203
Useful Insights from Writings on Military Strategy   204
Good Management Research as a Means to Useful Insights   205
    Mystery as Method   207
Getting Beyond the False Rhetoric   208

Postscript for Management Researchers   210
References   212
Index   225

Preface

The extraordinary complexity of management:
Getting the right people in place
Creating structures and lines of reporting
Correcting and adapting when things go wrong
Applying common sense. (Hamish McRae, Independent, 6 July 2005)

The essence of successful bullshit is that the really top-notch exponents not only manage to convince others but also manage to delude themselves. (Larry Elliot and Dan Atkinson, "Talk is Cheap", *Guardian* 18 May 2007)

As many of my colleagues know, I have rather a reputation for telling stories and, to some extent, maybe also embellishing them a bit. I remain a great believer in the power of the oral tradition but in more recent terminology it is rather a narrow-casting process! Some management gurus who are much more skilful than I have managed to convert it effectively into other media such as audio. Perhaps from my point-of-view the pre-eminent practitioner of this approach is Charles Handy who seems to have the uncanny knack of turning a vignette into a message, which in the end leaves the listener not actually with an answer but with an insight and therefore a more meaningful question.

In 1987 I was at a small rather informal launch of a book, edited by Barbara Stocking, which was a festschrift for one of my key colleagues Tom Evans, who sadly died much too early from stomach cancer. In introducing Charles Handy to say a few words, Barbara, who stepped down as Oxfam chief executive in February 2013, commented that with Charles you never knew whether you were going to get an insight into management or the text of "Thought for the Day". In posing the question she did, however, recognise the answer: that you got both!

In my case, there has been consistent encouragement, some might say badgering, particularly from Kiren Shoman, who is now Sage Executive Director of Editorial Books in London. It is no exaggeration to say that this book would never have seen the light of day without her enthusiasm and encouragement. I have finally succumbed to the pressure to put my stories and analytical insights into a coherent and more widely distributable but still rather traditional format – a book.

As always in writing a book, I am indebted to many colleagues and friends from whom I have often learnt so much. In particular I much appreciated the time and effort that a small group of individuals put into reading and commenting on an earlier draft of the overall book: Professors Geoff Easton, Gordon Murray and Peter McKiernan, as well as particularly to balance the academic input, Alan Morrison and Paul Denyer. They all provided insightful and useful comments but, as always, I reserved the right to choose how to incorporate them and therefore remain solely responsible for errors and omissions in the final text. Perhaps inevitably, reputedly rather like a first novel, the book is somewhat autobiographical: as a Masters student at London Business School I was an unpaid research assistant on the background work for Harold Rose's 1970 NEDO Report[1] on Management Education, and rather later my first article in *Journal of Management Studies* considered the forms of relationship between analysis and strategy.[2]

Over the last more than 40 years I have benefited from innumerable conversations and discussions, but I would particularly wish to mention: Paddy Barwise and Jules Goddard at LBS, George Day at Wharton, Bart Weitz at Florida, Richard Rumelt at UCLA, Mark Moore at Harvard, Bill Starbuck at NYU, Phil Stern, John Bennington and Colin Crouch at WBS. Finally, two other groups deserve mention: over the last eight years I have learnt a great deal from all the Fellows involved in the AIM initiative (the full list is still available at www.aimresearch.org) and last, but definitely not least, I have been very lucky to have had an outstanding set of doctoral students who have kept me thinking, particularly those with whom I have published, Sally Dibb, Liu Hong, Alex Faria and Ianna Contardo.

Inevitably this short book is a summary of many ideas and indeed some disputes. I have signalled in the text where any reader might follow up on the internet many of the approaches and techniques. Equally more can be found through Google (or another search engine) and Google Scholar. As I write this at the end of a rather extended winter, I also note we are in the middle of another controversy in the analysis and interpretation of economic data: this time on the disputed relationship between total national public debt and overall economic growth[3], which will no doubt develop further!

Leamington Spa, England
April 2013

[1]Harold Rose, *Management Education in the 1970s: Growth and Issues*, NEDO, London: HMSO, 1970.

[2]"The Effective Strategic Analyst", *Journal of Management Studies*, 16(3), 1979.

[3]www.peri.umass.edu/236/hash/31e2ff374b6377b2ddec04deaa6388b1/publication/566/

About the Author

Robin Wensley is Emeritus Professor of Policy and Marketing at the Warwick Business School.

He has been a Professor at Warwick since 1986 and Chair of the School from 1989 to 1994, as well as Chair of the Faculty of Social Studies from 1997 to 1999. Most recently, he was Director of the AIM Research initiative from 2004 to 2011. He was previously with RHM Foods, Tube Investments and the London Business School and was visiting Professor at UCLA (twice) and University of Florida. He was Chair of the Council of the Tavistock Institute of Human Relations from 1998 until 2003 and a member of the Sunningdale Institute (2008 to 2011)

He is a Fellow of the British Academy of Management (FBAM), the Chartered Institute of Marketing (FCIM) and The Academy of Social Sciences (FAcSS). He was awarded the BAM Richard Whipp Lifetime Achievement Award in 2012 and previously awarded the 1981 and 1988 Alpha Kappa Psi prize for the most outstanding article in the *US Journal of Marketing* and the Millennium Prize for the best paper in the *Journal of Marketing Management*.

He was appointed to the Council of the ESRC from 2001 to 2004 and was a Board member of the ESRC Research Grants Board from 1991 to 1995. He is a member of the Advisory Board of the Warburg Institute and the Academic Advisory Board of the Chartered Management Institute. Over his academic career, he has been involved with consultancy and management development for many major organisations.

Introduction

There is something odd with the word "management". It may have something to do with its rather prosaic etymology but somehow or other it seems to encompass two very different world-views. At one extreme we have the "leadership" (some might say heroic leadership) school of management with its emphasis on visionary approaches, stretch targets and winning against the odds, which rather discounts most of the historical evidence since even the SAS does not have a comprehensive record of "wins" (for instance, see Newsinger 1997). On the other hand, we have that expression beloved at least by those English who delight in understatement, "just managing", with its connotations of just about keeping one's head (above water?): sufficers more than heroes. This book is dedicated more to the latter than the former particularly in recognising that they most often have to get the actual job done and that we need to focus our academic insights on this rather than purvey a universal fantasy around heroic leadership which will only make management more difficult.

The most recent manifestation of misplaced confidence in heroic leadership in the UK is to be found, hardly surprisingly, in the banking sector. Fred Goodwin went from hero to villain in the wake of the collapse of Royal Bank of Scotland, as his leadership – which a number of us had previously extolled (Delbridge et al 2006) – became seen as overbearing and threatening. More recently he has become the benchmark for poor management, but to quote recent press comment, the trio of leaders at Halifax Bank of Scotland (HBOS) were recently described as "Worse than Fred Goodwin! The verdict on the bank bosses who presided over the £40bn collapse of HBOS" (Moore 2013). Where are the counter examples of those who just got on with the business of prudent banking? Inevitably they are much less high profile. As John Kay (2012a and 2012b) in his review for the UK government put it: "people now want their banks to be 'boring'"!

In this book I provide various forms of analysis that along with a commitment to critical questioning will enable most managers to be more effective and possibly less boring as well!

The Four Starting Issues

The overall focus in this book on analysis and its role in informing action comes from the interplay between four rather different issues in both type and

style. However, they are also to some considerable degree interlinked: to influence others we need to be aware of our audience. It is almost always a heterogeneous collection of individuals who start with differing sets of assumptions.
Often times we just fail to establish rapport and, finally, whilst there is often
pressure for novelty the most useful insights come from a well-grounded and
soundly developed stream of both research and practice.

Issues of Audience and Translation

This is unashamedly a book written by a management academic – and
indeed I hope the word "management" is a qualifier which refers to content
rather than quality! However, it is also an attempt to communicate with a
wider audience and in particular those who have been or wish to be exposed
to a rather idiosyncratic collection of ideas which in my view are an important part of a more informed, analytical and grounded approach to the challenges facing managers in a wide range of human organisations.

Groups of people and individuals are central to the book: not only are they
embedded in all aspects of management but they also comprise the intended
audience, or audiences, as well. This is not a book about "managing people"
but it is a book intended to be read by people! It is also a book which
attempts to be at the interface between those who undertake various forms
of academic studies of management and those who practise management.
Taking the intended readership seriously also poses an important challenge:
how do I avoid falling down the gap between academe and practice?

Throughout my academic career I have been both interested in and wary of
this "gap" notion. There are about as many ways of representing the gap as
there are commentators on it but some of the most common are: different
words, different languages, different values, different assumptions, different
world-views. On top of this it must also be admitted that much more is written
and said about the gap amongst academics than practitioners – the latter often
indeed seem to regard it as a non-problem or at least an unimportant one.

My own exposure to the issue of the gap has been throughout my teaching
and more recently in my various engagements with the two professional
bodies most closely allied to my academic interests: the Chartered Institute of
Marketing and the Chartered Management Institute. Even more recently, from
2004 to 2011, in my role as Director of the Advanced Institute of Management
Research (AIM), I was directly involved in many actual instances of linking
high-quality social science research to issues of policy and practice.

Over this period I have continued to believe that some degree of distance has
to be maintained between the worlds of academe and practice and that to some
degree at least this is an important and desirable state: management academics,

as an overall collective, should not be seen as merely responding to the demands of their practitioner clients but, equally, practitioners should not just be seen as passive subjects for academic studies. To some extent I fully appreciate the assertion by the German sociologist Niklas Luhmann that academe and practice inhabit two fundamentally different worlds, based respectively on truth and profit, and the attempts to intervene from one of these worlds to another will be seen by the recipient community as an "irritation". We will return in Chapter 3 to this debate in more detail and in particular the extent to which one way to achieve some worthwhile degree of interaction between these two worlds is for the practice world to act on the fiction that the knowledge is indeed relevant. By working on the knowledge in this way it does indeed become relevant but not necessarily in the way in which the academic originators intended or expected (see Rasche and Behnam 2009).

However, I wish to start from a rather different but related perspective: that of the nature of the audience and the process of translation. In many ways this encapsulates the challenge in writing this book: given that it is grounded in my own and, more importantly by far, others' academic studies in management I am mainly setting out to produce a manuscript that communicates to those who practise management, informed again to a significant extent by my own experience in the management practice of university departments, research institutes and, what we rather quaintly term in business school jargon, post-experience management teaching and development. This itself is a significant translation challenge and in the end the only arbiter of my success or otherwise in this endeavour is the reader individually and collectively, but I can I think identify what can be seen as three more starting conditions or assumptions which will need to be agreed between any reader and myself if we are to get to, let alone go beyond, first base.

Coping with Multiple Truths and Some Untruths

I, along with many others, learnt in my executive teaching career that it could be important to confront the popular canard "it's not like that in the real world" early on in many a particular module. Such a confrontation process requires in one way or another surfacing individual assumptions about the specifics of the "real world" and realising that there are at least as many different "real worlds" as there are active participants in the discussion.

Without going into a minefield, from this point-of-view, of social constructivism or critical realism to name but two theories, it is a pretty good working assumption that we will only be able to make progress in understanding, let alone intervening, effectively in organisational processes if we start by recognising that there are going to be a wide range of truths in circulation. Working hard to understand the particular issues from someone else's point of view is a key step in achieving an effective means of intervention but does not mean adopting wholeheartedly their beliefs. However, we should also be willing to suspend disbelief at least for a time as part of this process. Whilst there is no doubt that sometimes a clear case of untruths is being propagated it is much more common for there to be at least some degree of truth in many of the conflicting assertions and we will return often to the notion of the "balance of probabilities" as enshrined in civil law.

Impact and Horse Kicks

In reviewing the impact on practice of the research we funded through AIM, Della Bradshaw of the *Financial Times* summarised my overall comments as "Impact on practice is a very hit-and-miss thing." This was a fair but rather brutal summary. The basic point is that at the collective level management practitioners are subjected to a vast range of suggestions for action, based on varying levels of evidence, on a daily basis. On this basis the likelihood of any particular suggestion achieving collective impact is very low. Those with some degree of statistical knowledge may note some similarity between this situation and the classic story of the application of the Poisson distribution.

Perhaps the most famous application of the Poisson distribution was made by the Russian statistician Ladislaus Bortkiewicz (1868–1931). At the end of the nineteenth century, cavalry units formed a component of most armies and once in a while someone in a cavalry unit would be killed by a horse kick. Bortkiewicz took the record of such deaths for ten cavalry units of the Prussian army over a period of 20 years, from 1875 to 1894, and analysed them statistically and showed that the number of deaths per cavalry-unit year followed a Poisson distribution, with an average of 0.61.

The only major difference perhaps between this situation and that of the likely impact of any piece of management research is that it is very much less than 1 in 100. The resultant Poisson distribution for impact is inevitably going to produce an outcome where significant and widespread impact per item is very rare – more just a "miss" affair. Indeed the key point about the Poisson distribution is that there are literally countless instances of misses.

In the case of evaluation of the impact of management research, there is one obvious avenue to achieve a higher measure of impact performance and that is in changing what we might term the unit of analysis. There are two separate mechanisms operating here but both go in somewhat the same direction: one based on proximity to the research itself and likely improvement in communication generated by a longer term relationship; the other, given the context specific nature of management research, is moving from a broad context of

Table 0.1 Mapping collaborative research against five dimensions

WORK STAGE	Theory Driven		"In the Middle"		Problem Driven
INITIATION	Enquiry driven by theory (A journals)	Research agenda adapted to organisational interests	Research questions derived from dialogue	Organisation identifies broad issues and seeks academic collaboration	Organisation defines questions and hires researchers
FIELDWORK	Researchers use external data sources	Researchers get permission to survey managers or employees	Interviews held with emergent sample, some jointly	Academics act as advisors in sorting sample and data collection	Sample and questions determined by organisation
DATA ANALYSIS	Researchers do it all	Draft findings checked out with organisation	Initial findings discussed; lead to further data	Organisation interprets and checks out with academics	Organisation takes data and makes up own mind
CONTACTS	Contact only with gatekeepers	Contact with subgroup (e.g. SMT)	Wider contact and sharing of basic questions	Work with practitioner community and share questions	Respond as facilitator to community's questions
OUTPUT	Academics write for A journals	Organisation people contribute but academics write	Joint output in practitioner press	Organisation dissemination in practitioner communities; academics help	Internal dissemination by organisation only

© Mark Easterby-Smith

application to a more defined sub-group – industry sector, service business or size/frequency of transaction being some of the more obvious categories.

Getting down to the detail of the research process itself, Mark Easterby-Smith (2012) developed a way of mapping shown in Table 0.1 which provided a measure of the degree of co-production at the various stages of the research process between theory-driven and problem-driven activities. And we need to recognise that it is often true that the balance of engagement between research-ers and those working at the site of the research inevitably varies both over time and also in terms of the level of detail and content.

On the Shoulders of Others

It is a general principle of this book that it mainly involves putting together, contrasting and interpreting the work of others. I have often commented to academic colleagues that I generally find the scholarly work of others more interesting than my own and this book also reflects this view. There is one inevitable consequence of this which makes the text somewhat unusual. Almost all the works I refer to are, as indeed should be the case, ones where I believe those who are interested should read further "in the original". For this reason, when it comes to summarising their results, conclusions and interpretations, I believe this should be done as much as possible in their own words – after all, they have already gone to considerable trouble to do this themselves and I believe it is only right to quote them as far as possible ver-batim. However, there is an irony in the standard arrangements related to the copyright on text. Strictly what is defined as "fair dealing" is restricted in various ways including the fact that it should be no more than 300 words and should be subject to some level of critical scrutiny. This has meant that to some degree I have had to incorporate important works into my text while restricting, and of course clearly indicating, where I am quoting verbatim.

The Four Strands

There are four strands which run through this book. They are developed and repeated at various stages but it is useful to highlight them now.

The Importance of Questions

Questions and questioning are central to the analytical process espoused in this book, so much so that indeed the book itself could well be sub-titled "The Interrogative Approach". The process of questioning (and of course answering) can and often does serve a number of purposes: for instance eliciting information, testing particular assumptions and interpretations, and establishing commitment.

What happens if we abandon an interrogative approach? Inevitably the main effect is that we have no additional information upon which to make our own judgements on a range of critical aspects including those listed above. A classic example was the strategic choices that George W. Bush made in 2002 in the context of the Iraq invasion. With the failure later to find weapons of mass destruction (WMD) there has perhaps been some re-writing of history – or at least historical accounts – but even so, there are strong suggestion that part of the problem was that in key briefing meetings the President did not seem to want to question his informants in any great depth. For example, Colin Powell described a key meeting between himself, Condoleezza Rice and the President:

> I went to the President in August of 2002 after coming back from a trip and seeing all the planning that was underway and we had a long meeting upstairs in the residence. Dr. Rice was there but it was essentially a conversation between President Bush and myself. And for the better part of two and a half hours I took him through not only the military planning that was being done in the Pentagon but I took them through the consequences of going into an Arab country and becoming the occupiers. ... I did say to him, once you break it you are going to own it and we're going to be responsible for 26 million people standing there looking at us. And it's going to suck up a good 40 to 50 percent of the army for years. And it's going to take all the oxygen out of the political environment. And you need to understand this and the expense is going to be enormous. And he took it all aboard and he said, "What should we do?"
>
> And I said, "Well, we should take it to the United Nations. Because they are the offended party. It is their resolutions that have been offended ..."

He then went on to outline the aftermath of the meeting:

> And we worked for seven weeks after taking it to the UN in September and got a resolution unanimously approved by the Security Council with some get-out clauses for Saddam Hussein to avoid the conflict. And I said to the President, if we can solve this diplomatically are you prepared to accept that outcome, even if it means that we have a "changed regime" in Baghdad with Saddam Hussein still there, but no longer a danger or a threat but we wouldn't have a "regime change." And it was not something that he was immediately attracted to. But he said yes, he would have to. (Aspen Institute 2007)

The difference between this approach by President Bush and that taken by John F. Kennedy 40 years earlier during the Cuban Missile Crisis seems very clear particularly in view of the more recent material that has been de-classified. We now know that:

Kennedy resisted pressure from aides advising that he cede nothing to Moscow and even consider a pre-emptive strike. He instead engaged in intense behind-the-scenes diplomacy with the Soviets, other countries and the U.N. secretary-general.

Attorney General Robert F. Kennedy met secretly with the Soviet ambassador on Oct. 27 and conveyed an olive branch from his brother: Washington would publicly reject any invasion of Cuba, and Khrushchev would withdraw the missiles from the island. The real sweetener was that Kennedy would withdraw Jupiter nuclear missiles from U.S. installations in Turkey, near the Soviet border. It was a secret pledge known only to a handful of presidential advisers that did not emerge until years later.

Nevertheless, the brinkmanship myth persists, with President George W. Bush in 2002 citing the missile crisis as a historical lesson in fortitude that justified a pre-emptive invasion of Iraq. (Orsi 2012)

As we might expect there is also another side to the story of the Kennedy brothers in that, as Weiner observes overall "The two men unleashed covert action with an unprecedented intensity … 163 major covert operations in less that three [years]." (2008: 207)

Being Critical

The word critical has rather a multiplicity of meanings. The closest meaning to the approach I am espousing relates to "critical thinking":

the intellectually disciplined process of actively and skilfully conceptualizing, applying, analysing, synthesizing, and/or evaluating information gathered from, or generated by, observation, experience, reflection, reasoning, or communication, as a guide to belief and action. (Scriven and Paul 1987)

Or in more direct terms, "thinking about our thinking". In the case of management research, critical realism has a more focused meaning. We often need to recognise that whilst it may be reasonable to assume that there are indeed underlying causal processes they can only be clearly discerned by a rigorous analysis of the mental framing incorporated in our informants' own accounts and then a similarly rigorous analysis of our own interpretations.

Learning from Military Practice

There have been various attempts to incorporate insights from military writing and analysis into our understanding of management, particularly in the context of managing and leading organisations. This is hardly surprising given the long history of various approaches to the organisation of the military. However, there are also important differences between the nature of military organisation and management practice in the multitude of private, public and third-sector organisations.

So we will focus on military practice and writing in only two particular areas: organising for both central command but also with local agility and the nature of leadership. The former of these topics also relates closely to notions of strategy which are crucial to various stages of analysis in this book.

Insights from Research

Much has been already written about the need to encourage evidence-based management and this relates strongly to one of the key themes in this book. In my critical analysis of situations and action choices I look to apply any insights we can obtain from management research. This often proves to be a challenge, particularly because I must recognise to start with that the research itself is almost always to a lesser or greater degree context specific. On top of this, when there is a concern to introduce some actual notion of performance the more generalisable implications can also tend towards the trite. In this sense the classic example is probably the recommendation to "be lucky" to which I will return later.

Indeed, given the often pre-eminent demand that the key dependent variable should be organisational performance, there is also a need to appreciate the cautions most ably outlined in the paper by March and Sutton which focused on this particular issue. Their somewhat poetic overall advice is basically to live with the ambiguous relationship between scholarship and practice:

> If we remind ourselves, from time to time that standards of influence, like standards of imperial fashion, are more temporary approximations than eternal verities, we do not demean our allegiance to them but we reduce the risk that we will overlook the occasional beauty of cloth woven from invisible threats. And if we remind ourselves, from time to time, that what we are doing is the work of sustaining a belief in the emperor's clothes as a social mythology and a confession of weakness, we do not demean that work but we reduce the risk that we will come to believe in the emperors clothes as a literal reality. (March and Sutton 1997: 705)

The Chapter Sequence

Chapter 1: Extending Analysis in Effective Management

This book is to encourage those who both study and practise management to recognise that effective management means combining an ability to motivate and lead people with an ability to make sound choices grounded on robust and reliable evidence. In more modern parlance it means achieving the benefits of putting together both soft and hard skills. It also implies developing a set of analytical skills that facilitate an engagement with others in the organisation, not a process of abstraction and obfuscation which leaves others frustrated and marginalised.

I outline some of the basic issues involved in putting together different forms, of evidence and the importance of effective questioning. I consider some of the issues that arise with specific forms of representation – particularly the ubiquitous two-by-two box – and some of the possible pitfalls. I also consider the additional general questions of time and movement and some of the possible pitfalls of "mapping" or, in management terms, planning the future. Finally, I look at two central issues: the extent to which the abstraction that implies that decisions always act as a precursor to action actually holds up in practice and the various ways in which we can "simplify" the complexity of many choice situations.

Chapter 2: Never Stop Learning

The key challenge in any educational process is to enable participants to develop and extend their understanding and critical thinking long after the end of a particular programme. It could be argued that this is particularly important in the field of management, where new approaches are constantly being invented or re-invented, in a process often seen as more about fads and fashions rather than improvement. Part of such a "learning to learn" process is aided by considering critically the nature of any particular form of analysis while in the education process itself. However, it is at least as important to continue with reflection and critical evaluation of any approaches after the end of a specific programme to achieve full understanding. This book is intended for both groups: those currently in such educational programmes and also those who wish to undertake a further process of learning and development by visiting or revisiting some of the key analytical elements in their previous experiences – be they primarily in terms of education or indeed practice itself.

In so doing I will consider a number of ways in which our analytical insights can be grounded more effectively on the nature of good practice and how we can benefit more from reflection on our own experience as well as some of the issues in learning from other experience. I also consider critically some of the assumptions underlying the notion of "organisational learning".

Chapter 3: Evidence and Engagement

Extending the role of analysis involves ensuring that as much as possible of the appropriate empirical evidence is incorporated and that there is an active engagement with the nature and challenges of the management practice. The latter ensures a proper connection between the insights generated from the analysis and the management actions, or interventions, that are taken.

The concept of Evidence-based management is considered critically alongside the important distinction between risk and uncertainty. The degree to which consensus can and should be achieved is set alongside the so-called dialectical approach. The importance of folk wisdom and its relationship to scientific knowledge is compared with the nature of academic practice. Finally, some comparisons are made with clinical medical experience in the area of evidence-based practice.

Chapter 4: Tools for Thinking

The analytical tools and the useful insights that are covered in this chapter are based on various ways of representing the nature of the interconnections both within and outside the organisation between a particular choice and its wider context. This covers the use of various "tree" structures to represent choices and the use of modularisation based in particular on loose – tight linkages to help balance coherence with autonomy. The particular approaches are informed by systems thinking and also cover the general notions of closed, open and dynamic systems, and the insights we can glean from game theory. Finally, I look at the more particular issues that arise from some of the more simple experimental games.

Chapter 5: Making Sense of the Numbers

For those of us brought up on the classic monograph *Facts from Figures* – or at least the 1964 version – it is inevitable that M.J. Moroney occupies a rather special position in our thoughts and understanding about the role of statistical analysis. Of course much of what Moroney wrote about was the detail of conducting any statistical analysis by hand before the advent of user-friendly computer programs let alone more sophisticated forms of statistical analysis and algorithms. However, he was also keen for users of statistics to see beyond just the mechanics of, say, calculating a correlation coefficient by hand.

This chapter focuses on the interpretation of various forms of statistical analysis and in particular considers a range of specific issues: outliers, statistical significance, types of error and finally the interpretation of more complicated forms of analysis which incorporate intermediate variables and attempts to establish causal relationships.

Chapter 6: Returning to Practical Wisdom: The Frameworks for Analysis

In any domain of practical activity the central importance of what Aristotle originally termed "practical wisdom" is evident. However, such a form of wisdom should not be confused with what is commonly termed "common sense". Depending on the nature of the context and the evidence, so-called common sense can be of very limited validity. This, for instance, was inherent in Keynes' analysis of the so-called "fallacy of composition": it might be "common sense" to treat a national economy like the problem of balancing the household budget, but actually this can result in a set of major dysfunctional imbalances between supply and demand at a national level.

On the other hand, to the extent to which common sense genuinely embodies experiences grounded in evidence and analysis, it can be a useful guide and to some degree might also be seen to represent informed understanding. Equally, it can provide a basis to critique some of the implicit assumptions in particular forms of analysis and representation. Introducing the time dimension and the dynamic nature of most situations increases the analytical complexity and on top of this we need to recognise that in many competitive markets success can come from contrarian behaviour which contradicts the collective wisdom.

Chapter 7: The Central Role of Stories

The chapters of this book have moved from understanding the particular nature of any managerial knowledge through the analysis of empirical and numerical data, to the use and application of particular frameworks. This chapter moves to the least codified but perhaps most common approach: that based on individual stories and the presentation of arguments that convince others; what in academe is often refered to as the development of a "plausible narrative" and a convincing rationale for a particular course of action. It will also consider how the issues around the nature of such narratives are reflected in a form of teaching that most encounter at various times in their MBA or similar studies: the case study.

Chapter 8: Linking the Classroom to the Workplace

In this chapter the focus extends from the traditional nature of case-study teaching to the wider question of the links, or indeed sometimes lack of them, between much of what is taught in terms of theory and evidence in management and the range and types of experience in managerial practice.

There are many types of both "classrooms" and "workplaces" and hence, as with any aspect of management, "what works" inevitably varies with each individual context.

Chapter 9: An Ongoing Decision Process of Questioning and Dissonance

There is now a much wider recognition that to appreciate the nature of managerial decisions there is a need to go beyond the explicit cognitive approaches and recognise, in one form or another, the intuitive as well.

Various contributors have expressed this in different ways but most are clear that in such a situation it is not a matter of either/or but an appropriate mix of the two. The critical problem is, however, as Daniel Kahneman (2011: 416) puts it: "it is much easier to identify a minefield when you observe others wandering in to it than when you are about to do so".

The need for a balanced treatment of the cognitive and the intuitive also reflects the need for a simultaneous process of thinking "within and outside the box". One analytic way of representing the "outside" aspect is by allowing or even encouraging multiple economic metrics as David Stark (2009) illustrates in his notion of a sense of dissonance. His detailed study resonates in this respect with the equally detailed study by Hensmans et al. (2013), which identified a tradition of contestation as one of the three traditions illustrated by those large commercial organisations which had changed radically and successfully over time but without one or more serious crises.

In terms of thinking within the box, I return to the critical importance of a process of questioning: the interrogative approach and indeed the individual and shared assumptions about the intended outcome of such a process.

Chapter 10: Putting the Masters Back into Management Education and Development

Mastery in management involves both practical skills and analytical thinking. The critics of an exclusively analytical perspective are right in that management involves getting things to happen through people and this can never be purely an analytical process, but sometimes they seem to draw the wrong conclusions. The classic example of McNamara moving from Ford to the Secretary for Defense is not itself so much an example of the failure of an analytical approach but more the failure to consider issues from a range of analytical perspectives.

Equally, analytical skills can be applied to some of the current vogue areas in management: much of the espousal of entrepreneurship can be framed as "thinking outside the box" whilst an analytical approach can raise some critical questions around the research evidence and rhetorical claims in much writing on leadership.

Postscript

Finally, there is a postscript which considers how the underlying approaches developed in the book might influence the nature and interpretation of management research.

1   Extending Analysis in Effective Management

The Legacy of the Sixties

I believe the approach I have adopted in this book can be seen as the true inheritance of the oft-maligned Foundation Reports[1], both produced in 1959 and both highly critical of the quality of students and faculty in many US business schools at the time, as well as the nature of the underlying pedagogy which often relied on descriptive "war stories" from seasoned campaigners. The Foundation Reports not only recommended a substantial improvement in the quality of both students and faculty but also the development of a pedagogic approach which encouraged the twin application of sound theory and robust empirical evidence. In the later case, the reports clearly assumed that a more analytical approach would be completely compatible with a significant improvement in the nature and impact of management practice. Although the reports themselves have often been identified as a key influence in a shift towards a form of academic study which is seen as unworldly and of little use to practising managers, this was clearly not their intention. This book is an attempt to put the more analytical aspects of management back on the course which was originally charted for them by the two Foundation Reports: to play a key role in enhancing and developing the practice of management.

To do this, however, we need to recognise the essential flaw in the previous approach which was very much of its time. The sixties were a time of optimism – at least in Europe and North America – about not only the beneficial impact of technology but also of the burgeoning fields generally described as the social sciences. There was great optimism that many complex social and societal issue would succumb to effective policy initiatives based on a range of theoretical and empirical investigations.

> The discussion about the need for a social science research council began in earnest as the Second World War was drawing to a close. It was a time when the thoughts of policymakers and academics alike were turning to how to achieve the changes in society clearly required in the wake of two

---

[1]Foundation Reports was the colloquial term for the combination of Gordon and Howell (1959) and Pierson (1959).

destructive world wars. It was also a time of optimism, with a belief that all social problems were ultimately soluble. As Michael Young, the first Chairman of the Social Science Research Council (SSRC), reflected: 'there were high hopes, even among some normally cautious administrators, about what social sciences should do to illuminate public policy'. (ESRC [formerly SSRC until 1983] 2005: 4)

However, it was some considerable time after the war before the SSRC was actually established. After various "false starts" the Heyworth Committee was set up in 1963 and was a key committee in recommending the establishment of the SSRC in 1965:

> The Introduction (to part two of the report) set the scene for the recommendation that an SSRC should be established. The chapter stressed the need for more research ... After wide discussion there was as remarkable amount of sympathy with the aims of social scientists and appreciation of the benefits to be gained ... Much larger resources could be absorbed in social science research. "All" agreed on the need for more research on the social sciences, and much more utilisation of the results was required. The aim of the research could be seen as to increase knowledge of how society worked. (Nicol 2001: 81–82)

However, the net result was nicely summarised later and very much after the event by the notion of the "Moon Ghetto Paradox" – on the one hand the ability of a developed human society to succeed in achieving the complex technical task of landing a man, or more strictly men, on the moon, yet on the other hand singularly failing to overcome the social challenges inherent in the urban ghetto (Nelson 1974).

The underlying principle therefore of this book is that our forms of analysis should start from two assumptions that were almost always missing from or at best marginalised in the analytical treatments that informed developments in the sixties. These two assumptions are: first, the nature of the phenomena we study is such that in a broad sense appropriate analysis and action is inevitably context dependent in a way which cannot be captured adequately by any form of simple or indeed complex contingency framework; and, second, that useful forms of analysis and analytical insights are much more likely if they start from current management practices and understandings. A nice illustration of the problems of adopting the opposite approach – starting by redefining the problem so it becomes more amenable to our preferred forms of analysis – is to be found in the short fable on teaching the prince how to play chess (Petersen 1965).

Extended Analysis: Both Analysis and Synthesis

Analysts should therefore set rather more realistic objectives for their analytical investigations. Whilst they should still be true to the essential etymology of the word and develop understandings based on a closer look at constituent parts of the issue and the use of appropriate theory and empirical evidence, they should expect to arrive at insights rather than general prescriptions and at further questions rather than answers. Perhaps yet again it is worth recalling that one of the key elements in the Toyota Production System (TPS) is the notion of "asking the five whys". Invented in the 1930s by Toyota founder Kiichiro Toyoda's father Sakichi and made popular in the 1970s by the Toyota Production System, the five whys strategy involves looking at any problem and asking: "Why?" and "What caused this problem?" The idea is simple. By asking the question "Why" one can separate the symptoms from the causes of a problem. This is critical as symptoms often mask the causes of problems. In this way one should also ensure that analysis is combined with synthesis: achieving benefits from analysis requires recognising the equal need for some form of synthesis.

Meta-Analysis and Systematic Review

Such a synthesis should in general involve balancing analysis from different perspectives but also relying on differing forms of empirical evidence – both qualitative and quantitative. I have a number of techniques and processes to facilitate doing this and I will review and contrast them in more detail later in this book. In general, two challenges often get intertwined: incorporating different analytical perspectives on the nature of the "problem" situation alongside introducing evidence from public or private sources which relate to previous analogous situations. Here it is convenient to follow the terminology used by the Cochrane Collaboration, developed in the field of medical research, and use "meta-analysis" to refer to statistical methods of combining evidence, leaving other aspects of "research synthesis" or "evidence synthesis", such as combining information from qualitative studies, for the more general context of systematic reviews. In the latter case, I reserve the term "systematic review" for the wider integration of differing sources of data as well as differing analytical frameworks. Hence, meta-analyses are often, but not always, important components of an overall systematic review procedure.

In general, there are better-defined procedures for conducting a meta-analysis on quantitative data but when it comes to qualitative studies, although at some higher level the need to compare, contrast and evaluate is similarly important, there is less consensus about the most appropriate forms to adopt. This is at least partly a function of the wider range of forms of empirical data. Barnett-Page and Thomas (2009), in reviewing the various methods, partly focus on the underlying assumptions of the researcher[2]:

- *Subjective idealism*: there is no shared reality independent of multiple alternative human constructions.

- *Objective idealism*: there is a world of collectively shared understandings.

- *Critical realism*: knowledge of reality is mediated by our perceptions and beliefs.

- *Scientific realism*: it is possible for knowledge to approximate closely an external reality.

- *Naive realism*: reality exists independently of human constructions and can be known directly.

    Thus, at one end of the spectrum we have a highly constructivist view of knowledge and, at the other, an unproblematized "direct window onto the world" view.

They then note that such differences influence the choice of analytical tools for synthesis:

    Our methods split into two broad camps: the idealist and the realist [see Table 1.1 for a summary]. Idealist approaches generally tend to have a more iterative approach to searching (and the review process), have less a priori quality assessment procedures and are more inclined to problematise the literature. Realist approaches are characterised by a more linear approach to searching and review, have clearer and more well-developed approaches to quality assessment, and do not problematise the literature.

Unfortunately whilst their distinctions along the individual dimensions are useful, their labels are confusing: in their earlier analysis they have already recognised that in this context the terms "idealist" and "realist" can cover a range of research methods when it comes to interpreting the nature of a particular context.

Hence, whilst in overall terms realism reflects a belief that reality exists independently of any observer, whilst idealism in essence maintains that experience is ultimately based on mental activity, the different forms of both

---

[2]They refer in particular to Spencer et al. (2003).

Table 1.1   Summary table

	Idealist	Realist
Searching	Iterative	Linear
Quality assessment	Less clear, less a priori; quality of content rather than method	Clear and a priori
Problematising the literature	Yes	No
Question	Explore	Answer
Heterogeneity	Lots	Little
Synthetic product	Complex	Clear for policy makers and practitioners

N.B.: In terms of the above dimensions, it is generally a question of degree rather than of absolute distinctions.
(Copyright © 2009 Barnett-Page and Thomas. Reproduced with permission)

these frames of reference are more to be seen as differing assumptions within the framework of two conflicting philosophies as to the extent to which, in the case of idealism, there are or are not shared understandings and, in the case of realism, our understanding of the real is achieved directly or more mediated by our perceptions and beliefs. The distinction is further complicated by the fact that in the philosophy of mind, idealism is more the opposite of materialism, in which the ultimate nature of reality is based on physical substances but we should not assume that materialism and realism are strict synonyms.

As so often in these situations we encounter the issue of incommensurability: the degree to which particular theories can or cannot be compared to determine which is more accurate. In this sense most would argue that it is not possible to conduct a direct comparison between idealism and realism but it is possible at least to some extent to conduct such comparisons between different "variants" of each.

This helps to explain the rather confusing nature of Table 1.1 in that it is implied that each dimension is continuous and at least implicitly correlated but in practice the issues are more complex:

- At a philosophical level any dispute between idealism and realism cannot be resolved by pure empirical means. Again, in practice this may be less of a problem than in theory since both distinct views might support rather similar choices and actions in a particular context.

- The comments above apply most strongly to what might be termed naive realism and naive or subjective idealism but there becomes a form of partial convergence when we consider in the former case a shift towards critical realism and in the latter a shift towards objective idealism. For instance Byrne (2002) provides a constructive critique from a critical realist perspective on the issue of interpreting quantitative data.

- When it comes to the issue of the product of any research exercise, it is true that a form of naive realism helps to generate clear answers for policy makers and practitioners and in many ways this is linked to the real or apparent positivism of much policy research. On the other hand, as I will argue later in this book, if we look more for better questions rather than answers we may be able to avoid some of the traps of naive realism whilst still being seen as of genuine value to both policy makers and practitioners.

Beyond Naive Realism

Moving away from a perspective of naive realism also means moving away from the positioning of all five dimensions on the right-hand side of Table 1.1. However, it would be very misleading to suggest that the further one move towards naive idealism the more one shifts along all of these dimensions. It is more appropriate to see the critical realist or the objective idealist in a world which tends to have the dimensions of:

- iterative search;

- quality assessment based on content rather than method;

- a critical evaluation of prior literature;

- exploratory questioning;

- heterogeneity and complexity.

If this is most likely to be the output from an analytical and systematic review, where does it lead us in informing choice and action?

The basic analytical approach presented in this book is that of a further two-stage process as illustrated in Figure 1.1.

The final process to resolve remaining differences has to be based on judgement, experience and rhetoric. We also need to recognise that such an extensive and extended process is often unrealistic in terms of normal management practice and indeed even in policy contexts. As a necessarily anonymous example, I was in discussion with a group of civil servants about the evidence background for a new policy paper for UK ministers. As the most senior of the civil servants noted, his personal role was to produce the conclusions in consultation with the ministers concerned whilst, as he put it, the most senior

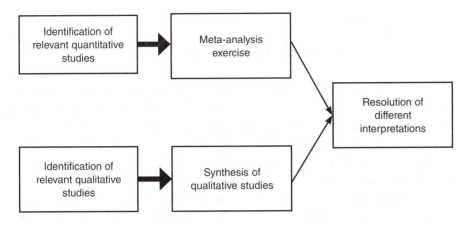

Figure 1.1   **Basic two-stage process**

© Robin Wensley

analyst, who was also present at the meeting, would work with a team to produce a synthesis of the relevant evidence for the appendix!

This means that analytical "interventions" must be timely and effective (rather than delayed, irrelevant and unrealistic) and so it is crucial to have a good sense of the basic assumptions and robustness of our analysis and ways of representing and presenting it which others will find convincing alongside an ability to refute what we see as flaws in alternative approaches. Later in this book, I will therefore compare the broad analytical approach with what is known about the nature of managerial wisdom, which we can describe as tied up more in what others have called "folk wisdom", as well as the issues in both process and analytical terms of the "onus of proof" in providing a means to achieve a clear resolution.

Whilst the discussion above is primarily framed in more philosophical terms I now wish to treat this more as a backdrop to the subsequent text: I will shift the focus to the key aspects in ensuring my analytical approaches, broadly defined, achieve real practical impact on action and choices.

The Relationship between Analysis and Process

Finally, as background it is important to recognise that analysis and process are not direct opposites; in the context of management choices and action, not only can most analysis be seen as also a process but analytical thinking is often embedded in the process itself. This inter-relationship underlies my emphasis on "extended analysis" looking beyond just the assumptions and limitations of particular analytical tools and approaches to the ways in which they can be used in particular contexts and the role they therefore might play in what is often described as the process of choice and action. Even this rather broad description of choices and actions could still be seen as rather misleading. Others would argue that it is much more of a chaotic flow of events and interventions and that many of the descriptions of choices made and actions decided upon are to a lesser or greater extent post-hoc rationalisations, at an individual or collective level. I am reminded of an aside made by Charles Snow, at a retrospective event to consider the 30-year legacy of the seminal paper by Miles and Snow (1978), when he said something to the effect that "we never saw the world as this complex – we just tried to start from what managers did"!

So we find that in many ways the original critique that managers should be better informed, in terms of both evidence and theory, and should be able to apply this knowledge more effectively through a process of analysis, remains valid today. The major difference is that we now know that there is neither one right way either in terms of theory or analysis so that we need to think much more carefully about what theories, what evidence and indeed what analysis is appropriate in any particular context. Not surprisingly our understanding of what makes for effective leadership and management, has evolved in the fifty years since the Foundation Reports, much as our understanding of both the benefits and the limitations of work measurement and control foreshadowed in the work of F.W. Taylor has similarly evolved over the last hundred years, but in both cases there remains still much to learn and apply.

F.W. Taylor is often seen as the initiator of the scientific management approach. In this he gave particular emphasis to two aspects: labour specialisation, much along the lines of Adam Smith's pin factory, and careful, accurate and fine-grained measurement of the work components in a similar manner to that espoused by the experimental scientists. This later aspect can, however, result in what might be termed "the tyranny of measurement". In particular, whilst Sir William Thompson, later Lord Kelvin, is commonly regarded as the source of the quotation:

> When you can measure what you are speaking about, and express it in numbers, you know something about it; but when you cannot measure it, when you cannot express it in numbers, your knowledge of it is of a meagre (sic) and unsatisfactory kind. (Thompson 1883: 80)

There is another side to this aphorism, perhaps best encapsulated in the story of one of his contemporary scientists, James Joule. The two of them were involved in a slightly bizarre experiment in 1847, when Joule, actually on his honeymoon, attempted to show that when water falls through 778 feet it rises one degree Fahrenheit in temperature. One of them was positioned at the top and the other at the bottom of the Cascade de Sallanches in Switzerland. However, in practice the flow was "too much broken into spray" to yield any results.

The Interrogative Mood

The essence of the approach developed in this book is well summarised by the title of Padgett Powell's 2009 book, although perhaps with a greater emphasis on the words before the colon. The full title is "The Interrogative Mood: A Novel?" but its form – a collection of questions which on the surface appear to be unrelated – helps both to emphasise the insights that can be achieved by a process of interrogation but also that the process of questioning even in a 164-page book does have to come to an end sometime!

The process of analysis that I have been outlining above requires a significant degree of interrogation: of the evidence, of others perspectives and of the forms of analysis that might and can be used. How far should this process go? Should we take the Toyota Production System (TPS) five whys as gospel, even when various introductions to this approach themselves note that it is much more important to get to a useful action point rather than slavishly always repeat the question why five times? Padgett Powell's book, however, also reminds us that the nth question, particularly if it is from what our American colleagues term "left field", can still provide a valuable new insight.

For me, this harks back to some early empirical research that I did with three colleagues at London Business School – Paddy Barwise, Paul Marsh and Kathryn Thomas – on the process of strategic investment decisions within a few large diversified corporations. In one case we were debriefing the chief executive officer and the chief financial officer after an executive committee meeting which had given the go-ahead to the particular project we had been following. In the meeting I was struck by the fact that one way of looking at the process of the meeting was that initially it was carefully staged by the project team but it was the supplementary questions by committee members that often elicited useful additional insight.

There seemed to be an analogy between this process and that to be found in Minister's questions in the House of Commons – the first response being a carefully crafted one to a prior question but the supplementary questions being a much severer test. Given that at various times in the executive committee process we had observed the CEO had decided to stop a particular line of questioning by one of his colleagues, I asked whether rather like the Speaker he had some general views as to the appropriate "stopping rule" on which he based his intervention. When I tried to explain as best as I could the analogy I encountered serious, blank expressions! I never did get an answer but I hope readers of this book will maybe have a better sense of their own when they have finished reading.

Indeed, the House of Commons Speaker has also very rarely pronounced – for good reason – on any universally applied number and relied more on his or her absolute discretion. Often the maximum in practice is around three from any one member but in response to a query during an extended exchange in December 1912 between Lord Beresford and Winston Churchill, then First Lord of the Admiralty, on the resignation of Admiral Sir Francis Bridgeman as First Sea Lord, the then Speaker indicated clearly that he would never allow more than eight questions (see Hansard 1912) – slightly less than the number employed in rather different circumstances by Jeremy Paxman, who in interviewing Michael Howard famously asked the same question 12 times (BBC 1997).

Issues of Representation

Throughout this book I will give significant emphasis to the particular ways in which we may choose to represent the outcome of any specific analysis. At this stage I will consider three exemplars: lists, boxes and arrow diagrams. Maybe we should actually start by considering what has almost become the generic representation form itself, not the two-by-two box diagram, but the mere process of listing has a longer history.

Lists and Columns

One exercise often used in management development programmes, but also to be found in use in many practical group situations, is to start or indeed sometimes summarise a discussion by providing a list of issues or considerations, often in columns which can be labelled in various ways: Good/Bad; Option A/Option B and so on.

This form of representation, as with any other, has some potential biases; the most obvious being that the option with the longest list of positives and/or, where relevant, the shortest list of negatives is often assumed to be the dominant one. This creates a form of game playing which encourages producing various phrases as separate items, with little consideration as to both the extent to which the new aspect is distinctly different from those already listed and the nature of the evidence claims in putting forward this particular aspect. This is why business-school professors often start a case discussion by encouraging the class to participate in some form of collective list writing so that they can then use such a diagram to develop and extend the overall case analysis to consider the degree of both the similarity and separateness of the items that have been listed.

Technically speaking we can resolve some of these analytical challenges by resorting to various more complex – and often number-based – forms of analysis but, as we will discuss further in the book, techniques such as cluster analysis and the analytical hierarchy process (AHP) can often mean we have to make prior assumptions and many users find the interpretation of the analysis more challenging than illuminating.

The Two-by-Two Box

Perhaps the most common medium used to translate management research into descriptions and prescriptions for management practice is the two-by-two matrix or similar device. George A. Miller (1956) wrote a paper entitled "The Magical Number Seven, Plus or Minus Two: Some Limits on Our Capacity for Processing Information", which asserted that the number of objects an average human can hold in working memory is 7 ± 2. Hence, an average limit on an individual's one-dimensional absolute judgement could be characterised as an information channel capacity with approximately two to three bits of information, which corresponds to the ability to distinguish between four and eight alternatives. More recently, Cowan (2000) also noted a number of other limits of cognition that point to a "magical number four" which might at least help to explain some of the sustained attraction of the two-by-two matrix! It is often suggested that a lecture course on management analysis could consist merely of one two-by-two box for each lecture with the only difference being the specific labels on the axes for each lecture. There are a number of key questions about this general form of representation that are almost always overlooked; in particular not only the extent to which the two basic dimensions are independent (orthogonal[3]) but also the degree to which the actual observations are really widely distributed in the matrix or concentrated in limited clusters or even only found close to the centre of the matrix.

Figures 1.2–1.7 show how the underlying representation might be altered to reflect the actual degree of orthogonality between the axes of the box or the actual dispersal of individual observations. Figures 1.2 and 1.5 are the "ideal" but in practice it is likely that we will often encounter both of the complications represented in the other figures.

---

[3]In mathematics, two vectors are orthogonal if they are perpendicular, i.e. they form a right angle. The word comes from the Greek (orthos), meaning "straight", and (gonia), meaning "angle".

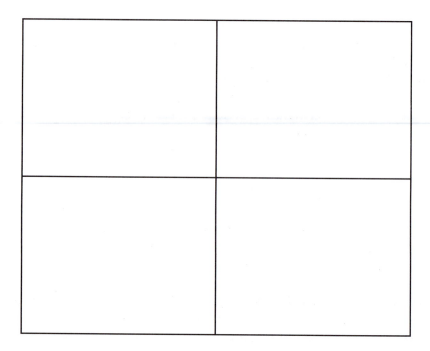

Figure 1.2   A matrix with fully orthogonal dimensions

© Robin Wensley

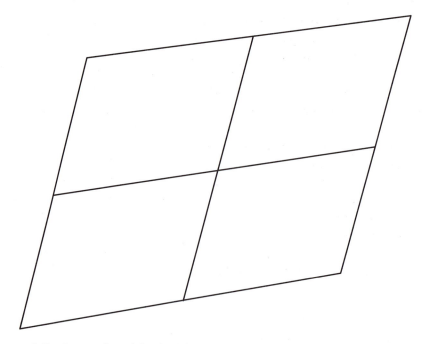

Figure 1.3   A matrix with significant orthogonality

© Robin Wensley

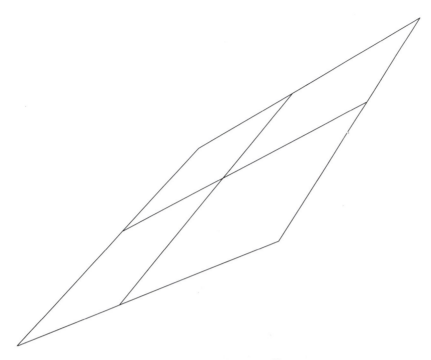

Figure 1.4   A matrix with limited orthogonality

© Robin Wensley

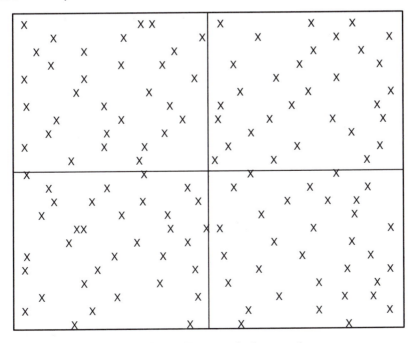

Figure 1.5   A matrix with fully dispersed observations

© Robin Wensley

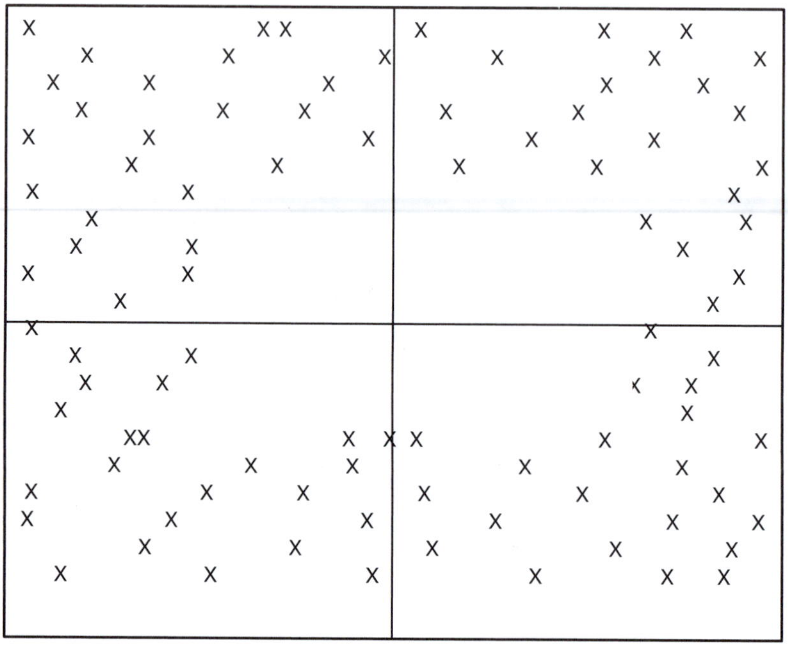

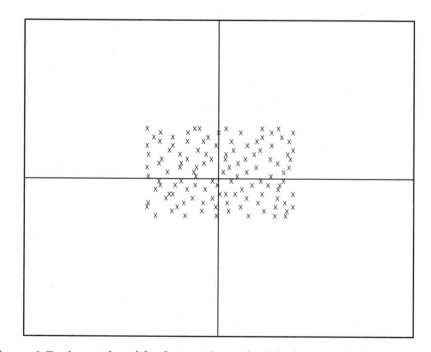

Figure1.6   A matrix with observations clustered at the extremes

© Robin Wensley

Figure 1.7   A matrix with observations clustered at the centre

© Robin Wensley

In general, each of these limitations can result in a misleading analysis of the available options:

- In the case of limited orthogonality, we may assume that any position within the whole of the two-dimensional space within the box is at least feasible, but in fact we are much closer to only having a single dimension to operate along which is actually more like the diagonal of the box diagram itself.

- In the case of clustered dispersion we face a different issue: in discussing the positioning options, we may again assume that at least to a certain extent any position is feasible when the empirical evidence is that this is not apparently the case. Perhaps the severest error is when in practice observations are clustered near the centre of the matrix but the analysis of options is conducted and explained as if the options were clustered at the extremes. In such cases the archetypal unit in any one quadrant is represented as one close to the extreme end and the relevant managerial prescriptions developed on the basis of such an archetype. Such a prescription is then applied to those units that map into the quadrant even if they are actually much closer to the middle rather than the extreme.

Introducing Time and Movement

Two-by-two boxes and similar representations focus our attention on the position of the entities, be they, for instance, a range of the firm's offerings or indeed a set of our own and competitors' offerings at a particular point in time. Most times in my analysis I am also interested in how such positions have moved and then will move through time. For instance, in one particular presentation by a senior colleague to an executive audience this was perhaps carried to its logical conclusion in that he labelled the axes in terms of "Hi" and "Lo", in the opposite manner to the direction of travel he proposed for the new strategy. When asked afterwards about this he responded that the proposed direction should always be represented as upwards and rightwards whatever the axes said; this would ensure the audience were more convinced of "progress"! In this particular case the audience appeared to be quite satisfied with the initial presentation.

In more academic terms, the problem in answering questions about movement through time is often that, to quote a rather well-known expression, the map is not the territory. The aphorism itself is commonly attributed to Alfred Korzybski who coined the expression in "A Non-Aristotelian System and its Necessity for Rigour in Mathematics and Physics", a paper presented before the American Mathematical Society at the New Orleans, Louisiana, meeting of the American Association for the Advancement of Science, 28 December 1931. The paper was reprinted in the book *Science and Sanity: An Introduction to Non-Aristotelian Systems and General Semantics* first published in 1933 and more recently in 1958. "A map *is not* the territory it represents, but, if correct, it has a *similar structure* to the territory, which accounts for its usefulness" (Korzybski 1958: 58). Although he did use a number of geographic examples, he focuses mainly on spatial sequencing in an essentially two-dimensional world and in particular does not really develop the topographical perspective, where often the direct route from A to B is blocked by mountains and chasms whilst the indirect route is much more feasible. On top of this, he generally defined maps and mapping very broadly, particularly when considering the role of language:

> If words *are not* things, or maps are not the actual territory, then, obviously, the only possible link between the objective world and the linguistic world is found in *structure, and structure alone*. The only usefulness of a map or a language depends on the *similarity of structure* between the empirical world and the map-languages. If the structure is not similar, then the traveller or speaker is led astray, which, in serious human life-problems, must become always eminently harmful. If the structures *are similar*, then the empirical world becomes "rational" to a potentially rational being, which means no more than that verbal, or map-predicted characteristics, which follow up the linguistic or map structure, are applicable to the empirical world. (Korzybski 1958: 61)

In discussions about management theory, a rather different approach has been popularised by writers such as Karl Weick, who have focused attention more on the ambiguity of the relationship between maps and reality combined with the importance of action rather that the importance of similarity in structure. His most quoted example is:

> A small Hungarian detachment was on military manoeuvres in the Alps. their young lieutenant sent a reconnaissance unit out into the icy wilderness just as it began to snow. It snowed for two days, and the unit did not return, The lieutenant feared that he had dispatched his people to their deaths, but the third day the unit came back. Where had they been? How had they made their way? Yes, they said, we considered ourselves lost and waited for the end, but then one of us found a map in his pocket. That calmed us down. We pitched camp, lasted out the snowstorm, and then with the map we found our bearings. And here we are. The lieutenant took a good look at this map and discovered, to his astonishment, that it was a map of the Pyrenees. (This story was related by the Nobel Laureate Albert Szent-Gyorgi and was turned into a poem by Holub, 1977.)

My favourite moral of the Pyrenees story is the advice, if you're lost any old map will do. For people who study maps, as well as those who claim to use them, a map provides a reference point, an anchor, a place to start from, a beginning, which often becomes secondary once an activity gets underway. Just as a map of the Pyrenees gets people moving so they find their way out of the Alps, a map of the wrong competitor can get people talking so they find their way into the right niche. (Weick 1990: 4)

Not surprisingly Weick's use of this example has raised some important questions. First, perhaps inevitably, there has been a long running debate as to whether in the way he told the story Weick was also guilty of plagiarism in failing to acknowledge the extent to which he copied Holub's poem word for word.[4]

But the more interesting question is the extent to which "any old map will do". Maybe we can find further enlightenment from Lewis Carroll who can be relied on to provide a rather contrarian view on many issues. As Tosey points out: "In the poem [The Hunting of the Snark], the Bellman's chart is, delightfully, entirely blank. This was much appreciated by the crew, who found it 'a map they could all understand'" (2005: 338). The efficacy of an analysis based solely on blank sheets is, however, something we might wish to challenge!

On top of the question of what might reasonably be termed the landscape is the further issue in many cases of the likely actions and reactions of our competitors and how they might intend to move their own offerings as well. I will return later to the ways in which we may be able to find useful insights in dealing with such a complex, interactive and path-dependent situation.

Choices, Decisions and Action

Weick, amongst others, reminds us that in a managerial context there is almost always an issue of action as well as understanding. The most common way of representing this analytically is a time sequence:

---

[4]Some have claimed that in his book he "straightforwardly plagiarizes Miroslav Holub's 'Brief Thoughts of Maps'". (http://hdl.handle.net/2381/3745) but Weick himself claims imperfect memory and archiving rather than any dubious intent (www.ephemeraweb.org/journal/6-2/6-2weick.pdf), and some of us suspect another academic descent into the grey world of asserted plagiarism. I once found myself on an examination appeals committee where the critical plagiarism case revolved around a single missing quotation mark. However, we should not underestimate the possible consequences of such accusations in certain cases; see the Jonah Lehrer case covered later in this book.

- choices: in which the discrete choices or options are identified;

- decisions: in which various forms of analysis are conducted to enable a particular choice to be made;

- action: in which action is taken to implement the choice which has been made.

Throughout this book we will encounter a significant number of limitations with this particular way of understanding what is going on. In some cases there are analytical approaches which can at least ameliorate these limitations; in other cases beyond recognising at least analytically speaking there is little we can do except recognise the limitations of a particular analytical framework being used.

Generally speaking the basic issue is that to conduct pretty much any useful analysis, the choice or action under consideration in both space and time. But any particular action is but one in a stream of actions through time and each such action can have direct and indirect consequences outside the particular analytical frame. It was for good reasons that A.J.P. Taylor suggested that it was the way the rail timetables for the mobilisation of the various armies were constructed that meant that there was no going back!

In his 1969 book *War by Timetable*, Taylor examined the origins of the First World War, concluding that though all of the great powers wished to increase their own power relative to the others, none consciously sought war before 1914. Instead, he argued that all the great powers believed that if they possessed the ability to mobilise their armed forces faster than any of the others, this would serve as a sufficient deterrent to avoid war and allow them to achieve their foreign policy. Thus, the general staffs of the great powers developed elaborate timetables to mobilise faster than any of their rivals. When the crisis broke in 1914, though none of the statesmen of Europe wanted a war, the need to mobilise faster than potential rivals created an inexorable movement towards war. Thus, Taylor claimed that the leaders of 1914 became prisoners of the logic of the mobilisation timetables and the timetables that were meant to serve as deterrent to war instead relentlessly brought war.

It will not, of course, come as surprise that a number of other commentators have contested A.J.P. Taylor's interpretation: not least because he was a vocal critic of the then current strategy of MAD (mutually assured destruction), which formed the rationale for nuclear deterrence.

In the less cataclysmic world of business decisions, however, it remains true that individual decisions are almost always to be seen within the context of a sequence of choices and interventions both within and also outside the organisation. Inside the organisation Nils Brunsson (1982) suggested in his research that one of the only things one can assert is that decisions are very rarely made at the point at which they are formally endorsed. After all, the first rule of organisational politics might be said to be to canvass support well before the formal decision. Indeed, in the research we (Paddy Barwise, Paul Marsh, Kathryn Thomas and myself) undertook on the nature of strategic investment decisions, we noted that in some cases key project sponsors had built in broad outline commitments in plans that had been approved one or more years earlier.

Rationality in Practice: Simplification Approaches

Another key aspect in interpreting the process of decision making is the extent to which the complex cognitive structure that underlies a full picture of any specific choice means that in practice a simplification approach such as that of "bounded rationality", as defined by Herb Simon (1991), is required. I note two particular strategies.

First, that of simplifying the structure of the choice map itself through some form of modularisation: we can in principle modularise in either or both space and time. There is an implicit assumption that in doing this the interactions that are being ignored are second order compared with those retained in the analytical framework.

Second, an approach based on a particular process of decision making employing so-called procedural rationality rather than more complex substantive rationality. In its simplest form procedural rationality requires us to start by focusing on ends or objectives and then gradually and consistently moving towards the specific current choice. In its more complex forms there is some form of check-list which we are required to follow. It should, however, be noted that it is in principle an empirical question whether particular decisions derived from a rational procedural approach are consistently "better" than those generated by other often less systematic procedures.

However, we need to recognise that this particular way of simplifying the analytical task embodies various assumptions about the nature of the choices themselves and indeed the role and form of analysis.

In two key papers, Brunsson (1990, 1993) went further in his analysis. In one paper he argued that organisational decisions sometimes play one or more of three other roles: mobilising organisational action, distributing responsibility or providing legitimacy. Different roles imply different designs of decision processes, different usages of information, different costs and different needs for making decisions at all. The degree of rationality in decision processes tends to vary according to the roles adopted. High degrees of rationality can be interpreted as attempts to prevent action, evade responsibility or support organisational legitimacy in a complex environment. In the other paper, he argued that irrationality is a basic feature of organisational behaviour. Organisational decision making tends to be irrational, and organisational ideologies bias organisations' perceptions. Much effort has been spent on prescribing how organisations should achieve more rationality. However, rational decision making affords a bad basis for action. Some irrationalities are necessary requirements for organisational actions. Choices are facilitated by narrow and clear organisational ideologies, and actions are facilitated by irrational decision-making procedures which maximise motivation and commitment.

Brunsson's focus on so-called irrationalities, which of course could also be seen as rational if we allowed a wider context to be considered that recognised clarity, co-ordination, commitment and motivation, are all essential elements in ensuring that actions taken are indeed effective. This relates rather closely to the observations made by Ed Lindblom (1959, 1979) in the field of public policy, where he argues that to achieve consensus it is often more effective to eschew an approach based on procedural rationality and focus attention on means rather than ends.

The other key assumption underlying the bounded rationality approach is that the choice process is to be seen from an analytical perspective as cognitive rather than intuitive. There has been a recent increased interest in the role of intuition in management decision making (Dane and Pratt 2007; Hodgkinson et al. 2008) and with the advantage of hindsight it is clear that the US Foundation Reports with which this chapter started did not really consider the role of the intuitive in analytical management. The specific word "intuition" is not to be found in either report but there are some illuminating comments on "intuitive" aspects of management. The most direct are:

> The critical change will be the increase in the clarification of variables that need to be considered in making decisions, the increase in the use of carefully obtained quantitative information concerning these variables, and the increase in rigorous analysis weighting and combining the variables involved. We all know that in some vague intuitive way this is what we must be doing when we make decisions now. The change I am predicting is, therefore, one of clarifying and of bringing to the surface the variables and implicit logical models our minds must be using now in decision making, and of persistently improving the logic of these models. (Bach 1959: 322)

"In Peter Drucker's words, 'The days of the "intuitive" managers are numbered.' Since the closing decades of the nineteenth century, the problems facing the businessman have become increasingly complex" (Gordon and Howell 1959: 12). This general assertion is combined with a rather vague notion of what is called "semi-intuitive":

> The management of economic resources takes place in a continually changing environment. It must try to anticipate a future that can be but imperfectly foreseen. It must not only react to past and current change but also try to anticipate future change. Imagination, the ability to make decisions on the basis of incomplete information, and a semi-intuitive skill in anticipating the future all have to be combined with the kinds of knowledge we have described. (Ibid. 1959: 68)

As will be discussed later in the book, it has become much clearer that not only does intuition play a significant part in many actual choice situations, but also that this aspect can be subjected to some degree of analytical scrutiny alongside the more cognitive approach around forms of bounded rationality.

Conclusion: Coping with Complex Rationality

So I end up with a rather complex notion of rationality, one which might, or might not:

- simplify the analytical task by either or both bounding the problem domain (in terms of space and time) and focusing attention more on a so-called rational process rather than analysis itself;

- extend the notion of rationality to include the critical factors such as commitment, motivation and co-ordination;

- focus attention more on achieving consensus around the next action to be taken rather than the long-term desired end-state.

Of course in practice I will choose to emphasise rather different elements of these three choices in different specific contexts. I now turn to the critical issues of how we might learn to operate more effectively in such an ambiguous environment and some analytical perspectives that might help us to do so.

2   Never Stop Learning

Give a man a fish and you feed him for a day. Teach a man to fish and you feed him for a lifetime. (Chinese Proverb)

Some Basic Ideas

Many years ago a colleague of mine, who was marketing director of a medium-sized UK book publisher, tried a new technique in the annual process of reviewing divisional marketing plans with the relevant executives. Instead of the usual process in which they would present their plans and then be subject to questioning on the detail, he started with a rather different question: "In the context of the marketing approach for your division what have you learnt that you did not know a year ago?"

The initial response was slight confusion – after all the previous regime had put much store on a "no surprises" approach which meant all developments were represented as part of an earlier and established understanding of the relevant marketplace – but the subsequent discussion was much more insightful.

Surprises, Conjectures and Refutations

Equally, of course, it was not the sort of intervention that can be simply maintained over a number of years yet still retain its surprise impact. Like many such changes in auditing and performance management it is subject to Goodhart's Law, originally formulated by Professor Charles Goodhart, who was Chief Adviser to the Bank of England, in the context of government attempts to control monetary policy via different measures of the money supply. It can be framed in various ways. One of the original versions is the statement that: "Any observed statistical regularity will tend to collapse once pressure is placed upon it for control purposes." Hence there will be a limited number of rounds before gaming behaviour dominates and, in this case, the learning value of the intervention is considerably reduced.

Some have argued that it is the social science equivalent of the well-known Heisenberg uncertainty principle in physics which asserts that the very process of measuring an entity actually modifies it. At some level this is true but it should also be noted that the order of magnitude in the Heisenberg equation for the error term is actually a very small number – plank's constant – and in this sense in the social sciences we also have to recognise the effect is significant on a day-to-day scale rather than just at the sub-atomic level.

In fact the issue of surprise value arises more widely when considering issues of learning. In general, we can argue that our understanding about the nature of any situation or problem will only be enhanced when we encounter a surprising event and then reflect on how we should incorporate this in our overall understanding. We might well say that a key element in learning is both the ability to recognise surprising events and then also to reflect on them. There is an interesting contradiction here with the style of management and leadership which ostensibly operates on the "no surprises" principle. If this is used as a means to emphasise that strategic issues and problems should not be hidden from senior management then it is a generally positive perspective but if, on the other hand, it is seen to mean that the principle is that all events must be fully anticipated then this is more a recipe for limited learning and hence failure.

It may be both rather a cliché and also of dubious provenance but one is inevitably reminded of the lesson incorporated in the remark allegedly made by Harold Macmillan, when asked by a young journalist after a long dinner what can most easily steer a government off course. He answered "Events, dear boy. Events."

Recently, Alvesson and Kärreman (2011) have argued very persuasively that management researchers need to develop their further understanding by first identifying what they term the "mystery" in the empirical data that they are considering. Indeed, we might well argue such advice extends from researchers to practitioners as well. One might also interpret this as a technique to overcome the common occurrence of confirmatory bias: the tendency to search for evidence which supports rather than challenges our prior assumptions. Indeed, we might also see this as rather consistent with what Karl Popper noted in *Conjectures and Refutations*:

> "The criterion of falsifiability is a solution … for it says that statements or systems of statements, in order to be ranked as scientific, must be capable of conflicting with possible, or conceivable, observations." (Popper, 2002: 51).

However, espousing an approach which is nicely summarised by Winch (2010: 238) as having the central requirement that "The arrogance of conjecture needs to be coupled with the humility of refutation" proves not to be the same as actually behaving in such a balanced manner. In the (in)famous incident of *Wittgenstein's Poker*, Philip Davis (2002) notes in his review of the book of the same title by David Edmonds and John Eidenow (2001) that "Popper was brilliant, insecure and arrogant, self-righteous, disputatious. Supremely egotistical, he had to win an argument at whatever the cost." Just for balance he also says "Wittgenstein was brilliant, eccentric, egotistical, and ascetic".

We are quite often likely to be found somewhat wanting when our prescriptions for the behaviour of others are applied critically to our own behaviour![1]

Double-Loop Learning

A different but perhaps somewhat analogous perspective is provided by the notion of "double-loop" learning initially popularised by Chris Argyris and Donald Schön (1978). They saw that it was important to encourage a learning process which not only refined the ways of currently performing any management task but also at the same time some way of challenging or validating the assumptions underlying the way in which the task itself was framed.

They argued that double-loop learning is necessary if organisations and its members are to manage problems effectively that originate in rapidly changing and uncertain contexts.

Argyris and Schön distinguished three levels of learning in organisations:

1 Single-loop learning: Adaptive learning focuses on incremental change. This type of learning solves problems but ignores the question of why the problem arose in the first place.

2 Double-loop learning: Generative learning focuses on transformational change that changes the status quo. Double-loop learning uses feedback from past actions to question assumptions underlying current views. When considering feedback, managers and professionals need to ask not

---

[1]"Popper was especially unyielding in public argument. He would even occasionally demand that his graduate assistants ask prepared questions at his lectures, rather as if he were speaking at a plenary session of the Moscow Communist Party, and would then berate them in public if the wording of their questions strayed from their prepared text or, worse, so much as hinted at any inadequacy in his views. This obnoxious habit prompted one wag to claim that Popper's most famous book, *The Open Society and Its Enemies*, should instead have borne the title The Open Society by One of Its Enemies" (www.firstthings.com/article/2007/01/problems-or-puzzles-35).

only the reasons for their current actions, but what to do next and, even more importantly, why alternative actions are not to be implemented.

3 Deutero-learning: Learning how to learn better by seeking to improve both single- and double-loop learning.

Individual's mental maps provided guidance on the processes of planning, implementing and reviewing actions. Learning was based on the detection and correction of errors given a current set of norms, the applied action strategy and the realised outcome.

Others have, however, challenged the relatively simple assumption that mental maps tacit or otherwise provide a full explanation of the underlying rationale for specific actions. In particular Malle (2004), to whom we will return later in this chapter, argues that when people explain their own behaviour and the behaviour of others they are using the explanation to manage a social interaction – by offering clarification, trying to save face, or casting blame.

Argyris and Schön (1978) regarded individuals as the key to organisational learning. People constructing and sharing mental maps make the development of organisational memory and learning possible.

There are many pictorial representations to illustrate the difference they see between double- and single-loop learning. A common version is provided in Figure 2.1, which also helps to illustrate the board link between a notion of double-loop learning and the oft-used entreaty in popular management books to "think outside the box".

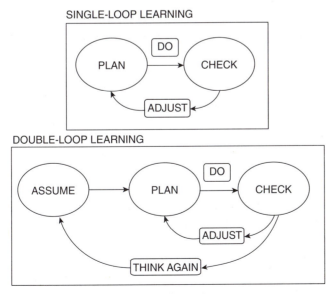

Figure 2.1 Single- and double-loop learning

(Copyright © 2009 Luc Galoppin. Reproduced with permission; source: www.reply-mc. com/2009/10/26/what-about-chris-argyris/)

Boxes, Boundaries and Questions

However, we might also ask: What box? And how far? We noted earlier that on issues of both analysis and organisation, Herbert Simon (1969a) emphasised the strong advantages of the related notion of modularity which implies recognising the benefits of boundaries and boxes.

This provides a rather different approach to the inevitable question as to why thinking outside the box so often does not actually happen and takes us in a rather different direction from that pursued by Chris Argyris (1985) himself, who tended to explain what he saw as a dysfunctional lack of learning on the existence of defensive routines.

An alternative but somewhat related view is, of course, to be found in the "five whys" approach, which has already been mentioned as a key part of the Toyota Production System (TPS). Interestingly Toyota itself notes that the acronym TPS can also stand for "Thinking People System"!

The Reflective Practitioner

Whilst Chris Argyris focused his attention on the problems as he saw them of dealing with defensive routines, which inevitably lead also to the critique that he himself was exhibiting a defensive routine in not adapting his underlying model to recognise more clearly why individuals focused so much attention on what he termed "single-loop" learning, Donald Schön shifted his focus rather differently to understanding the nature of what he called the "reflective practitioner". Schön (1983) argued that such a reflective practitioner:

> "also reflects on the understandings which have been implicit in his (sic) action, understandings which he surfaces, criticizes, restructures, and embodies in future action. It is the entire process of reflection-in-action which is central to the 'art' by which practitioners sometimes deal well with situations of uncertainty, instability, uniqueness and value conflict." (p. 50)

Reflective practice is widely espoused but it would seem rather less commonly achieved. This may be because, in the ways in which Schön and others describe it, it requires time, commitment and a significant mentoring and professional supervisory role. Overall, it is noteworthy that the general notions attached to the process of supervision are very different if we are framing it in the context of professional development rather than solely management control. The practice has historically been applied most in the educational and medical field and it is a further challenge to apply it in what might be termed quasi-professional fields such as management.

There are various models that can be used to facilitate the process of reflection and action; one of the most established ones is the Kolb (1984) learning cycle which is illustrated in Figure 2.2. Together with some variant of the TPS five whys this in broad terms covers the suggested approach although there are, of course, many other variants.

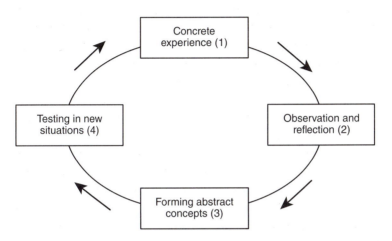

Figure 2.2   A Representation of The Kolb (1984) Learning Cycle

(Copyright © 2002 Lynne Montrose. Reproduced with permission)

Finally, suggested ways for professionals to practise reflective management include:

- keeping a journal;
- seeking feedback;
- view experiences objectively; and
- taking time at the end of each day, meeting, experience, etc. to reflect on actions.

Sources of Learning Beyond One's Own Practice

Of course as we continue in our management practice we have other opportunities to add to our learning (or of course to some considerable extent help us to un-learn as well!) beyond reflection on our own actions and choices.

Learning from others can be very much a personal issue and to a significant extent is outside the direct remit of this book, but often we aim to learn from others' experience mediated by communications in books, pamphlets, articles, blogs, briefings and indeed the internet as a whole. On top of this the multiple experiences of many others are often partially incorporated into various analytical tools of one sort or another.

At this stage I want to focus attention on some of the more generalised accounts of the experience of others: in the next chapter I will look more closely at some of the approaches and issues that arise when we attempt to introduce what is currently known as evidence-based management (EBM) in a more systematic and formal manner as well as the various ways in which we might apply some theoretical insights as well.

However, in the context of learning the lessons from other practitioners, we face some challenges from both empirical and theoretical work, where I suspect if we are honest to ourselves the result is one which actually reflects what many of us have always suspected. Sims et al. (2009) in their empirical work focus on the evidence that the presentations of practice are themselves often a set of connected but only loosely connected anecdotes and this to an audience which internalise different individual elements of the presentation to produce a useful and meaningful – but also individual – understanding of the message. Such a critique is reinforced by much of the work of Malle, which was referred to earlier.

Indeed, we should be equally honest about our own academic practice. It is often the case that we trawl through various papers and reports on empirical work to find pieces of support for our own arguments without paying too much attention to the more detailed context and framework around the piece of theory or empirical research that we are considering. So it is also true that much of our scholarly practice is mainly guided by confirmatory bias.

Malle's (2004) work talks to another important form of bias in many situations: it can be seen as a major development and critique of the wide use of "attribution bias" as a means of interpreting reported outcomes for particular events which can be seen as caused by the interaction of internal and external forces; in management terms, by firm decisions internally or the competitive environment externally. The attribution bias explanation depends on the assumption that in general we tend to ascribe success primarily to our internal decisions and insight and failure to external factors beyond our control. One of the neatest pieces of empirical research on this is to be found by Bettman and Weitz (1983), in which they noted that corporate annual reports tended to ascribe successes to management judgement and other internal factors and at the same time failures to uncontrollable external events such as the weather even in situations in which both groups of companies had effectively operated in markets equally affected by the same external events and uncertainties. Despite the historical nature of research it seems likely that such behaviour remains widely true today as well.

Malle's essential argument was not that attribution bias did not exist but that the issue of explanations that individuals or groups give for their actions and those of others was much more complex than a simple attribution model implied. In particular he argues that behavioural explanations exist not only in the mind but that they are also overt verbal actions used for social purposes. Such purposes include clarification, saving face or casting blame. Broadly he distinguishes between behavioural events which are interpreted as actions influenced by intentions and "mere behaviours" that are treated as unintentional. In the managerial context individual actors will more often provide intentional interpretations rather than mere observations. We might also note that Malle is substantially widening the context in which we interpret explanations for a particular form of behaviour, much as Brunsson was widening the framework within which we interpreted the nature of decision making.

Hence, we are more interested in approaches that have to in one way or another incorporate the intention(s) of the actor(s) in explaining the reason something happened. Malle invokes what he terms the folk concept of intentionality to develop his analysis further. He distinguishes between explanations which mainly rely on enabling factors that facilitate the link between intention and action and those which incorporate reasons that "explain" these particular intentions. As he notes, in some cases interpretations of the intentions of the actors are solely provided by what he terms the "causal history of reason" (CHR) approach, which he defines as:

> Causal History of Reason explanations cite factors which lay in the background of an actor's reasons and typically brought them about thereby helping explain the background of the action. Causal history factors are not themselves reasons, so the agent does not form an intention in the light of or on the grounds of causal history factors. (Malle 2004: 86)

And he illustrates the difference, with Table 2.1.

We will return to two particular aspects of this analysis later in the book. First, there is the issue of intentionality itself and the ways in which we anticipate the actions of others in our own actions and strategies. Second, there is the ways in which we interpret and understand the lessons we can learn from others – either through interaction and communication with specific informants or, even more difficult, through surveys or other more impersonal means of accessing and aggregating the experiences of others.

Table 2.1   Reasons and causal histories for why the chicken crossed the road

Reason explanations

Captain James T Kirk: to boldly go where no chicken had gone before
Plato: for the greater good
Ernest Hemmingway: To die. In the rain

Causal history of reason explanations

Aristotle: It is the nature of chickens to cross roads
Hippocrates: Because of an excess of phlegm in its pancreas
Darwin: Chickens, over a great period of time, have been naturally selected in such a way that they are now genetically disposed to cross roads

(Copyright © 2004 MIT Press. Reproduced with permission)

What about "Organisational Learning"?

Much has also been written to advocate the development of a so-called "learning organisation"(LO). However, it would seem that this is an area where we need to be particularly careful about shifting the unit of analysis from the individual even to a team let alone a whole organisation, both in the private sector and perhaps even more so in the public sector. As Simon commented:

> we must be careful not to adopt too strict a definition of organizational learning, or we will define our topic out of existence, thereby denying the legitimacy of this conference. All learning takes place inside individual human heads; an organization learns in only two ways: (a) by the learning of its members, or (b) by ingesting new members who have knowledge the organization didn't previously have. But what is stored in any one head in an organization may not be unrelated to what is stored in other heads; and the relation between those two (and other) stores may have a great bearing on how the organization operates.

> What an individual learns in an organization is very much dependent on what is already known to (or believed by) other members of the organization and what kinds of information are present in the organizational environment. As we shall see, an important component of organizational learning is internal learning – that is, transmission of information from one organizational member or group of members to another. Individual learning in organizations is very much a social, not a solitary, phenomenon. (1991: 125)

In terms of organisational level learning this leads to a number of insights, such as those due to March, that there was a

> tendency to substitute exploitation of known alternatives for the exploration of unknown ones, to increase the reliability of performance rather more

than its mean. This property of adaptive processes is potentially self-destructive. As we have seen, it degrades organizational learning in a mutual learning situation. Mutual learning leads to convergence between organizational and individual beliefs. The convergence is generally useful both for individuals and for an organization. However, a major threat to the effectiveness of such learning is the possibility that individuals will adjust to an organizational code before the code can learn from them. Relatively slow socialization of new organizational members and moderate turnover sustain variability in individual beliefs, thereby improving organizational and average individual knowledge in the long run. (1991: 85)

This approach led others to place emphasis on the extent to which accumulated organisational knowledge was embedded in various forms of routine – or standard operating procedures – which, however, meant that significant changes required actions outside the realm of such procedures and this led to a notion of punctuated equilibrium in the longer development and evolution of the organisation: periods of relative stasis and incremental developments followed by shorter periods of radical change. Others, however, such as Feldman and Pentland (2003), have more recently noted that in practice so-called organisational routines were themselves evolving and subject to modification and hence it was much less clear how far the actual performative routines were adequately represented by the ostensive form in which they were often represented.

Weick was, as often, also more challenging of the overall attempts to extend individual learning to the organisational level. He argued the need for a redefinition of the basic nature of organisational learning:

A more radical approach to redefinition would be to take the position that individual learning occurs when people give a different response to the same stimulus, but organizational learning occurs when groups of people give the same response to different stimuli. (1991: 121)

This leads him, perhaps rather unsurprisingly, to argue the need to move the frame of reference from learning per se to interpretation and sense-making. In a separate but related commentary he notes:

Previous efforts to grasp the phenomenon of organizational learning have mixed together change, learning, and adaption, with only casual attention to levels of analysis and to referents for the activity itself. One way to untangle this mixture is to designate an explicit anchor, which I have done by constructing this review around a traditional psychological definition of learning, and then ask, when do conditions necessary for traditional learning occur in organizations? Having asked that question, I then began to see potential non-learning sources of change in organizations as well as novel forms which learning itself might take. (1991: 122)

de Holan and Phillips (2004) too start from a perspective which differenti-
ates between organisational and individual level learning but they develop
a different emphasis:

> Given that organizational knowledge is differentiable from the knowledge
> of its members, there must be some form of organizational memory system
> responsible for the management of the processes of knowledge storage and
> retention ... In this paper, we ... define organizational memory broadly as
> "sets of knowledge retention devices that collect, store, and provide access
> to the organization's experience" (Olivera 2000, p. 815). Given our view of
> organizational knowledge, these storage retention devices include a broad
> range of organizational processes that store both behavioral and cognitive
> elements of knowledge. (2004: 1605)

Hence, it might be more appropriate to consider the ways in which from
one perspective information is codified and made accessible to others in
the organisation, or indeed team, concerned and from the other the ways
in which individuals are encouraged to access such data and use it to
further their understanding of the particular situations they find themselves facing.

Such twin topics can and do justify a whole book on their own. Indeed, as
Easterby-Smith et al. note in their introductory review paper for another
special issue:

> In this paper we attempt to map the development of organizational learn-
> ing as a field of academic study by examining the rise and fall of specific
> debates. This does not pretend to be a comprehensive review of the field
> since there is now far too much material available to allow full coverage in
> any single publication. (2000: 783)

So here I will focus on two aspects only: first, the extent to which individuals are not only encouraged to access such data but also the extent to which
they are motivated to do this in a systematic and challenging manner; and,
second, the ways in which the practical nature of organisational "learning"
can often constrain rather than facilitate this process, which has led some to
argue that we should encourage organisational level forgetting as much as
learning.

There has also been a parallel and only somewhat related academic
field of study with the specific notion of the LO, which itself has been
subjected to a range of criticisms. To some significant extent the key
popularisers of this particular approach – Senge (1993) – saw it as directly
related to a systems perspective on the nature of organisations. In fact, he
used a systems dynamic perspective rather than the aggregation of

individual learnings and understandings. In a sense it approaches organisational learning from a "top-down" broader systems view rather than a bottom-up individual knowledge and cognition view. This leads to a series of further criticisms of which the most significant are linked in one way or another to the degree to which it not only privileged structure over agency but also treated as relatively unproblematic the allied notion of distributed leadership unconcerned by issues of the distribution of power.

In this sense at least one might reasonably describe Peter Senge as an optimist about the nature of organisational learning. My only personal recollection of him is distinctly more trivial but perhaps illustrative. I was one of at least 1000 in an audience he addressed at the annual Academy of Management conference in the US. He came onto the "stage" and announced that he wanted his session to be a "conversation", which seemed a little unlikely given the size of the audience. The whole session became more surreal when it became clear that the PA system was not working properly. Senge suggested that as the technicians were available in the hall to make adjustments those who were unable to hear clearly should raise their hands. This meant the most memorable aspect of the session was a sort of continual but randomised Mexican wave!

More recently Senge's work has been subjected to a number of trenchant criticisms, both on grounds of theory and practicability. In his synopsis of one of the most sustained critiques, Eijkman (2011) comments:

> In a most coherently argued theoretical critique of the LO concept, Jim Grieves (2008, p. 463) makes a strong case for jettisoning the idea of the learning organization, "on the grounds that it was an imaginative idea that has now run its course". The concept is "a metaphor too far"; so inherently flawed that it is best to abandon it altogether. He succinctly, and convincingly, argues that the concept of the learning organization is not only inherently contradictory (because organisations are about stable and ordered structures while learning is about transformation and change), but is also naively apolitical in that it ignores organizational power arrangements as well as, for instance, exploitative work practices and socio-cultural diversity (Weick and Westley 1996). The bottom line, as Jim Grieves (2008) points out, is that while its decidedly radical rhetoric draws people in, the actual concept of the LO is predicated on a conservative functionalist consensus-based view of the world which ignores the critical issues of politics, power, and difference. The concept discounts if not denies differences in power between a managerial elite and the bulk of ordinary employees; differences in the objectives of public, private, and voluntary organizations; and differences in stakeholder values and expectations. (2011: 166–167)

Grieves, to whom he refers, notes:

> the concept is caught in a tension between commissioned improvement, by which consultants sell its very intangibility, and a type of critical discourse that seeks to transcend the present. The ideal of the learning organization, to which organizations could aspire, is an impracticable and unobtainable myth precisely because it is constructed as a social fact. That is, as an entity with assumed objective evidence based knowledge. Consequently, it is committed to the fallacy of scientific discourse by pretending to be objectively neutral. It is weak in demonstrating the type of knowledge it seeks to pursue and it is unable to provide rules for its discourse which should clarify what type of problems it seeks to explore in the organizational world and what type of methodology it requires for doing so. This is my dangerous idea. To be provocative, this is why I believe we should now abandon the idea of the learning organization. (Grieves 2008: 472)

And Caldwell asserts there are inherent analytical flaws:

> [there are] two major analytical flaws of Senge's work. First, the learning organization rests on a flawed concept of 'structure' that cannot explain the organizing practices and learning processes by which systems as feedback structures come into being and change. Without a practice-based exploration of how learning organizations emerge and change through social practices, systems thinking lacks a credible theory of organizational change and organizational learning. Second, 'agency' as a form of practice, combining intentional action and iterative behaviour with unintended consequences, is subsumed within the behavioural regulation of system thinking structures, archetypes and cognitive models, thereby undermining an analysis of how human action and learning is produced and reproduced through social practices. (Caldwell 2012: 161)

Using Internal Data in a Systematic and Challenging Manner

The most basic model in communications theory is one in which the "sender" encodes the information and the "receiver" then decodes it. In the context of using internal data this raises two further questions: the extent to which the way in which the data has been encoded facilitates the receiver being able to use it effectively to address their specific issue of interest; and the degree to which the user has confidence in the authenticity of the data or indeed sometimes even the trustworthiness of the initial provider.

A very interesting study conducted on GPs by John Gabbay and Andrée le May found strong evidence of such considerations at work. They noted that:

Clinicians rarely accessed and used explicit evidence from research or
other sources directly, but relied on "mindlines" – collectively reinforced,
internalised, tacit guidelines. These were informed by some brief reading
but mainly by their own and their colleagues' experience, their interactions
with each other and with opinion leaders, patients, and pharmaceutical
representatives, and other sources of largely tacit knowledge. Mediated by
organisational demands and constraints, mindlines were iteratively negoti-
ated with a variety of key actors, often through a range of informal interactions in fluid "communities of practice", resulting in socially constructed
"knowledge in practice". (2004: 1013)

A somewhat different but related piece of empirical research in this area is
to be found in Levin and Cross (2004), who in their analysis of the strength
of ties and the mediating effect of trust, note that "the structural benefit of
weak ties emerged. This finding is consistent with prior research suggesting
that weak ties provide access to non-redundant information… competence-
based trust was especially important for the receipt of tacit knowledge"
(2004: 1477).

In a rather different context, many of those who have tried to apply reliable national data to key economic phenomena, such as the growth and
development of the services sector of the economy, have bemoaned the fact
that such data has often been collected and presented in the context of a very
historical view of the nature of a national economy so that, say, the scope of
the service sector in the Office of National Statistics (ONS) data has been
described as "a residual notion embracing all that is not agriculture, mining,
construction, utilities or manufacturing" (Castells and Aoyama 1994: 8). This
observation reflects a common problem with much data that is collected
over a significant period of time, be it within the organisation concerned or
on a wider scale; as the context changes the most appropriate way of classi-
fying and coding the data itself often changes. On the other hand, we need
to adopt stable categories if we are to be able to make valid longer-term
judgements about trends and changes.

Obviously, there is no generic way in which we can overcome this data
problem: as new situations emerge and the critical elements of the context
changes the issue of the appropriateness of the data structure, classification
and aggregations will inevitably arise. It should come as no surprise now to
readers of this book that the general recommendation is to ask further questions: Where does the data actually come from? How has it been coded and
classified? What is the specific nature of the respondents?

For instance, we can see the importance of diagnostic questioning in the
case of a widely used innovation survey which is generally known as the EU
Community Innovation survey. Obviously, how the elements of innovation

(both qualitative and quantitative) are measured at the firm level is rather critical yet often the survey is subject to various statistical analyses without much critical commentary on the nature of the measurement protocol. In fact, data collection takes place under what is known as the Oslo Protocol and depends on one or more key respondents. On this particular matter the protocol notes:

> Choosing the unit's most suitable respondent is particularly important in innovation surveys, as the questions are very specialised and can be answered by only a few people in the unit, often not those who complete other statistical questionnaires. In small units, managing directors are often good respondents. In larger units, several people are often involved, but one must be responsible for co-ordinating the replies. It is highly recommended to make a special effort to identify respondents by name before data collection starts. (OECD/Eurostat 2005: para 450)

Whilst this is undoubtedly good advice in terms of administering firm-level questionnaires in general, we need to recognise some of the accumulated research evidence about the relative reliability of estimates provided by key informants. Not only are there often issues around attribution bias and the other aspects raised by Malle, but also the concerns raised by Starbuck and Mezias (1996) that even those who should have available reliable quantitative answers to particular performance questions often appear to be unreliable informants.

Conclusion: Reprise on the Reflective Practitioner

Donald Schön himself elaborated on the two very different perspectives on the nature of management:

> The field of management has long been marked by a conflict between two competing views of professional knowledge. On the first view, the manager is a technician whose practice consists in applying to the everyday problems of his organization the principles and methods derived from management science. On the second, the manager is a craftsman, a practitioner of an art of managing that cannot be reduced to explicit rules and theories. The first view dates from the early decades of the twentieth century when the idea of professional management first came into good currency. The second has an even longer history, management having been understood as an art, a matter of skill and wisdom, long before it began to be understood as a body of techniques. But the first view has gained steadily in power. (1983: 236)

But he also saw the reflective professional manager as someone who in their own practice was able to achieve a synthesis between these two competing views:

> We might begin to heal the split in the field of management if we were to recognize that the art of management includes something like science in action. When practicing managers display artistry, they reveal their capacity to construct models of unique and changing situations, to design and execute on-the-spot experiments. They also reveal a capacity to reflect on the meanings of situations and the goals of action. A more comprehensive, useful, and reflective management science could be built by extending and elaborating on what skilful managers actually do. Practitioners might then become not only the users but the developers of management science. But extending and elaborating on artistry means reflecting on artistry and its limits, that is, on the ways in which managers do reflect-in-action and on the theories-in-use and organizational learning systems that constrain them. (Ibid.: 266)

In a number of ways Donald Schön's guidance directly relates to the central theme of this book and I will consider a number of ways in which skilful management practitioners can and do operate effectively.

3   EVIDENCE AND ENGAGEMENT

Economists and econometricians are redefining traditionally qualitative fields ... into quantitative domains. While this can offer new perspectives, it can also create a situation where journal articles become patently impenetrable – certainly to practitioners. (Peters 2012)

While round him voices rise and fall in oral goulash, Occam's call Leaches his vision of variety: He mumbles, "In all likelihood An n-dimensional matrix could succinctly summarise society" ... (Poor Kim Tarvesh – we must recall He's an economist after all), (Seth 1986: Stansa 11.10)

One way of characterising the crucial aspects of attempts to extend the role of analysis in informing management practice is around the twin notions of evidence and engagement. This reflects the concern that as much evidence as is feasible should be brought to bear in the analysis and that a process of engagement between the academic perspective and management practice should ensure that the evidence itself has impact on the choice under consideration.

Both of these aspects have been the subject of much scrutiny and debate over the last several years and this chapter will cover a number of key aspects of the debate and some of the underlying issues.

Evidence-Based Management

In academic circles there has been a determined attempt to give greater emphasis to what has become termed "Evidence-based management" (EBM). In the public policy field there has perhaps been an even wider espousal of the closely related notion of "evidence-based policy". In the UK particularly this was encouraged by Tony Blair's assertion that the key basis for policy interventions should be "what works". In practice, however, the actual nature of various key policy interventions has led some commentators to quip that it has been more a case of "policy-based evidence" in that prior policy choices seem to have dominated the selection of evidence itself.

It starts from the very reasonable assertion that we should ensure that previous experience and evidence both from our own organisation and others should inform current management choices. In practice, however, it would seem that the critical questions are often around what is to be regarded as relevant previous evidence as well as the ways in which it should be incorporated into the analysis of the current situation. Overall, it would seem it is much easier to identify bad and misleading practice rather than good and useful approaches! So much so indeed that some commentators have rather mischievously pointed out that the advocates of EBM often rely on assertion and faith to support their own case rather than sound evidence of the efficacy of their preferred approach!

As I have noted already, much of the problem can be put down to the fact that whilst it is often quite difficult to determine "what works" itself it is much more difficult to answer the further questions such as "why it works?" or "will it work again?" in a way which helps us to decide how far and in what way the past evidence can be applied to the current situation. As will be discussed later in the book, this means even with the best intentions we have to find a middle way between, on the one hand, focusing all our attention on one particular theory, instance or indeed analytical framework and, on the other, discounting all previous evidence as being of limited if not nil value. How is it that we can only ever expect to represent a series of partial pictures of the particular issue that we are considering?

The basic issue lies in the irreducible context dependency of the situation, which is reflected in the basic uncertainties in terms of both time and space.

Risk, Uncertainty and Profit

There are two approaches which perhaps give us a more applicable insight into the issues when we are operating on what might be termed a human scale. The first is a distinction which goes back a long way in our understanding of the way an economy operates – at least on what might be broadly termed a market basis – and clearly enunciated by Frank Knight in his seminal book *Risk, Uncertainty and Profit*, published in 1921, between "risk" and "uncertainty". The second is the development of a conceptual framework which helps us appreciate the necessary conditions to achieve a position of sustainable profits. Self-evidently the analytical framework employed is applicable more to the private sector but elements of it are also very applicable in a public and policy-making context.

Risk and Uncertainty

From a Knightian perspective:

> Uncertainty must be taken in a sense radically distinct from the familiar
> notion of Risk, from which it has never been properly separated. The term
> "risk," as loosely used in everyday speech and in economic discussion, really
> covers two things which, functionally at least, in their causal relations to the
> phenomena of economic organization, are categorically different. ... The
> essential fact is that "risk" means in some cases a quantity susceptible of
> measurement, while at other times it is something distinctly not of this
> character; and there are far-reaching and crucial differences in the bearings of
> the phenomenon depending on which of the two is really present and operat-
> ing. ... It will appear that a measurable uncertainty, or "risk" proper, as we
> shall use the term, is so far different from an immeasurable one that it is not
> in effect an uncertainty at all. We ... accordingly restrict the term "uncer-
> tainty" to cases of the non-quantitative type. (Knight 1921: 19)

Much more recently critical situations have arisen in which risk has been
confused with uncertainty, particularly in the financial crises related to the
failure of, first, LTCM in 1998. LTCM was founded in 1994 by John
Meriwether, the former vice-chairman and head of bond trading at Salomon
Brothers. Board of directors' members included Myron Scholes and Robert
C. Merton, who shared the 1997 Nobel Memorial Prize in Economic
Sciences. Initially successful with annualised returns of over 40 per cent
(after fees) in its first years, in 1998 it lost $4.6 billion in less than four months
following the Russian financial crisis and the fund closed in early 2000. The
second and more emblematic failure was, of course, the collapse of Lehman
Brothers in 2008, as a result primarily of the sub-prime mortgage crisis.

Rather ironically Lehman Brothers had contributed $100 million in the
previous LTCM bail-out and in a commentary on the earlier bailout in its
annual reports, Merrill Lynch observed that mathematical risk models "may
provide a greater sense of security than warranted; therefore, reliance on
these models should be limited". This was sound advice which was clearly
ignored by the financial markets in the subsequent decade.

Very broadly speaking, the existence of various forms of financial derivatives has meant that the effects of risk-adjusted valuation models could be
tested to "destruction" and that at least one problem with such models was
that they made strong normality assumptions in terms of the risk profiles
rather than "fat tail" assumptions to be discussed later in the book. To this
extent at least the demise of LTCM in 1998 bore some striking similarities to
that of Lehmann Brothers ten years later. What should we learn from not just
one but two major financial catastrophes?

Besides the strong evidence of some level of mendacity within the banks themselves, it has also been suggested that we need to be much more cautious about blind trust in computer valuation models, however sophisticated. When dealing with a large number of individual agents whose own actions are informed both by their intentions and their anticipation of others' likely behaviour we have a very complex modelling problem, which I will also come back to later in this book.

The Wisdom of Crowds (Sometimes)

Ever since the publication of James Surowiecki's book *The Wisdom of Crowds* in 2004, there has been much comment on his general, and rather counter-intuitive, assertion that in many instances the collective judgements of a large group of relatively ill-informed individuals is often better than that from a single or a much smaller group of well-informed experts. Interestingly, perhaps given the comments on the two financial crises above, Surowiecki writes the "Financial Page" column in the *New Yorker* and indeed commented on the opposite notion of "the madness of crowds" in his analysis of the more recent crash:

> Explanations for the crash often focussed on the hysteria and panic that periodically seem to seize investors. But the madness of crowds wasn't the whole story. In a healthy market, there are countercyclical forces—mechanisms and institutions that go against the general market trend and encourage diversity of thinking—that make it harder for feedback loops and vicious cycles to take hold. Lately, though, many of these institutions and mechanisms have become procyclical: instead of countering trends, they amplify them. (Surowiecki 2008)

To be fair, in his original book, he identified four conditions to be met:

- diversity (to ensure that different information is used to make the decision);

- independence (individual opinions aren't determined by the opinions of those around them);

- decentralisation (to ensure that no one person is dictating the decision and that people are using their own private information);

- aggregation (a way of summarising the different opinions into a collective view).

And it is very clear that in the financial crisis that these conditions – particularly that of independence – were not met. Indeed, even in relatively simple cases, the profit or loss that accrues from a particular action or choice is itself critically dependent on the expectations and choices of others. When it comes to business or management decisions, the benefits of independence would strongly suggest that genuinely decentralised decision making would be a more effective way of exploiting a wider and more localised knowledge base.

Isomorphism and Lemmings

A different perspective on the rather broad notion of the wisdom of crowds is provided if we consider more the wisdom of competitors – a much smaller but maybe better-informed group. A rather basic version of the "rational expectations" assumptions is that one's competitors are on average about as smart as each other and indeed as oneself. The average response across the range of competitors therefore provides a reasonable estimate of the scale and impact of any market opportunity or threat.

In the early 1980s, Paul DiMaggio and Walter Powell published a foundational work in the neo-institutional school of organisational theory (1983), in which they argued that institutional as well as competitive pressures produce sameness in many organisations, that sameness can be traced not only to the need to find efficient structures but also to the need for organisations to legitimate themselves in their institutional environments. It is no surprise therefore that we often observe such a phenomenon for which they coined the term "structural isomorphism". Their analysis clearly suggests this is not necessarily an irrational response at the individual firm level but it does ignore the additional benefits in competitive situations where there may be greater rewards to be gained from not behaving like "the pack" but taking a more individual approach.

Of course this is particularly true when the collective wisdom creates what might be described as lemming-like behaviour. In passing it is worth noting that the species lemmus lemmus has had a bad press. It would appear that the reputation of the species for collective mass suicide by herding themselves off sea cliffs owes much more to a Walt Disney natural-history film than actual empirical evidence, which suggests that lemmings are both quite good swimmers and in such situations are mainly responding to population pressures on their food resources.

Unexpected Events and Isolating Mechanisms

Indeed in competitive market situations we face an analytical dilemma: over-all we should reasonably conclude that the response of our competitors defines a collective estimate of the most likely opportunity but, on the other hand, the more the market is properly competitive the less likely we are to achieve economic rents or above average profits by merely imitating our competitors. After all, in much economic commentary it is often forgotten that a theoretical outcome of a situation of pure competition is indeed one in which no producers make any above average – that is the cost of capital – returns.

The route to such real returns is through what are termed contrarian strategies. A contrarian approach is one which regards the collective or conventional wisdom in any particular situation to be flawed and therefore an inappropriate basis for action. It can perhaps be most clearly identified in the area of financial investment where a contrarian believes that certain crowd behaviour among investors can lead to exploitable mis-pricings in securities markets. For example, widespread pessimism about a stock can drive a price so low that it overstates the company's risks, and understates its prospects for returning to profitability. Identifying and purchasing such distressed stocks, and selling them after the company recovers, can lead to above-average gains. Conversely, widespread optimism can result in unjustifiably high valuations that will eventually lead to drops, when those high expectations don't pan out.

Ideally, what we are trying to achieve is "controlled contrarianism" where we take the general notion of the conventional wisdom seriously but at the same time recognise that we are searching for specific situations where there is good reason to believe that the conventional wisdom is flawed. On top of this we need to always be aware of what Rumelt originally referred to as "isolating mechanisms", which provide a basis to ensure that our choices are made in a way in which it is difficult for our competitors to directly imitate. As Rumelt notes:

> Thus Table [3.1] presents a simple theory of strategy: a firm's strategy may be explained in terms of the unexpected events that created (or will create) potential rents together with the isolating mechanisms that (will) act to preserve them. If either element of the explanation is missing, the analysis is inadequate. (1984: 568)

Hence, we need to focus on twin questions: On what basis do we believe that our specific perspective is both counter to the conventional wisdom but also correct? In what ways can we temporally protect ourselves from imitation by our competitors if we turn out to be right?

Table 3.1   Elements of strategic position

Sources of Potential Rents	Isolating Mechanisms
Changes in technology	Causal ambiguity
Changes in relative prices	Specialised assets
Changes in consumer tastes	Switching and search costs
Changes in law, tax, and regulation	Consumer and producer learning
Discoveries and inventions	Team-embodied skills
	Unique resources
	Special information
	Patents and trademarks
	Reputation and image
	Legal restrictions on entry

Source: (Copyright © 1984 Richard Rumelt)

Dialectic, Rhetoric and Consensus

In practice, the analytical approach outlined above calls for some form of process or procedure which allows the participants to explore the case for action along both the dimensions of credibility and sustainability. In the private-sector case sustainability may be primarily around achieving relative isolation from competitive response, whilst in the public sector it is often around stability in user requirements and sustaining public support as outlined in the notion of "public value" developed by Mark Moore (1995).

This points us in the direction of a process which is both dialectical in nature and directed towards achieving some form of consensus. Dialectic (also dialectics and the dialectical method) is a method of argument for resolving disagreement that has been central to Indian and European philosophy since antiquity. The word dialectic originated in Ancient Greece, and was made popular by Plato in the Socratic dialogues. The basic method is dialogue between two or more people, holding different points of view about a subject, who wish to establish the truth with reasoned arguments. Dialectics is to be seen as different from debate, wherein the debaters are committed to their points of view, and mean to win the debate, either by proving their argument correct, or proving the opponent's argument incorrect – thus, either a judge or a jury must decide who wins the debate. Dialectics is also different from rhetoric, wherein the speaker uses logos, pathos or ethos to persuade listeners to take their side of the argument.

In practice, the clear philosophical distinction between a formal dialectical approach and the application of rhetoric is rarely reflected in the actual process of making decisions but there is a clear need to have a significant component of the dialectic built in to the overall process.

Formalising the Dialectic Approach

Advocacy of a formalised dialectic approach in strategic planning goes back to the late sixties and in particular an article by Richard Mason called "A Dialectical Approach to Strategic Planning", in which he concluded:

> there is a need for a planning technique which serves to "test" the assumptions of a plan by exposing "hidden" assumptions and, ideally, by suggesting new and potentially more relevant assumptions upon which the manager can base his future plan. It was argued that the traditional "expert approach" to planning fails to adequately test assumptions and that the Devil's Advocate approach, while in a sense testing assumptions, also tends to destroy the plan without replacing it with an improved plan. Hegel's triad-thesis, antithesis and synthesis, was drawn upon in order to design a dialectical approach to planning that averted the deficiencies of both the expert and Devil's Advocate approaches. It was proposed that the resulting counterplanning problem technique would stimulate a new and embroadened concept of the planning problem, the synthesis. (1969: B413)

However, it would perhaps be fair to say that it has remained a minority taste! Mainstream practice seems to have remained focused on either the expert approach, often supplemented by management consultants, or a process of general questioning and challenge more like the devil's advocate procedure.

It may be that the reason for this lack of general development is the organisational and individual challenges of introducing what Mason and others would have regarded as a true dialectical inquiry approach and that it is more realistic and sustainable to refine a process grounded more on a mixture of expert assessment and critical challenge.

The Nature of Consensus

Most discussions around the notion of consensus and particularly consensus decision making tend to be in the context of wider issues such as macro-economics, public policy or social activism. However, in the more restricted context of organisational decision making it is still important to recognise some critical issues.

In particular, it is generally agreed that consensus seeks to improve solidarity in the long run. Accordingly, it should not be confused with unanimity in the immediate situation which is often a symptom of groupthink. Studies of effective consensus process usually indicate a shunning of unanimity or "illusion of unanimity" that does not hold up as a group comes under real-world pressure and dissent reappears.

Whatever one thinks of the merits of seeking a unanimous agreement in a particular situation, in general unanimous, or apparently unanimous, decisions have numerous drawbacks. They may be symptoms of a systemic bias, a rigged process (where an agenda is not published in advance or changed when it becomes clear who is present to consent), fear of speaking one's mind, a lack of creativity (to suggest alternatives) or even a lack of courage (to go further along the same road to a more extreme solution that would not achieve unanimous consent).

Most models of consensus specifically exclude uniformly unanimous decisions and require at least documentation of minority concerns. Some state clearly that unanimity is not consensus but rather evidence of intimidation, lack of imagination, lack of courage, failure to include all voices, or deliberate exclusion of the contrary views. Indeed it is worth recalling the four prior process conditions within the notion of the "wisdom of crowds": diversity, independence, decentralisation and aggregation.

Traditions for Sustainable Transformation

The analysis above links quite closely with a detailed comparative and historical case study on those rare UK organisations in the private sector that have continued to perform at high levels over an extended period of time even as they substantially modify their strategies.

The researchers identified the need to develop what they called "traditions for transformation", to enable companies to sustain high performance and transform their strategies based on the need to foster alternative management coalitions and value constructive tension and challenges to the status quo. Two of the eight recommendations that they developed for accelerating these changes are particularly relevant to our analysis at this point:

Ensure that decision making allows for dissent. There's a fundamental difference between an organization built to maintain consensus around a dominant logic and one where managers naturally challenge it. Butler, the former Unilever director, recognized that Unilever "had many layers of people that were clever enough to think of many reasons why a new idea wouldn't work." Tesco's Malpas, on the other hand, described Tesco as an organization where new ideas took on momentum across different levels of managers: "You have bright people who have ideas and want to mold the business their way, so an initiative gets to the boss at the next level who embraces it, and it becomes his scheme; it gets to the next level and he embraces it, and it becomes his scheme. How the hell do you stop it?" A decision-making process that allows for dissent and challenge works only among people who can live with, and indeed welcome, challenge.

Create enabling structures that encourage tension. Creative tension between opposing views can also be fostered structurally. When Smith & Nephew bought an R&D facility from another company, and when Tesco gave responsibility for demographic profiling to the marketing department rather than the real estate department, the companies ensured that there would be new and different perspectives. Such changes alone will not guarantee that alternative views will be heard and taken seriously — that will depend on the relevance of the views and who in the organization promotes them. But changing the structure can make a difference in how people see ideas internally. (From Johnson et al. 2012: 31)

Engagement and Management: Scientific Knowledge and Folk Wisdom

So far this chapter has focused more on general rules and theoretical frameworks for analysis of the evidence for a particular course of action but I now return to examine the essential context dependent elements of any action choice.

The issue of context dependency also arises in a rather different form when we consider what might be termed the nature of managerial knowledge. Chia and Holt (2008) have argued that much of the problem of relevance of business-school knowledge can be explained by the privileging of what they term management-by-representation over management-by-exemplification. However, their critique goes beyond the analysis here. They combine a number of elements to argue that their preferred form of knowledge representation portrays knowledge in the moment rather than reflection and reflexivity and focuses on the need for both more inductive reasoning and also a wider appreciation of context.

Street Mathematics and the Issue of Wider Context

The idea of management knowledge as more akin to folk wisdom links to the notion of vernacular knowledge. Whilst the more detailed analysis of "vernacular knowledge" has often been restricted to the activities of anthropologists looking at primitive or exotic tribes, it is also to be found in some education research. One particularly interesting area is that of everyday mathematics as studied by Lave (1988) amongst shoppers and in so-called "street mathematics" (Nunes et al. 1993).

"Street mathematics" can be seen as a form of vernacular knowledge which is not just a very focused set of procedures for dealing with particular practical problems but also capable of some degree of extension and implicit generalisation. The claim is not that in "street mathematics" there is an equivalent degree of formalisation and conceptual complexity as compared with the more codified "school mathematics" but that the boundary between the two is less rigid than is often assumed. In this sense "street mathematics" could be seen as to some degree an alternative form of codification of mathematical knowledge compared with the more "common" form of mathematics as it is taught in schools.

Interestingly and importantly there is also an extent to which these two forms of knowledge can interact in unexpected ways. For instance, Nunes et al. note that an apparently simple arithmetical reasoning question such as "There are 10 birds on a line, two are shot, how many remain?" requires a form of suspension of practical knowledge to arrive at the answer eight – in most normal circumstances the remaining birds would have flown away!

The process whereby knowledge derived from practical problem solving becomes codified and generalised might be seen as analogous to the development of what has been termed folk wisdom in management practice. Two particular aspects of this analogy are of interest: the nature of formalisation and the context dependency of experience. Not surprisingly the formalisation of management problems represented by most econometric and statistical modelling reflects a very similar basic approach to that used in "school mathematics", and therefore we might expect that just as with street mathematics the formalisation implicit in folk understanding of management would be quite different. However, we need to be aware that the effects of formalisation and the effects of context specificity are often confounded in many of the critiques of "school mathematics":

> 'Everyday mathematics' as it is found in Lave's studies and, we would argue, in other comparable studies, appears to postulate two different kinds of reasoning, those of a 'formal' sort which are taught in school, and those of an 'informal' sort which grow up wild (to borrow from Levi-Strauss). We hold that this postulate is stretched, if not invalid, depending on a very narrow interpretation of 'what is taught in school' contrasting with a very liberal one of what is 'developed independently of school mathematics.' We do not deny the differences between the two

situations, for example, between doing formal school tests (at one pole) and supermarket shopping or carpentry (at the other), but argue that the differences are precisely there: in the situations. (Greiffenhagen and Sharrock 2008: 15)

To some extent certain ethnographic and qualitative studies of managers and management provide some hints as to the nature of this alternative formalisation. We might note, for instance, Watson's comments that:

managerial competence or effectiveness is indeed a subtle, multi-faceted and context-bound thing. It does not just involve skills and attitudes, but encompasses knowledge even if that knowledge is stored in the form of intuitions and is manifested in what Donald Schön calls reflection-in-action. (1994: 223)

Whilst in a quantitative framework we attempt to characterise context with a number of specific variables, this again rarely equates with the way in which individual managers would define the specifics of the situation they face. In such situations it is therefore hardly surprising that the nature of what might be called knowledge transfer is individual and idiosyncratic, and often based on stories and anecdotes. I will return in much more detail to the issue of storytelling later in the book.

Folk Wisdom and Common Sense

Oaksford and Chater (1998, 2002) have consistently argued against the emphasis on the principles of logical inference in understanding the nature of human thought. Their central proposition is that we need to shift our perspective on human reasoning towards a probabilistic perspective to recognise the inherent uncertainties of thought and action. They start from the basic proposition that the key characteristic of folk theories is the degree to which they generate inferences that are defeasible, in other words capable of being readily defeated by further information. This is in contrast to the nature of scientific inference that requires a much higher level of robustness to further information. Hence, they argue that judged against normal criteria, folk theories will always be bad science in domains that are well understood scientifically but elsewhere:

Folk theories must allow us to make the best possible sense of our everyday world and guide our actions as successfully as possible: to do this they must face up to the full complexity of the everyday world, which, we

suggest science rightly prefers to avoid ... [folk theories] must deal with
domains in which good science is more or less impossible and rough and
ready generalisations must suffice. Thus the fact that folk explanations do
not stand up to scientific scrutiny should not be viewed as a criticism of
folk theories: it is an inevitable consequence of the fact that folk theories
must venture where science cannot. (1998: 166–167)

They also link their overall analysis to the extent to which the development
of knowledge through common sense is more appropriately seen as an
inductive rather than a deductive process, as well as recognising the link to
a number of issues originally developed by Simon under the general framework of bounded rationality. The related Simon proposal that procedural
rationality was a more appropriate objective in complex situations than
substantive rationality also underpins the design-science approach (van
Aken 2005) which is argued to be one route available to improve the practice
relevance of management research.

It is indeed true that in systems terms the application of procedural rules
is likely to be underdetermining of outcomes compared with substantive
rules. However, as Hahn and Chater (1998) remind us, if the basic elements
of either types of rule remain ambiguous it may just be that we achieve
apparent validity only because the evidential conditions for refutation of the
rule are less well defined.

This leads to more of a dual-process perspective on the nature of choice
making where analytical and intuitive processes are seen as distinct and
therefore competing rationalities which can perhaps reflect the Oaksfield
and Chater distinction between "science" and "folk theories".

The Nature of Academic Practice: Statistical Analysis and Evidential Claims

Oaksfield and Chater (2002) provide a closely worded and logical argument
that demonstrates a common problem in much empirical work around
human cognition and behaviour, which also bedevilled much of the research
in management, to the extent that it is perfectly understandable that, as
Huberman (1990: 378) notes, practitioners often "felt that social scientific
research was half common sense and half nonsense". It should, however, be
noted that this expression or at least the equivalent is to be found rather
earlier in Gilbert (1982: 56), where he notes wryly that when he was awarded
his PhD in the 1940s his mother "scornfully described psychology as half
nonsense and half common sense".

In response to this implicit dilemma, management researchers have taken one of two dominant methodological routes. The first is what might be seen as an effort to extend the understanding that is usually encompassed within the notion of "common sense". As others have of course commented before, such "common sense" is not necessarily that common and is often actually rather ambiguous. Equally, a re-reading of "That's Interesting" (Davis 1971) helps to provide a framework within which to locate more systematically the conditions under which we may expect to avoid the "just common sense" response. Such an approach has in general required getting close to manage-ment practice, often subjecting it to direct observation, and then inducing more general principles. Given the inevitable context dependency of much managerial practice there is a danger that much of this research is then seen as "just common sense", although there are indeed classic studies that clearly transcend this critique such as Weick (1993) in the Mann Gulch Disaster.

In the most recent manifestation of the debate around practice–research "dichotomy" in management research, we have yet again wit-nessed a set of propositions which broadly span from a view that these two worlds are self-contained and effectively incommensurate (Kieser and Leiner 2009) to the view that they are already substantially inter-penetrated by the application of particular tools, such as the structured use of empirical evidence particularly in areas such as recruitment and appraisal (Hodgkinson and Rousseau 2009) or design science (Starkey et al. 2009). If perhaps we were to apply a more practice-based perspec-tive to our own research activity we might expect that the search for a clear and unambiguous answer to the question "Is there a divide?" is likely to be both context specific and contingent. Of course it must be admitted that many of the contributors to this (academic) debate them-selves recognise that they occupy the rather grey area in the middle of the dichotomy (Fincham and Clark 2009) but perhaps also see the advan-tages of the dialectical rhetoric, at least in terms of stereotyping the position of the "other".

Indeed, the bald assertion that "bridging ... is already happening" in the title of the paper by Hodgkinson and Rousseau (2009) is accompanied by an admission that two key assertions by the "other side" have validity: the fact that the overall issue is more than just a question of language and style differences and the extent to which both key groups, academics and prac-titioners, have a socially constructed and relatively homogeneous view of the other.

Equally, Kieser and Leiner (2009) imply in the title of their paper that the "gap ... is unbridgeable" but go on to define the nature of such a bridge in a particular way which they equate very much with the so-called linear model; after all, to be literal, at least most bridges allow two-way traffic! Rasche and Behnam (2009) provide a rather more nuanced interpretation of both the nature of the relationship between the two systems and also the application of Luhmann's framework. They focus more on the observation that that given the relative separateness of the worlds of practice and academe, interactions between the two are best seen as "irritations". So for such "irritations" to have any effect on practice it is necessary for the practice world to act on the fiction that the knowledge is indeed relevant. By working on the knowledge in this way it does indeed become relevant but not necessarily in the way in which the academic originators intended or expected.

> Research can be relevant. However, relevance is nothing that is decided by academics or practitioner–academics teams prior to application. Research relevance is decided where it occurs: in the system of practice. To produce relevance we do not need bridges or translations but insightful practitioners who do not quickly follow the latest management fad and instead understand the necessary "emptiness" (i.e., noncontext-specific nature) of scientific knowledge as an opportunity to modify this knowledge according to their specific circumstances. (Rasche and Behnam 2009: 249)

Learning from the Clinical Medical Experience of Evidence-Based Practice

As discussed earlier, there has recently been a resurgence of interest in evidence-based management even in such august practice journals as the *Harvard Business Review*. Much emphasis is given to experience in the clinical medical field and indeed some of the mechanisms available for consolidation and comparison of empirical evidence are undoubtedly impressive (compared to our own in management!), such as the Cochrane Collaboration.

The Cochrane Collaboration (2013) describes itself as:

> an international network of more than 28,000 dedicated people from over 100 countries. We work together to help healthcare providers, policy-makers, patients, their advocates and carers, make well-informed decisions about health care, by preparing, updating, and promoting the accessibility of Cochrane Reviews – over 5,000 so far, published online in the Cochrane Database of Systematic Reviews, part of The Cochrane Library. We also prepare the largest collection of records of randomised

controlled trials in the world, called CENTRAL, published as part of
The Cochrane Library.

However, existing experience in this so-called exemplar area can be used to
further challenge the apparent assumption that its application is unproblematic. The disembodied meta analysis of data, which underlies proposals
for greater attention to the role of systematic reviews based on the medical
experience in the management field (Tranfield et al. 2003) can be balanced,
somewhat ironically, with significant discussions in the health field as
to the extent to which evidence-based improvements can be difficult to
achieve in practice because of the problems of organisational change (Grol
and Grimshaw 2003).

In the medical context we can, at least in principle, organise an experiment in which the treatment group receives the intervention and the
control group does not. A large enough sample will ensure that even a
small effect on outcomes can be measured and identified as statistically
significant.

Indeed, despite a relatively clear agreement on what actually consti-
tutes legitimate evidence (the gold standard of the double blind experimental design) and an expert-informed evaluation agency (the UK
National Institute for Health and Care Excellence – NICE), issues arise
about the degree to which individual variation should be recognised let
alone the way in which costs and benefits should be valued. Life gets
more difficult when we wish to test the efficacy of particular interventions. At first pass we can compare relative costs per average level of
improvement, but how can we be sure the same patients are benefiting in
both cases? Of course we cannot do so with complete confidence so we
rely on proxies.[1]

The relatively recent public debates about the recommendation by NICE
that three Alzheimer's drugs – Aricept, Exelon and Reminyl – should only
be available on the National Health Service (NHS) to patients with moderate
symptoms, reveals clearly the difficulty of using even well-structured evidence to come to an unambiguous conclusion. On top of this there is an
active methodological and statistical debate about the nature and scale of the
placebo effect or perhaps more correctly, the placebo response (Kienle and
Kiene 1997; Hróbjartsson and Gøtzsche 2006; Miller and Rosenstein 2006).
No wonder Gabbay and Le May (2004) draw our attention to the unpredict-
able, non-linear and contingent nature of research impact on practice even
amongst medical professionals.

---

[1]For a much fuller analysis of some of the underlying issues with the "double-blind"
design see Byrne (2002).

From Medical to Social Science

In the social sciences we face a much more substantial problem in handling empirical evidence. In most cases the "best" we can do analogous to the double-blind experiment is based on some form of natural experiment accompanied by that well-known process of statistical inference. A basic description of the process of statistical inference is provided by the *Encyclopædia Britannica*:

> Economists typically begin by describing the area under study according to what they feel to be important. Then they construct a "model" of the real world, deliberately repressing some of its features and emphasising others; they abstract, isolate, and simplify, thus imposing order on a world that at first glance appeared disorderly. Having evolved an admittedly unrealistic representation of the real world, they then manipulate the model by a process of logical deduction, arriving eventually at some prediction or implication that is of general significance. At this point, they return to the real world to see whether or not the prediction is borne out by observed events.

Certainly, in a world in which most of the relevant outcome variables are substantially influenced by factors we neither control nor measure and where context is crucially important, statistical inference provides us with a way of simplifying in an intellectually defensible yet also often relatively unhelpful manner.

It is by definition most useful when we are genuinely interested in the aggregate performance of the average but even here we need to be careful in interpretation since it is often the case that the average is more a statistical artefact rather than a realistic mode. Often we are interested more in the specific than the general but in a high variance world the broader statistical measures such as variance itself tell us little.

Overall it may be much more pragmatic to assume that some form of policy and practice relevance is more likely to be achieved in one of the ways identified by Weiss (1968) in her analysis of social science research utilisation as related to what she termed "enlightenment" rather than, for instance, "problem solving". Similarly, with his fine ability to encapsulate the whole argument in the title of a paper, Aaron Wildavsky with Jack Knott (1980) used the title "If Dissemination Is the Solution, What Is the Problem?"

In a wider, comprehensive and critical evaluation of the "evidence-based movement", Morrell (2008) considers the extent to which the movement has attempted to define relevance as synonymous with this particular methodology. He notes that much of the espousal of the general approach is more about the effective use of language and narrative itself rather than a more substantial attempt to build on an established scientific methodology; as he terms it perhaps a case of physician envy rather than physics envy!

Indeed, there is a rather interesting partial symmetry between the way in which Morrell critically deconstructs the attempt to establish evidence-based management as the way to achieve relevance, at least in policy if not practice terms, and the way McCloskey has consistently challenged the economics discipline seen to many in social sciences as the most evident source of disciplinary rigour. McCloskey (1986, 1994) argues that the legitimation of a particular form of generally quantitative analysis is to be seen as, no more and no less than, an effective rhetorical device. Rigour, by implication therefore, is not to be seen, in a disciplinary sense, as some form of objective criterion but the outcome of a wider political debate within a discipline about the preferred forms of argumentation.

Return to Managerial Relevance and the Issue of Timeliness

If we go back to the initial framing comments in the debate then it is clear that much of the contradiction might have been better framed in terms of the nature of knowledge and knowledge claims alongside their usefulness in a managerial context.

As we have seen, the notion of relevance itself cannot be treated as an objective construct independent of a definition of the recipients, their interests, role and context. In a similar vein Starkey and Madan (2001) previously recognised the centrality of some notion of stakeholders in any attempt to operationalise usefulness. Not surprisingly, if we subject any particular definition to critical scrutiny we also have to recognise that there is no reliable measure of what might be termed general relevance.

This is even truer when we consider the extent to which context dependency often gets extended into some notion of the criticality of the present. Because the accumulation of knowledge and the enactment of practice takes place in very different time cycles it is often common to imply if not indeed assert that somehow only the most recent or contemporaneous research can yield any relevant insight. We can recognise various processes which might help to overcome both the substantive problems underlying these different time cycles. One obvious approach is to pretty much collapse the academic cycle-time into the practice cycle-time by using a process of small group discussions amongst a set of participants consisting of a mixture of academics and practitioners and using a very constrained period for further research between two such meetings (see Schiele et al. 2012).

An alternative approach is to see the whole process as a joint development activity based on a sequence of meetings which identify important issues at each stage and then reconvene with new relevant information provided by all parties. Finally, we can intentionally look for aspects where we might expect there to be much less dramatic changes in short time periods and build on our understanding of these to address what is initially seen as a novel problem.

Overall, however, attention should be focused on a set of related but distinct elements, which themselves start from a less rigid application of the Luhmann notion of two systems.[2] In doing so we would continue to recognise that both the academic and the practice systems have their own processes of knowledge generation and practice development. This means we must consider as much the relationship between practice-knowledge generation and research practice as the relationship between research-knowledge generation and, in our case, managerial practice.

Conclusion: Getting the Best out of Engagement

Any conclusion which repeated a utopian perspective that all empirical evidence should be considered and there should be full integration between the perspectives of practitioners, policy makers and academics would be highly naive and indeed probably more dystopian than utopian. One of my practitioner colleagues espouses the view that whilst managers have to get on and do things (or indeed stop things) in a complex and messy world, academics are more concerned about proving themselves right and others wrong on fine points of rather esoteric research.

Whilst we are all prey to stereotypes, my own perspective is more along the lines of the latter view. Engagement between theory and practice has significant benefits but only where it works. This means management academics need to prepare the ground beforehand – or what my colleagues in industrial relations used to call "attitude structuring" – as well as represent the empirical evidence in an appropriate manner. On top of this some form of critical distance needs to be maintained between academe and practice even whilst searching to achieve constructive engagement.

---

[2]An alternative perspective which places much more emphasis on the long-run permeability of such system boundaries between disciplines and by extension between academe and practice is to be found in Abbott (2001b).

Finally, we need to recognise that there are very often other parties involved in such debates, in particular in the private sector, management consultancies and in the public sector think tanks. Indeed, management consultancies have extended their reach considerably into the public sector as well. This can have two dysfunctional consequences in terms of the issues we have discussed in this chapter. It can be seen as an excuse for academics who otherwise would find any engagement with practice uncomfortable and at the same time transfer the responsibility to communicate the evidence to a group more concerned about what the client wishes to hear rather than any assessment of the robustness of the empirical conclusions.

4   Tools for Thinking

We find that most aspects of life and its interactions with its surroundings all interconnected into complexes. No powerful action can be expected to have only one consequence, confined to the thing it was primarily directed at. It is almost bound to affect lots of other things as well. Our old-fashioned common sense has not had to face such situations before, and is not well adapted to doing so. We need nowadays to be able to think not just about simple processes but about complex systems. (Waddington 1977: xii)

Introduction: Comparing Perspectives in 1975 and 2009

In 1977, a book entitled *Tools for Thought* was published by Paladin. However, the author, C.H. Waddington, had died on the 26 September 1975 shortly after completing his revisions but before he was able to see the proofs. Much more recently, in 2009, Mike Pidd, at Lancaster, wrote the third edition of his book entitled *Tools for Thinking*, which in broad terms covers a very similar set of themes to *Tools for Thought*. To illustrate this consider the following quotation from Waddington's introduction:

We have been trained to think, or have accepted as common sense, that what goes on around us can usually be understood as some set of simple causal sequences in which, for instance, A causes B and B then B causes C, then C causes D and so on. This is only good enough when A causes B but has very little other effect on anything else, and similarly the overwhelmingly most important effect of B is to cause C. Many of our own individual actions still have this character. That is really because they are in some ways relatively feeble compared to the whole mass of things and processes of which they are part. The change which has occurred, or is occurring now, is that the effects of human societies on their surroundings are now so powerful that it is no longer adequate to concentrate on the primary effects and neglect all secondary influences. (1977: xi–xii)

And compare it with the following from the first page of Pidd's initial chapter:

Our lives are increasingly complex, whether we consider only our individual lives, sharing with our families or working in some kind of organization.

Those of us in the Western world depend on artificial aids for our survival. We travel long distances by car, boat or plane; we cook food on devices fuelled by gas or electricity; and we take for granted that computers enable us to communicate instantly across the globe. We are very much part of an interconnected world in which our decisions and those of others can have major consequences for us and for other people. This became very clear in the second half of 2008, when over liberal availability of credit, reckless lending, little understood and complex financial instruments and an out of control bonus culture, led to the effective insolvency of large banks and finance houses. These symptoms, which first appeared in the USA and the UK, quickly affected all nations in our global economy and then blighted the lives of millions, possibly billions. We live in a complex, fast moving and highly interconnected world in which we must make better use of resources or face a very uncertain future. (2009: 3)

However, when it comes to the detail of the tools themselves the emphasis in the two books is significantly different. Waddington focuses on broad illustrations to reinforce the text in representing the nature of the problem. Indeed, he goes so far as to say:

This book is therefore provided with a large number of diagrams. These are not intended to express facts about quantities of things, like the usual graphs one sees in scientific books. They are strictly illustrations of the ideas, and their purpose is to stimulate your imagination to seize the gist of what an idea is about. They are therefore not drawn in a way that has become conventional for illustrations in technical or most other intellectual books, but have been executed by someone whose main interests are in painting and design. (1977: xiii)

Pidd, on the other hand, gives an altogether more detailed and comprehensive coverage of a number of key analytical approaches in management science. In this chapter I will err towards the Waddington approach, particularly in the terms that Waddington says of his audience: "[the book] demands no mathematics from its readers!" Pidd's book focuses primary attention on what might be called the practice of modelling: interpretive, mathematical and logical, and also assessment and validation, whilst Waddington is more concerned with more generic issues of systems: complexity, structures, processes, feedback, stabilisation and communication. However, not surprisingly Waddington overlaps with Pidd on the issues he raises for analysing systems and Pidd overlaps somewhat with the more philosophical issues with which Waddington starts his book. Even here, however, Waddington is determined not to be over-serious. He starts his first chapter on philosophies:

'For heaven's sake' you'll say 'just how systematic you have to try to be? Let's skip this and get on to something that matters'. Okay we could, but you'd come back to it. Philosophy does matter. It matters particularly to those – the great majority of mankind – whose life is devoted to bringing about changes of some kind or other in the world surrounding them even if these effects are no more important than selling more of Messrs. X's refrigerators than Messrs Y succeeds in unloading on to the market. (1977: 15)

Complexity and Chaos

Waddington's interest in complexity marks an early point in the development of what has become a key theme in much more recent writing about the nature of organisations, market systems and the range of managerial challenges. In the process the treatment of complexity, and its close cousin chaos, has varied between the purely analogical to the highly systematic informed by rigorous analysis and mathematical modelling. However, it is also important to note that there is often a tension between these two perspectives in practice. The best way I can illustrate this from my own experience harks back to the early nineties and a series of three research workshops co-organised by Professor David Rand and myself between the Mathematics Department and the Business School at Warwick to discuss and develop joint approaches in the area of complexity and chaos. After the workshops, which made rather little progress but which were also very good natured, he and I were reviewing what we had or had not achieved. He summarised it as, roughly, the fact that he saw my colleagues in the business school as wishing to model complex systems in which the individual "particles" (i.e. people) had both intentions for themselves and were forced to anticipate the behaviour of others. As an expert on modelling amongst other things turbulent flow in fluids, his comment was that this was "particularly difficult"! Good advice indeed.

It might therefore be more practical to look specifically at particular aspects rather than try to build a single comprehensive and integrated approach. This is, of course, a common strategy when facing complex systems: to go for some form of simplification and hierarchical modularity.

Herb Simon (1969b) emphasised above all that hierarchy was something profoundly natural. He viewed hierarchy as a general principle of complex structures – and not just of particular complex structures but of complexity in general. Hierarchy, he argued, emerges almost inevitably through a wide variety of evolutionary processes, for the simple reason that hierarchical structures are stable. To motivate this deep idea, he offered his most important example of hierarchy, a "parable" about imaginary watchmakers named Hora and Tempus. According to the story, both watchmakers were equally skilled, but only one of them, Hora, prospered. The difference between them lay in the design of their watches. Each design involved 1000 elementary components, but the similarity ended there. Tempus' watches were not hierarchical; they were assembled one component at a time. Hora's watches, by contrast, were organised into hierarchical sub-assemblies whose "span" was ten – he would combine ten elementary components into small subassemblies, and then he would combine ten sub-assemblies into larger sub-assemblies, and these in turn could be combined to make a complete watch.

The difference between the two watchmakers' designs became crucial in the wider context of their lives as artisans. Customers would call them on the phone, and when the phone rang they would be compelled to abandon their current assembly, which would fall apart. These interruptions did not bother Hora, who lost at most ten units of work: whatever sub-assembly he happened to be working on. Tempus, however, would lose (on average) much more: an entire partly assembled watch would fall apart. If interruptions are at all common, it can easily be shown that Hora will complete many more watches than Tempus.

The Structure of Systems: The Ubiquitous Tree

The notion of a tree diagram as a form of representation of the underlying structure of any particular system is very common. The form in which we will often see it is in terms of the hierarchical structure such as found in organograms for specific organisations.

Figure 4.1 is a representation of a relatively simple hierarchy. It is, of course, based on the obvious strong hierarchy found in a military structure, but following Waddington introduces some degree of roughness to emphasise that it is still a particular representation rather than overall reality. After all, Helmuth von Moltke the Elder – who was both a disciple of Von Clausewitz and who studied Napoleon's battles – asserted that "no military strategy survives the battle".

Moltke had worked out the conditions for the movement and supply of an army. Only one army corps could be moved along one road in the same day; to put two or three corps on the same road meant that the rear corps could not be made use of in a battle at the front. Several corps stationed close together in a small area could not be fed for more than a day or two. Accordingly, he inferred that the essence of strategy lay in arrangements for the separation of the corps for marching and their concentration in time for battle. In order to make a large army manageable, it must be broken up into separate armies or groups of corps, each group under a commander authorised to regulate its movements and action subject to the instructions of the commander-in-chief as regards the direction and purpose of its operations.

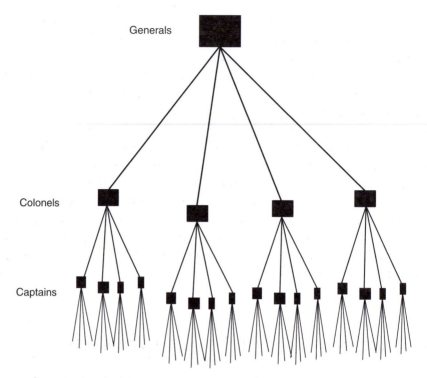

Figure 4.1   A simple hierarchy (after waddington)

© Robin Wensley

> Moltke's main thesis was that military strategy had to be understood as a
> system of options since only the beginning of a military operation was
> plannable. As a result, he considered the main task of military leaders to
> consist in the extensive preparation of all possible outcomes. His thesis can
> be summed up by two statements, one famous and one less so, translated
> into English as "No plan of operations extends with certainty beyond the
> first encounter with the enemy's main strength" (or "no plan survives
> contact with the enemy") and "Strategy is a system of expedients."
> (http://en.wikipedia.org/wiki/Helmuth_von_Moltke_the_Elder)

The latter of these aphorisms perhaps needs some further translation in
terms of modern usage; his use of expedients really combines an emphasis on making specific choices that are both advantageous in terms of
the overall objectives and pragmatic in terms of the specific situation at the
particular time and place.

In a number of ways von Molke's approach resonates rather well with
much more recent attempts in large complex organisations to achieve a
degree of both coherence and local entrepreneurship. He was in no sense an
anti-planner but recognised that once battle was joined local units had to

have the capacity and authority to act according to the local circumstances they confronted. In a rare reference to his approach to be found in a business-management journal, Hans Hinterhuber and Wolfgang Popp note that:

> Perhaps the greatest strategist of all time was not a business executive but a general. Helmuth von Moltke, chief of the Prussian and German general staffs from 1858 to 1888, issued "directives" to his officers rather than specific commands. These guidelines for autonomous decision making encouraged Moltke's subordinates to show individual initiative. … according to Moltke, strategy is applied common sense and cannot be taught … but even if managers have the potential to be good strategists, they must develop and hone their natural talents. And CEOs and top management can help by identifying and promoting such talents in their employees. Strategic managers provide subordinates with general guidelines, just as Helmuth von Moltke issued directives to his officers. And outstanding entrepreneurs create a corporate culture in which their vision, philosophy, and business strategies are implemented by employees who think independently. (1992: 105–108)

Von Moltke's approach might well be seen as rather more appropriate in many corporate management contexts than the more popular ones of Sun Tsu, more focused on unnerving and misleading the enemy, von Clausewitz, more concerned with the massing of resources to confront the enemy, or even Liddell-Hart and his emphasis on the indirect route to achieve success. However, we will return later in the book both to the contentious nature of common sense that Moltke sees as so crucial in making action choices on the field of battle and indeed also to some further insights we can get from Moltke's writings.

Cluster Analysis Trees

A more complex and sophisticated representation of the relationship between various items is to be found in the notion of cluster analysis. Here we can allow for different degrees of similarity and/or difference and also use particular statistical algorithms to generate the relevant graph(s). Figure 4.2 indicates a typical diagram.

However, as will be discussed later in Chapter 6, we need to make some simplifying assumptions in most instances before we can reduce what is often a complex situation into something as simple as a single tree diagram. In particular we need to decide how many "dimensions" we will use as the basis for the overall distance between the individual items as well as the extent to which we wish to weight these dimensions differently. Broadly speaking we have a set of further analytical tools relating to so-called factor analysis to aid us in doing this.

CLUSTER DISTANCE

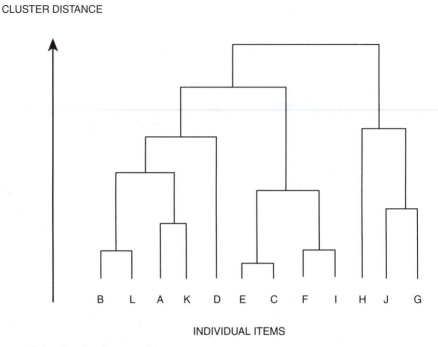

Figure 4.2   **Basic cluster diagram**

© Robin Wensley

Analytical Hierarchy Process (AHP)

Thomas Saaty, the prime developer of analytical hierarchy process (AHP), sought a simple way to deal with complexity. He also noted a common theme in the way humans often deal with complexity: the hierarchical structuring of complexity into homogeneous clusters of factors.

He developed the AHP as a highly scalable way of managing a group process intended to produce a clear preferred outcome. I will just give one relatively simple example but then consider the general principles involved. The brief introduction below is based on a particular worked example provided at: http://en.wikipedia.org/wiki/Talk:Analytic_Hierarchy_Process/Example_Leader.

An AHP hierarchy is a structured means of modelling the decision at hand. It consists of an overall goal, a group of options or alternatives for reaching the goal, and a group of factors or criteria that relate the alternatives to the goal. The criteria can be further broken down into sub-criteria, sub-sub-criteria, and so on, in as many levels as the problem requires. In the worked example there is a simple hierarchy for choosing a new CEO (Leader): see Figure 4.3.

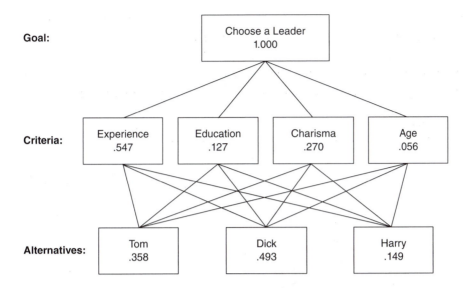

Figure 4.3   Basic AHP diagram for selecting a new CEO

(Copyright © 2010 Lou Sander. Reproduced under public domain rights release; http://
commons.wikimedia.org/wiki/File:AHP_TDHLeadImage.png)

The actual numbers in the cells are generated by a particular arithmetic process designed to ensure that the resultant scales have ratio properties rather
than just interval properties. The overall numbers at each level sum to unity
and require a particular pair-wise comparison estimation approach for every
pair within each level. Basically, the resultant weight attached to each criterion and the alternatives "score" on each criterion provided the basis for the
overall evaluation of the alternatives.

The AHP approach provides a considerably improved form of analysis
compared with the more common Human Resources approach which
relies on a more generic list of essential and optional elements in that it both
focuses on the specific individual options available and provides for a finer
grained weighting of attributes.

A much more comprehensive introduction and commentary on the AHP
is to be found in Forman and Gass (2001).

Decision Trees

Broadly speaking we can regard our cluster trees as a parsimonious way of
representing differences and similarities between items in a multi-dimensional
space. Of course we also often want to consider the time dimension and the

way in which choices are sequenced through time. For this purpose we often
use a different sort of tree diagram – a decision tree.

The basic structure of such a tree is normally involving a sequence of further
branching but the tree itself is represented "on its side". For standard decision-
tree analysis the diagram in Figure 4.4 illustrates the basic principles.

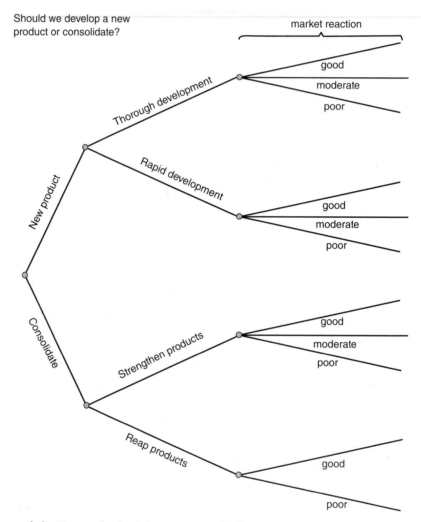

Figure 4.4   Example decision-tree analysis

(Copyright © MindTools.com; reproduced with permission from Figure 1 in www.mindtools.
com/dectree.html)

A decision tree consists of three types of nodes:

1 decision nodes – commonly represented by squares;

2 chance nodes – represented by circles;

3 end nodes.

Drawn from left to right, a decision tree has only burst nodes (splitting paths) but no sink nodes (converging paths). Therefore, used manually, they can grow very big and are then often hard to draw fully by hand.

A full decision-tree analysis involves working backwards from the end nodes to establish expected monetary values at the chance nodes (taking into account both benefits and costs) and then using these values to establish the best return at each choice node. This path then becomes the dominant one for the next stage of the backwards analysis.

Various further complexities can be introduced into the analysis including differing degrees of risk preference and a longer time sequence of decision nodes. The latter opportunity also raises difficult issues as to how and where we put a time boundary on the analysis. In formal analytical terms, as we go into the future the reliability of our outcome estimates decreases as nicely illustrated by spread diagrams as used by the Bank of England in, say, its forecasts of gross domestic product (GDP) growth (see Figure 4.5).

The diagram spread covers the 90 per cent range forecast. At some point in the future it becomes more sensible to treat the further end states as indeterminate until future data becomes available. Such an approach suggests considering these end states more as states in which a range of further decisions will be made in the future and which should be evaluated more in terms of options pricing, where, for instance, all other things being equal, a greater risk distribution of outcomes makes the option price itself more rather than less valuable.

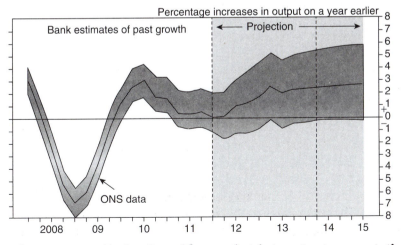

Figure 4.5 GDP projection based on market interest rate expectations and £325 billion asset purchases

However, as trees become more complex and the calculations more extensive, we can often create in practice a situation in which the preferred outcome seems more a result of complex analytical manipulation rather than based on an appreciation of the key factors at work in a particular situation. A still very current example of this is to be found in unresolved question of London's airport capacity. Much effort has gone in over the years to attempt a comprehensive and unbiased cost–benefit analysis. In particular:

> The Commission on the Third London Airport chaired by Mr Justice Roskill was set up in 1968 "to enquire into the timing of the need for a four-runway airport to cater for the growth of traffic at existing airports serving the London area, to consider the various alternative sites, and to recommend which site should be selected". According to David McKie, the problem was handed over to an impartial Commission "impervious to nobbling by pressure groups" which would look at the advantages and disadvantages of potential sites in a logical manner. (Helsey and Codd 2012)

In practice this has proved to be a rather unrealistic assumption. As John Kay notes:

> The commission concluded that a new airport should be built to the northwest of London at Cublington, between Aylesbury and Milton Keynes, with matching improvements to road and rail links ...

> Not that the excellence of the Roskill Commission's work did them or us much good. A government of different complexion rejected its findings immediately. A scheme to build an airport at Foulness, on Maplin Sands in the Thames Estuary, was chosen instead. This option had been considered by Roskill and decisively rejected ...

> Cublington was almost certainly the right answer in 1971 when Roskill reported. It might still be the right answer but the scale and complexity now involved in creating a wholly new facility in the English countryside would be orders of magnitude greater.

> [Nowadays the] models are more elaborate but less useful, and grossly misused. (Kay 2012a)

Beyond just the issue of increased complexity there are two particular areas of problem. The first relates to the input of various probabilities at the chance nodes. On a technical point, as in the example above, the distributions are in fact continuous rather than discrete for measures such as market reaction and this can introduce further problems when using two- or three-point probability estimates. More fundamental is the issue of the source of these probabilities themselves. Two little illustrations come to mind. Early in my own career

I experimented with decision-tree analysis in making decisions about test marketing various new retail grocery products. Given the very substantial pay-offs from a subsequently successful market launch it became clear that often I only had to make a marginal one- or two-point adjustment – say from 3 per cent to 5 per cent – in the prior estimate of the probability of success in the test market to justify going ahead. This leads one to the further question of the evidential basis for any such estimates.

There is a very appropriate vignette in Roger Graef's 1976 fly-on-wall documentary *Decision Oil*, which records the decision-making process that went on inside the American Occidental Petroleum company when faced with the uncertain advantages and major expenses of drilling for oil in a marginal North Sea oilfield. In the middle of a statistical analysis presentation by the relevant consultant, the senior manager makes an aside in which he notes that "the trouble with statistics is you need a reasonable number of previous cases to make a decent estimate but in this case we only have half one case"!

Influence Diagram

In view of the complexities discussed, it is often more useful to adopt an influence diagram representation (as in Figure 4.6), which is more compact

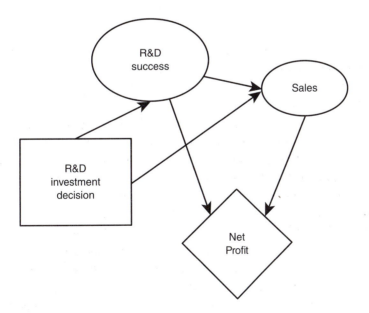

Figure 4.6 A basic influence diagram

(Copyright © 2006. A. M. Sheldon. Reproduced under Creative Commons. See http://en.wikipedia.org/wiki/File:Factory2_InfluenceDiagram.png)

and can be more effective at focusing attention on the issues and relationships between events. The squares represent decisions, the ovals represent
action and the diamond represents results.

Of course adopting this simpler representation risks losing some important elements and much of the time dimension in the analysis. As I will
discuss later, many of the single-direction arrows are in fact over time often
bidirectional.

Open and Closed Systems

In principle we can draw a clear distinction between two ways of considering any system. A closed system is entirely contained within some envelope
through which nothing passes either inwards or outwards. In an open system things pass into the system from the outside and something else is
extruded to the outside from within the system.

Whilst a simple distinction to draw in principle, in practice and for most
purposes we are considering degrees of openness or closeness rather than
absolutes. As for instance, Waddington notes:

> Spaceship Earth, which we are often advised to think of as a body
> completely isolated in space, dependent only on its stores of enclosed
> energy, is actually all the time receiving a very considerable supply of
> energy from the radiation of the sun. (1977: 65)

In terms of business and management issues we are almost always concerned with not so much the question whether any system we wish to study
is strictly open or closed – it is almost certainly to a greater or lesser extent
open – but with the more pragmatic question as to where in time and
"space" the boundaries are drawn and whether it can be assumed that the
first-order effects within the boundary dominate the phenomena that we are
studying to the extent that we can effectively treat this system as "closed".
This means that both within the organisation itself and between the organisation and its environment we accept some degree of non-optimal choices at
the boundaries as a way of making the overall managerial task feasible.
Examples include the macro – issues such as the difficulty of having a coherent and consistent policy with respect to areas such as CSR (corporate social
responsibility) across diverse contexts both political and economic to the
crude method of allocating resources between activities and divisions and
budgets. Without some form of prior budgetary system we would have to
reconsider all expenditure commitments whenever a single new demand
came along!

Growth

Most systems that we wish to study go through periods of growth – and often decline – over time. In the management of modern organisations, at least those in the commercial sector, there seems to be a strong bias towards growth sometimes of astronomic proportions. Of course this is partly achieved through mergers and acquisitions and therefore large entities but fewer of them result and there are also two other effects. The first, which has been well documented over a long period, is the continued growth in all forms of goods accompanied more recently by the growth in retail services and additional value-added elements to goods themselves. The second has been the more recent and faster growth in what has become termed the derivatives markets. Varying from fairly simple options trades to very complex financial instruments it has seemed in the recent past that the growth possibilities are almost inexhaustible. Indeed, further growth has been stimulated by the increased securitisation of novel sources of revenue. The *Financial Times* defines securitisation as:

> The creation and issuance of tradable securities, such as bonds, that are backed by the income generated by an asset, a loan, a public works project or other revenue source.

> Pooling of assets such as mortgages into securities that are sliced up and sold to different types of investor. Lenders pass on loans quickly, giving them few incentives to ensure they are repaid. Limited information on underlying assets makes them illiquid and hard to value. (http://markets. ft.com/research/Lexicon/Term?term=securitisation)

Figure 4.7 illustrates the relative growth rate in derivatives trades (from Blundell-Wignall and, Atkinson 2011). Not surprisingly, the dramatic relative growth rate in derivatives trades has stimulated a number of key empirical questions. For the lay person foremost among them would appear to be the welfare effects either positive or negative of these developments. In principle more active trading in derivatives should provide one means whereby the volatility of market prices is reduced. However, the empirical evidence appears rather mixed. As the then Chairman of the Financial Services Authority, Lord Turner observed:

> to the extent that complex structuring was driven by either tax or capital arbitrage, reducing tax payments or reducing capital requirements without reducing inherent risk, then it clearly falls in the category of the 'socially useless' (i.e. delivering no economic value at the collective social level) even if it generated private return. (2010: 22)

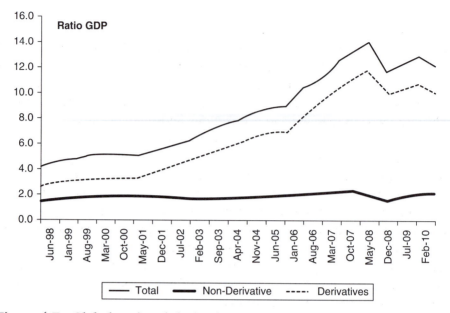

Figure 4.7   Global notional derivatives versus primary securities

(Copyright © 2010. OECD. Reproduced with permission)

However, a highly technical and sophisticated analysis concluded that:

> the benefits for improving real economic activity and reducing risk of this explosive growth are anything but evident. Primary assets that actually fund growth, and on which derivatives are based, have remained stable at around two times GDP through this period. A major reason why derivatives and leverage have built up since 1998 is because risk has been chronically underpriced. Had derivatives growth and leverage been more effectively constrained, the systemic risks would have been commensurately smaller. (Blundell-Wignall and Atkinson 2011: 198)

At a much more micro view it is worth considering how far we can make sensible judgements about medium- or long-term sustainable growth rates within a particular firm or indeed division. In one sense we can make the reasonable assumption that no firm can in the very long run expect to grow faster than the economy in which it is embedded. In general this constraint is likely to be even more binding in the public sector.

From another point of view others have attempted to derive sustainable growth rates for the firm on the basis of the level of retained earnings but such analyses tend to underemphasise the extent to which growth may be funded by new sources as well as loan financing and new equity investment. At the firm level, it would appear that on average it is advantageous to use some sources of funding beyond retained earnings even to the extent of using some level of derivatives trading:

> Using a large sample of nonfinancial firms from 47 countries, we examine the effect of derivative use on firm risk and value. We control for endogeneity by matching users and nonusers on the basis of their propensity to use derivatives. We also use a new technique to estimate the effect of omitted variable bias on our inferences. We find strong evidence that the use of financial derivatives reduces both total risk and systematic risk. The effect of derivative use on firm value is positive but more sensitive to endogeneity and omitted variable concerns. However, using derivatives is associated with significantly higher value, abnormal returns, and larger profits during the economic downturn in 2001–2002, suggesting that firms are hedging downside risk. (Bartram et al. 2011: 967)

The other crucial firm-level question relates to the sustainable growth rates that may be achieved in terms of new markets. It might be fair to describe the conventional wisdom in this area as one which favours the so-called "rapid follower" approach but this prescription is challenged in a large-scale empirical study which concluded:

> Based on an empirical analysis of a diverse set of consumer and industrial innovations introduced in the US over the past 100 years, we find that entrants during the pre-firm take-off stage (termed Creators) have higher survival rates than later entrants that enter between the firm and sales take-off (termed Anticipators), and both of these entrant types have higher survival rates than firms that enter after the sales take-off (termed Followers). Notably, survival rates for Creators and Anticipators do not depend on entry time within the cohort group, i.e., what matters is whether an entrant enters before or after the take-off, not whether it entered first in its cohort. Our results indicate that there is no real option value in waiting when one considers survival as a performance measure, which bodes well for firms interested in creating new industries. (Agarwal and Bayus 2004: 107)

Feedback

The notion of feedback provides us with a parsimonious way of characterising the time dynamics of a system. Broadly speaking, if modeling the system under study as transformation of input(s) into output(s), allows feedback to be used as a way of describing how a particular output affects the subsequent input and then the output. Positive feedback is when a part of the output is given back to the input so that the output increases more and negative feedback is when a part of the output is given back to the inputs so that the output decreases more.

In economic systems the most widely used feedback notion is that described as (dis)economies of scale often linked to marginal costs. The most common assumption for everyday economic systems is that the balance between negative and positive effects changes with the scale of operations: at small scales there are positive economies of scale but at large scales negative effects emerge and we have diseconomies of scale. However, in theory, even if not in practice, we should be able to avoid many of the diseconomy effects by merely establishing a parallel set of operations at the optimal scale.

Modularisation and Loose–Tight Linkages

As I have already outlined in principle, many systems in one way or another have to combine a number of desiderata including efficiency, adaptability and robustness. To achieve this we can identify two related approaches. Modularisation provides a means to produce products or services where there are a complex set of interactions within each module but much more simplified interactions between the modules. I have already considered the example used by Herb Simon of Tempus and Hora.

The "loose–tight" linkage approach considers the design challenge from a somewhat different perspective. Karl Weick (1976) suggested that one could view organizations as loosely coupled systems, and his insight has been developed by, amongst others, Moitra and Ganesh (2005) to argue that: "understanding an organization as a loose coupling of actors, rewards, and technology may help better explain how organizations adapt to their environments and survive amidst uncertainties" (p. 927). In their classic book in 1982, Peters and Waterman identified an analogous lens through which to view the performance of a number of excellent companies: the adoption of simultaneous loose–tight properties. A commonly occurring example in many organisations is to have tight central control of finances but much more autonomy in, say, market positioning and market development. In other areas such as employee relations, the impact of much legislation has been to required increased conformity and control at the centre.

As Peters and Waterman themselves noted, this was just a more recent manifestation, or perhaps more correctly, operationalisation, of the old centralisation–decentralisation dilemma. As such, this means we make choices explicitly, or implicitly, about the trade-off between the possible economic benefits of centralised coherence compared with localised autonomy adapted to appropriate specific conditions for a range of organisational activities. In between these two polar extremes there is the notion of procedural rationality previously mentioned, where there is standardisation in terms of process for choice-making but not the actual choices themselves. It is perhaps worth noting, however, that in the area of planning, Peters and Waterman claimed that they saw no evidence that their excellent companies demonstrated any superiority in terms of their planning processes.

Dynamic Systems and Emergence

So far this chapter has mainly adopted what might be termed an everyday perspective on the nature of systems albeit with a rather analytical bent. But there is now a rather challenging issue that must be faced, which was first indirectly brought to my notice by the almost legendary Professor of Marketing at Harvard Business School – Ted Levitt. I was sitting in my office at London Business School as a young(ish) Lecturer in Marketing, when my phone rang and the woman at the other end told me that a Ted Levitt wanted to have a word with me; he then came on the phone to say how much he liked the article I had just managed to publish in the *Journal of Marketing* and when I was next around Boston could I call him up and we could meet.

Later in the year, near Christmas, I was indeed in Boston and he said he would come and have breakfast at my hotel. The next morning it happened to be snowing rather heavily and he appeared fully kitted out in his all-weather gear. He sat down and said, "I have brought the only academic book you must read", and I expected to be given a copy of his most recent work. But no, what he gave me was Clifford Geertz's *Interpretation of Cultures*!

It took me a long time to work out what he was really getting at even though I much enjoyed the classic interpretation of the Balinese cock fight on first reading. It only began to properly dawn on me when I read much later Alicia Juarrero's book *Dynamics in Action* after I had also begun to take an interest in critical realism.

The essential part of the argument that Juarrero makes is that:

> When non-linear interaction result in inter-level relationships ... the meaning of individual events can be fully understood only in context: in terms of the higher level constraints (the dynamics) that govern them. I propose that explaining complex systems including human beings and their actions must therefore proceed hermeneutically, not deductively. Interpreters must move back and forth: the whole text guides the understanding of individual passages yet the whole can be understood only by understanding the individual passages. This inter-level reclusiveness characteristic of herme-neutics is thus "a continuous dialectic tacking between the most local of local detail and the most global of global structure in such a way as to bring both into view simultaneously". (2002: 222–223)

Geertz gives specific examples of this interpretative process:

> In order to follow a baseball game one must understand what a bat, a hit,
> an inning, a left fielder, a squeeze play, a hanging curve, or a tightened
> in-field are, and what the game in which these "things" are elements is all
> about. When … Leo Spitzer attempts to interpret Keats' "Ode on a Grecian
> Urn", he does so by repetitively asking himself the alternating questions,
> "What is the whole poem about?", and, "What exactly has Keats seen (or
> chosen to show us) depicted on the urn he is describing?"; at the end of an
> advancing spiral of general observations and specific remarks he emerges
> with a reading of the poem as an assertion of the triumph of the aesthetic
> mode of perception over the historical. In the same way, when a meanings-
> and-symbols ethnographer like myself attempts to find out what some
> pack of natives conceive a person to be, he moves back and forth between
> asking himself, "What is the general form of their life?", and, "What
> exactly are the vehicles in which that form is embodied?", emerging at the
> end of a similar sort of spiral with the notion that they see the self as a
> composite, a persona, or a point in a pattern. (1974: 44)

Not only does this process have substantial implications for how we undertake our research but also how we frame our interpretation of what can be
understood in what way. I will revisit some of these implications in terms of
causality – where the whole "common sense" notion appears to be rather
more doubtful than we might expect – in the next chapter and in terms of
our research itself – where despite her use of a term (hermeneutics[1]) most
commonly associated with biblical texts we find Juarrero is generally also
close to those who argue for an abductive approach – in the final chapter.

Networks

As the interconnectedness of many activities and organisations has become
even more evident it has become almost otiose to refer to the undoubted
importance of networks and networking. However, the network perspective
continues to provide important insights on the nature of many phenomena
we try to study and understand.

   In most actual systems the individual links do not simply get split up
along a whole set of diverging pathways like branches and twigs of the
tree diagram. Pathways along which things are processed may have this
as their major characteristic but it is often as important to consider the

---

[1]Hermeneutics is a widely defined discipline of interpretation theory; it includes the
entire framework of the interpretive process, encompassing written, verbal and non-
verbal communication.

interconnections between the branches and twigs on top of the rather simple tree-like pattern. Within such networks there will be the same tendencies to destabilise the overall behaviour by positive feedback or to stabilise
it by negative feedback, as was shown in the simple unbranched
sequences. Additionally, if one of the channels of communications
becomes constricted the flow will just go round, on one or more of the
alternative pathways the network provides.

Again, the level of some final output may act as the negative feedback,
repressing or even inhibiting some other link in the network, which need not
be directly on the sequence leading to it. Often in real ecosystems there are
indirect negative feedback loops which are likely to be more effective than
the direct, and this fact might be called a sort of inherent network buffering.
The more complex a network is and the more it is interconnected the more
indifferent it is to the severing of any particular link. This is, however, only
a very rough rule. The general theory of stability of networks remains little
understood.

One of the main results in attempts to compare network model outputs
with actual results is to note that complex networked systems behave in very
unexpected ways. As a simple example consider what actually happened
compared with the spread forecast for UK economic growth at the start of
2007, as shown in Figure 4.8 just before what is probably the largest economic recession in a century.

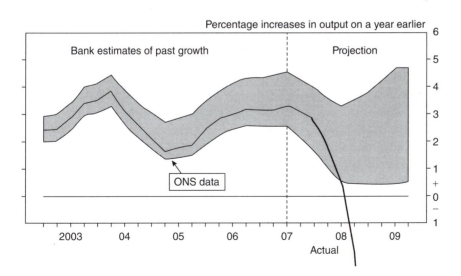

Figure 4.8   Bank of England modelled estimates of UK GDP Nov 2007

(Copyright © 2007 Crown copyright with additional annotation)

Their behaviour has been described as counter-intuitive in the sense that if one makes some changes to the system with the intention of producing a certain effect, the actual response often turns out to be something quite unanticipated. Sometimes these counter-intuitive results occur only in the short run; they may be caused by some parts of the system approaching a new equilibrium by an oscillatory path instead of a smooth path, or by some other transient phenomena of that kind. But sometimes they're due to a breakdown in some apparently unrelated but fragile part of the system.

Alterations in some places are likely to have more profound effects on the system than alterations at others; moving one particular item from a house of cards may bring the whole thing tumbling down, whereas removing many other items may have much less effect. Of course if one is trying to alter a system which has some in-built buffering, one of the first important steps is to try and locate these soft spots. There has been a good deal of theoretical discussion about how to locate them, or preferably how to measure the sensitivity of each particular link in the network. The most important result to emerge is that the sensitivity of a particular link is not a fixed characteristic of it, but depends on the state of the rest of the network. More recently there has also been much more analysis to try and understand how to interpret and design stable networks in various fields. This has amongst other things resulted in a plethora of terms and concepts, often used by different disciplines in rather different ways: dependability, fault-tolerance, reliability, security and survivability (see Al-Kuwaiti et al. 2009).

Basic Game Theory

A game-theory model is characterised by a set of rules which described: (1) the number of firms competing against each other; (2) the set of actions that each firm can take at each point in time; (3) the profits that each firm will realise for each set of competitive actions; (4) the time pattern of actions – whether they occur simultaneously or one firm moves first; and (5) the nature of information about competitive activity – who knows what, when. The notion of rationality also plays a particularly important role in models of competitive behaviour. Rationality implies a link between actions and intentions for each individual but not common intentions between competitors.

Models describing competitive activity are designed to understand the behaviour of "free" economic agents. Thus, these models start with an assumption of "weak" rationality – the agents will take actions that are consistent with their longer-term objectives. The models also assume a stronger form of rationality – the intentions of the agents can be expressed in terms of a number of economic measures of outcome states such as profit, sales, growth or market-share objectives.

Do the results of the game-theory model indicate how firms should act in competitive situations? Do the models describe the evolution of competitive interactions in the real world? These questions previously spawned a lively debate among management scientists concerning the usefulness of game-theory models. Kadane and Larkey (1982) suggested that game-theory models are conditionally normative and conditionally descriptive. The results do indicate how firms should behave given a set of assumptions about the alternatives, the pay-offs, and the properties of an "optimal" solution (the equilibrium). Similarly, game-theory results describe the evolution of competitive strategy but only given a specific set of assumptions.

The seemingly unrealistic and simplistic nature of the competitive reactions incorporated in game-theory models and the nature of the equilibrium concept led some to question the managerial relevance of these models (Dolan 1981). More recently, however, attention has in general shifted from attempts to predict actual behaviour to experimental work in which individuals in "playing" the relevant game reveal some of key logics that underpin their actual behaviour: a field which has become labelled as behavioural economics.

Principles: Normal Form Games

The normal (or strategic form) game is usually represented by a matrix which shows the players, strategies and pay-offs. More generally it can be represented by any function that associates a pay-off for each player with every possible combination of actions. In the accompanying example there are two players; one chooses the row and the other chooses the column. Each player has two strategies, which are specified by the number of rows and the number of columns. The pay-offs are provided in the interior. The first number is the pay-off received by the row player (Player 1 in this example); the second is the pay-off for the column player (Player 2 in this example). Suppose that Player 1 plays Up and that Player 2 plays Left. Then Player 1 gets a pay-off of 4, and Player 2 gets 3.

When a game is presented in normal form, it is presumed that each player acts simultaneously or, at least, without knowing the actions of the other.

As will be discussed below, it is such normal form games which often provide the basis for laboratory-based experiments in behavioural economics.

Table 4.1   Pay-off matrix of a two-player, two-strategy (normal form game)

	Player 2 chooses *Left*	Player 2 chooses *Right*
Player 1 chooses *Up*	4, 3	−1, −1
Player 1 chooses *Down*	0, 0	3, 4

Multi-Period and Multi-Player Games

We can obviously extend the normal form to both multi-period and multi-player situations: the longest established of such games are almost certainly war games which have been around in one form or another for hundreds of years.

The basic approach with such games is that whilst there are rules and limits to the nature of individual responses throughout the game there is not a sense in which the outcome is fully determined at the start. A good example of a relatively "simple" case is a chess match. Besides differences in the skill levels of the two players, each side has exactly the same level of resource. In such circumstances we might expect there to be at least a small advantage to the first mover (white) and this would appear to be the case with the total proportion of wins for white being in the range 52 per cent to 56 per cent. However, this is only a small difference and others have argued that in fact the most likely outcome amongst evenly matched expert players is a draw.

More recently, writers have argued that black has certain countervailing advantages. The consensus that white should try to win can be a psychological burden for the white player, who sometimes loses by trying too hard to win. Moreover, from a game theoretic point of view, playing second may be advantageous because white has to reveal their hand first. Some openings are thus considered good for black but less so for white, because white's extra tempo allows black to adjust in advance to the opponent's plans. Some symmetrical openings (i.e. those where both players make the same moves) can also lead to situations where moving first is a disadvantage, either for psychological or objective reasons.

Simulation

More complex war games are even less determined than a chess game in terms of end states. In such circumstances, we aim to develop a better understanding of the overall structure of the game and the likely implications by repeated experiments using either human judgement and agency or computer simulation based on approaches such as Monte Carlo simulation. The insights from such activities can sometimes be very illuminating even in situations in which the decision makers find the projected outcomes difficult to believe before the event.

Two examples of such situations are:

- A pair of war games in 1964 (SIGMA I and SIGMA II) tested the ideas that North Vietnam could be deterred by aerial bombing or by American land forces. How did that go?

> The game's results raised troubling questions about the viability of the Rostow thesis. After initiating a bombing campaign, the United States confronted "the question of what to do since escalation of the war into NVN [North Vietnam] had failed to achieve desired results in SVN [South Vietnam], and the enemy appeared to be raising the ante toward major ground warfare". The American "team", however, remained "anxious to continue trying to force the DRV [aka NVN] out of the war through air attack". Lincoln noted that once open hostilities began, consideration of "possible alternative strategies such as to negotiate" was minimal and the United States "followed through with escalation of pressures against North Vietnam to include wiping out all DRV industrial targets" and the mining of North Vietnamese ports. The bombing, however, had a minimal effect and actually stiffened North Vietnamese determination, as the Viet Cong used existing stockpiles and civilian support to sustain the insurgency in the South. General Wheeler seemed particularly impressed by the game's findings that the Viet Cong's low demand for supplies, coupled with the agrarian nature of North Vietnam's society, made the enemy resistant to the use of air power. (McMaster 1997: 156)

- Modelling the long-run behaviour of oil prices (see Figure 4.9) has involved both scenario planning and simulation approaches:

> Arie de Geus and Pierre Wack both worked for Shell and both emphasised the extent to which various techniques, particularly scenario planning, did not result in specific forecasts but did mean that Shell was better prepared to respond both to the severe oil price hike in 1973 and the subsequent collapse in the oil price in the early eighties. Peter Schwartz was head of scenario planning at Shell from 1982 to 1986. In 1982, Schwartz and Shell's scenario planners speculated that oil prices could collapse to $16 a barrel. They also foresaw the collapse of the Soviet Union years before it happened.

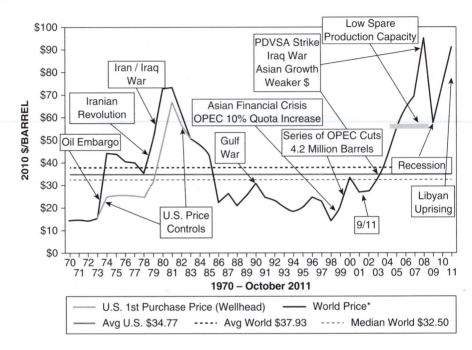

Figure 4.9   **Crude oil prices in 2010 dollars**

(Copyright © 1998–2011 James L. Williams, WTRG economics. Reproduced with permission. Source: www.wtrg.com/prices.htm)

As Schwartz explained it:

There is recognition that big complicated methodologies and elaborate computer models are not the optimal way. It [scenario planning] is a methodology for contingent thinking, for thinking about different possibilities and asking the question "what if?"

Schwartz also suggests that scenario planning moves the focus of thinking away from the external world toward the internal world of the executive. "This was Pierre Wack's big insight at Shell", he observed. "The objective is not to get a more accurate picture of the world around us but to influence decision making inside the mind of the decision maker. The objective of good scenarios is better decisions not better predictions." (Edited version of Management Lab Briefing 2009)

Insights from Simple Experimental Games

We now return to some simpler game structures which can be revealing both in terms of the nature of the dilemmas they pose and the evidence that accumulates as to how we respond to the choices provided.

Prisoner's Dilemma

Perhaps the best-known game theory model is that known as the "prisoner's dilemma". In this game the two players are partners in a crime who have been captured by the police. Each suspect is placed in a separate cell, and offered the opportunity to confess to the crime. The game can be represented by the following matrix of pay-offs (text and matrix from www.dklevine.com/general/whatis.htm and released under a creative commons attribution license).

	not confess	confess
not confess	5, 5	–4, 10
confess	10, –4	1,

Note that higher numbers are better (more utility). If neither suspect confesses, they go free, and split the proceeds of their crime which we represent by 5 units of utility for each suspect. However, if one prisoner confesses and the other does not, the prisoner who confesses testifies against the other in exchange for going free and gets the entire 10 units of utility, while the prisoner who did not confess goes to prison and which results in the low utility of –4. If both prisoners confess, then both are given a reduced term, but both are convicted, which we represent by giving each 1 unit of utility: better than having the other prisoner confess, but not so good as going free.

This game has fascinated game theorists for a variety of reasons. First, it is a simple representation of a variety of important situations. For example, instead of confess/not confess we could label the strategies "contribute to the common good" or "behave selfishly". This captures a variety of situations economists describe as public goods problems. An example is the construction of a bridge. It is best for everyone if the bridge is built, but best for each individual if someone else builds the bridge. This is sometimes referred to in economics as an externality. Similarly, this game could describe the alternative of two firms competing in the same market, and instead of confess/not confess we could label the strategies "set a high price" and "set a low price". Naturally, it is best for both firms if they both set high prices, but best for each individual firm to set a low price while the opposition sets a high price.

A second feature of this game is that it is self-evident how an intelligent individual should behave. No matter what a suspect believes his partner is going to do, it is always best to confess. If the partner in the other cell is not confessing, it is possible to get 10 instead of 5. If the partner in the other cell is confessing, it is possible to get 1 instead of –4. Yet the pursuit of individually sensible behaviour results in each player getting only 1 unit of utility, much less than the 5 units each that they would get if neither confessed. This conflict between the pursuit of individual goals and the common good is at the heart of many game theoretic problems.

A third feature of this game is that it changes in a very significant way if the game is repeated, or if the players will interact with each other again in the future. Suppose, for example, that after this game is over, and the suspects either are freed or are released from jail, they will commit another crime and the game will be played again. In this case, in the first period the suspects may reason that they should not confess because if they do not their partner will not confess in the second game. Strictly speaking, this conclusion is not valid, since in the second game both suspects will confess no matter what happened in the first game. However, repetition opens up the possibility of being rewarded or punished in the future for current behaviour, and game theorists have provided a number of theories to explain the obvious intuition that if the game is repeated often enough, the suspects ought to cooperate.

Win–Win?

We can also treat a particular representation of the prisoner's dilemma to critically address what is perhaps one of the most over-used expressions in the current management lexicon: the search for the win–win outcome. It is most commonly encountered in espousing strategies in bilateral negotiations of one sort or another, but also used to suggest better outcomes can be achieved if the situation is framed as a positive-sum rather than a zero-sum "game".

A classic example is provided by Stephen Covey in "The 7 Habits of Highly Effective People" when he gets to "Habit 4: Think Win–Win":

> Think Win–Win isn't about being nice, nor is it a quick-fix technique. It is a character-based code for human interaction and collaboration.

> Most of us learn to base our self-worth on comparisons and competition. We think about succeeding in terms of someone else failing – that is, if I win, you lose; or if you win, I lose. Life becomes a zero-sum game. There is only so much pie to go around, and if you get a big piece, there is less for me; it's not fair, and I'm going to make sure you don't get any more. We all play the game, but how much fun is it really?

Win–win sees life as a cooperative arena, not a competitive one. Win–win is a frame of mind and heart that constantly seeks mutual benefit in all human interactions. Win–win means agreements or solutions are mutually beneficial and satisfying. We both get to eat the pie, and it tastes pretty darn good! (Covey 1979: 1)

From one perspective (that is the two persons in the game above itself) there is a clear net benefit to going for the co-operative solution but does anyone outside these two lose? There is probably both an individual and a societal answer to this. First, and most obviously, what about the previous owner of what was stolen (and probably worth considerably more to her or him than the ten units that the criminals will get as the proceeds of the crime – say at least –20). What was previously a win–win solution has become a win–win–lose outcome.

There is probably also a more general and long-term loss to society as a whole if a win–win strategy is encouraged: the long-term societal effect could indeed be wealth destroying (although admittedly with some element of redistribution) rather than wealth creating.

Ultimatum Game

The ultimatum game is a game often played in economic experiments in which two players interact to decide how to divide a sum of money that is given to them. The first player proposes how to divide the sum between the two players, and the second player can either accept or reject this proposal. If the second player rejects, neither player receives anything. If the second player accepts, the money is split according to the proposal. The game is played only once so that reciprocation is not an issue.

Traditional game theory predicts that the play of this game will result in an outcome in which the second player plans to accept whatever she is offered and the first player offers virtually nothing. However:

In the first of many experiments on this and related games by numerous authors, Guth et al. (1982) found that the modal offer was ½ and that player I had roughly half a chance of being rejected if he offered about 1/3 of the sum of money available. Binmore et al. (1989) reported qualitatively similar results in their replication of the Ultimatum Game experiment. There have been many related studies in the interim, ...

Critics of traditional game theory have quoted these results (along with the early results on the finitely repeated Prisoner's Dilemma and games involving the private provision of public goods) as demonstrating that the optimizing paradigm on which game theory is based is fundamentally mistaken. Instead, so the story goes, people simply honor whatever social norm is appropriate to the situation. Frank (1988) is particularly eloquent on this subject. In bargaining games, for example, it is popular to assert that people "just play fair." (Gale et al. 1995: 57; some references excluded)

Penalty Game

As a final example, let us consider how a particular two-person game provides an insight into one of the critical biases in management behaviour: the so-called action bias or action/omission bias. There has been discussion as to whether either in general or specifically managers show a tendency to over-react to any changes in situations and therefore demonstrate what is known as an action bias which is at best merely "noise" in the system and at worst actually dysfunctional. For example, Leeflang and Wittink (1996) claimed that their data on competitive response patterns by brand managers suggested that over-reaction occurred more frequently than under-reaction. However, it is difficult to define accurately what is over-reaction and under-reaction given the nature of their data. To an Englishman, it is perhaps not surprising that a much clearer example of "action bias" is to be found in of all things the penalty taker/goalkeeper interaction in football (or soccer) penalties.

The English national side has a poor reputation with penalty shoot-outs, as indicated by the historic performance (Table 4.2), based on international tournaments for those nations that have played in a World Cup final, excluding Czechoslovakia, who have only competed in two penalty shoot-outs both of which they won, and Hungary, who have not appeared in a penalty shoot-out. Not surprisingly, we find that national scoring rates vary but shoot-out win rates vary much more and generally in line with scoring rates (R^2 is 0.74).

To return to the issue of action bias, the broader evidence of over-reaction from a much wider study is compelling (from Bar Eli 2007). A total of 311 penalty kicks were analysed based on searching various television channels for soccer matches in the top leagues and championships worldwide. For each penalty kick, three independent judges were asked to determine to which part of the goal the ball was kicked, to which direction the goalkeeper jumped (if at all), and whether he stopped the ball. After this classification 18 kicks were subsequently excluded from

Table 4.2   Penalty shoot-outs: % scored and % won

Nation	Scored %	Win/Loss %
Germany (inc West Germany)	85	71
France	84	50
Uruguay	84	50
Brazil	83	64
Argentina	80	73
Sweden	75	50
Spain	74	33
Italy	72	33
England	68	17
Netherlands	67	20

(Copyright © 2010 Jon Billsberry. Reproduced with permission. Source: www.penaltyshootouts.co.uk/countries.html)

the analysis because they were shot to the goalposts and the crossbar or outside the goal.

Table 4.3 shows that whilst there is relatively little evidence for strong "matching" behaviour there is a major difference between overall distributions of kick direction – roughly uniform – and jump direction – strongly biased against staying in the centre. This matrix can now be compared with Table 4.4's empirical outcome data (in terms of successful "saves": that is, situations in which the penalty kick was stopped).

Table 4.3   Joint distribution of jumps and kicks

		Jump direction			
		Left	Centre	Right	Total
	Left	18.9%	0.3%	12.9%	32.2%
	Centre	14.3%	3.5%	10.8%	28.7%
Kick direction	Right	16.1%	2.4%	20.6%	39.2%
	Total	49.3%	6.3%	44.4%	100.0%

Three things are clear from this data. First, stopping a penalty kick is a pretty rare event (14.7 per cent) or alternatively, there is an average scoring rate of around 85 per cent (which in passing is almost exactly the shoot-out rate achieved by the most successful national side (Germany)).

Table 4.4   Chances of stopping a penalty kick

| | | Jump direction | | | |
		Left	Centre	Right	Total
	Left	29.6%	0.0%	0.0%	17.4%
	Centre	9.8%	60.0%	3.2%	13.4%
Kick direction	Right	0.0%	0.0%	25.4%	13.4%
	Total	14.2%	33.3%	12.6%	14.7%

(Copyright © 2007 Elsevier. Reproduced with permission)

Second, as we might expect, there is clear evidence that matching behaviour does result in more successful saves but, third, that there seems to be no empirical evidence to support the over-emphasis of jumping (left or right) amongst goalkeepers.

Commenting on this, Bar Eli et al. observe:

> To reinforce the findings in the first study and our interpretation of them, we conducted a second study in which we elicited the attitudes and opinions of top professional goalkeepers. The results support our claim (which was based on the data collected in the first study) that the norm during penalty kicks is that the goalkeeper jumps to one of the sides and does not stay in the goal's center. The results are also compatible with our explanation for the tendency of goalkeepers to jump more than is optimal, which suggests that goalkeepers feel worse about a goal being scored when it follows from inaction (staying in the center) than from action (jumping). (2007: 616)

One is tempted to add what about the response from one's team-mates and the supporters as well!

In extending their own interpretation they note that:

> we may conjecture that if the economy has been doing poorly lately, the central bank or the government might be tempted to "do something" and change certain economic variables, even if the risks associated with the changes not necessarily outweigh the possible benefits. If things turn bad, at least they will be able to say that they tried to do something, whereas if they choose not to change anything and the situation continues to be poor (or becomes worse), it may be hard to avoid the criticism that despite the warning signs they "didn't do anything." On the other hand, if the economy has been doing well recently, policy-makers might have a temptation not to change anything, even if they believe that changes can improve the economy further. The reason is that if the economy becomes

bad, this might seem a result of their changes if they do something, but if they do nothing, they are less likely to be blamed for the sudden adverse change. Similar arguments apply to managers who consider whether to change the direction and strategy of their firm. (Ibid.)

Maybe in whole areas of management activity we should reconsider the benefits of inaction but it also might mean more difficulty in publically justifying material rewards such as high remuneration!

Perhaps we should also take to heart what Frank Partnoy has to say in promoting his recent book *Wait: The Art and Science of Delay*:

> The crush of technology is ruining our decision making. The relentless [sic] of email and social media and the 24-hour news cycle is speeding up our decisions. And the best thing to do is just to take a breath and be cognitively aware of what your own limitations are. Say, "You know what, I live in a fast-paced world and my computer screen is flashing at me and I'm subject to all this stimulus. What I need to do every once in a while is just take a break, take a deep breath, look outside, stare out into the distance and that will help us make better decisions." (www.marketplace.org/topics/life/big-book/art-and-science-managing-delay)

We will return to look in more detail at some of the evidence and implications that Frank Partnoy develops later in this book.

Conclusion: Bounded but Not Restricted

From an analytical point of view any of the forms of analysis or representation that have been considered in this chapter is itself a particular response to the cognitive problem of bounded rationality. As also considered in Chapter 3, this should mean that we make sure we always do two things:

- We use a number of approaches to ensure we generate a range of different insights. We must sustain a "mixed methods" analytical approach which avoids a one-dimensional perspective on any particular issue. During the 1989 UK budget debate the former Conservative Prime Minister Ted Heath constructed a devastating critique of government economic policy, likening fellow Conservative Chancellor Nigel Lawson to a "one-club golfer" stuck in a bunker. However, outside economic policy there are of course those contrarians who see this as an opportunity for a new version of the game itself: Thad Daber apparently holds the record for the lowest round with one club: a very creditable 70. (www.golf.com/tour-and-news/one-club-18-holes-event-less-more)

- We remain aware of what goes on "inside" the particular analytical approach. With increased analytical and computer power in many situations it is too easy to suspend critical judgement and assume that the computer "gets it right". Such "black box"[2] thinking can be disastrous if the assumptions upon which the approach has been developed are not valid in a particular situation.

---

[2]A black box is a device, system or object which can be viewed solely in terms of its input, output and transfer characteristics without any knowledge of its internal workings (http://en.wikipedia.org/wiki/Black_box).

5   Making Sense
of the Numbers

A statistical analysis, properly conducted, is a delicate dissection of uncertainties, a surgery of suppositions. (M.J. Moroney, 1964: 3)

In this chapter I will not try and repeat directly all the teaching material covered in what is often called a "quantitative methods" course but rather look at the more generic issues that arise in trying to apply insights from statistical analysis to actual decision making.

Concentration and Dispersion of Variables

To make any sense of a statistical analysis we need to start with some quantitative data itself, normally referred to as a dataset. At its simplest this dataset will consist of a number of observations which provide a specific value for a set of variables. Often the dataset will be cross-sectional in that all the observations are to be treated as independent of each other and as if observed essentially at the same time, more complex times series datasets are sometimes used where some or all of the observations consist of groups of the same variables measured at different specified times.

The first consideration is how we represent the variation in the values recorded for each variable: across observations, time periods or a combination of both. In general terms we can define this as the ways in which we may represent the concentration or dispersion of individual observations on the variables. It is also worth recalling that to later establish any statistical relationship between particular variables we need to have a reasonable level of variation in the actual values of all relevant variables.

The Problems of Averages

In a world of wide variability of specific observations, be it firm annual profitability or indeed academic citations, we have to be wary of the most common form of average: the mean. One response, particularly when there are significant outliers, is to look at measures such as medians or modes which are relatively robust to such extreme events.

Mean

The average value, calculated by adding all the observations and dividing by the number of observations.

Median

Middle value of a list. If you have numbers 2, 3, 4, 5, 6, 7 and 8, the median is 5. Other definitions include the smallest number such that at least half the numbers in the list are no greater than it.

Mode

For lists, the mode is the most common (frequent) value.

On the other hand, there are also two further general considerations:

- We may well be attempting to average over two or more distinct categories or groupings. Sometimes this can be rather misleading such as in Tony O'Reilly's brief encounter with a group of farmers in his early days with the Irish Dairy Board when, as he used to tell the story, they regaled him with the assertion that 75 per cent of them were above average – that is the average of the other 25 per cent!

- In a relatively high variance world any form of average figure on its own tells us little without some measure of dispersion. The most common dispersion measures are range, interquartile range, variance and standard deviation.

Range

The range is the simplest measure of variability to calculate, and is simply the highest score minus the lowest score.

Interquartile Range

The interquartile range (IQR) is the range of the middle 50 per cent of the scores in a distribution.

Variance

The variance is defined as the average squared difference of the scores from the mean.

Standard Deviation

The standard deviation is simply the square root of the variance. In the "normal" case 95 per cent of the distribution is within two standard deviations of the mean.

Forms of Representation: Frequency Plots and Box Diagrams

Of course as we encounter a wider dispersion of values and/or a larger number of observations we often have to consider other forms of data representation, in particular, frequency plots and box diagrams.

Frequency Plots: Normal and Fat-Tail Distributions

A fat tail is a property of some probability distributions (alternatively referred to as heavy-tailed distributions) relative to the much more commonly used "normal" which itself is an example of an exceptionally thin tail distribution. The term fat tail is a reference to the tendency of many financial instrument price and return distributions to have more observations in the tails and to be thinner in the midrange than a normal distribution.

Figure 5.1. illustrates the difference between a "fat tail" and a "normal" distribution which has a relatively lower proportion of extreme values. Quite a lot of management researchers let alone practitioners have often regarded the so-called "normal distribution assumption" (i.e. we start from the assumption that the underlying distribution of the relevant variable follows the normal curve and therefore we can use a range of statistical techniques which depend on the underlying normality of the population distributions)

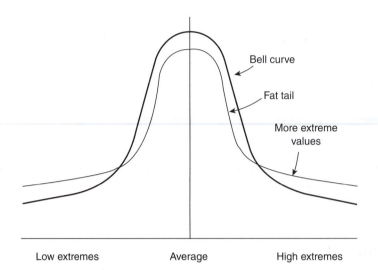

Figure 5.1   Normal (bell curve) and fat-tail distributions

(Copyright © 2012 Victor MacGill. Reproduced with permission; adapted from http://
complexity.orconhosting.net.nz/fattail.html)

as relatively unimportant and not of critical concern. Indeed, if you look at
the actual comparison of the overall distributions in Figure 5.1 you can see
why this might be regarded this as a relatively trivial simplification.

However, as often, the key question is the context in which such a simplification is applied and we now recognise much more clearly that at the extremes
of the distribution at both ends, the assumption can have critical limitations.
As can be seen in the diagram, whilst there is little difference between the two
distributions over much of the range close to the mean, at the extreme areas
whilst probabilities are low in both situations, in the normal case they tend to
zero whilst in the fat-tail case they tend towards a continued small but finite
number. This inevitably means that if we estimate the frequency of extreme
events on the basis of a normal curve when the more correct basis would have
been a fat-tailed distribution then we will underestimate the frequency of such
events. Further, our relative level of error with this estimation will increase as
we estimate frequencies for increasingly extreme events.

How much does this matter in practice? A great deal when in situations
in which there are a large number of observations and/or occurrences of
particular events. The most obvious examples in commercial terms are
economic measures such as prices for financial instruments and commod-
ity prices as well as natural events such as covered by insurance liabilities.
In such situations, as amongst others Nassim Taleb (2001, 2007) has noted,
the misuse of the "as normal distribution" assumption and a common

cognitive bias apparently to underestimate the occurrence of extreme events can mean that errors are made which have significant and much wider consequences.

However, other commentators have suggested this is less of a problem with statistical analysis itself and more an issue with how it is used and interpreted:

> Taleb's final major theme is skeptical empiricism. He likes plenty of observation, with minimal theorizing. He accuses statisticians of jumping in too quickly with models, discarding inconvenient observations as "outliers" and inconvenient results as "anomalies." No doubt there's plenty of that going around, especially with easy-to-use (and easier-to-misuse) statistical packages and too few introductory statistics courses taught by statisticians. But this is likely to be a sin of inadequately trained practitioners, not professional statisticians. (Brown 2007: 197)

Box Plots

Given the problems involved in building in the normal distribution assumption into the way in which we represent our data, there have been various attempts to come up with a more general, less restrictive form.

In 1977, John Tukey published an efficient method for displaying a five-number data summary. The graph is called a *box plot* (also known as a box and whisker plot) and summarises the following statistical measures:

- Median;
- upper and lower quartiles;
- minimum and maximum data values.

Figure 5.2 shows an example of a box plot. The plot may be drawn either vertically as shown, or horizontally.

The box plot is interpreted as follows:

- The box itself contains the middle 50 per cent of the data. The upper edge (hinge) of the box indicates the 75th percentile of the data set, and the lower hinge indicates the 25th percentile. The range of the middle two quartiles is known as the inter-quartile range.

- The line in the box indicates the median value of the data.

- If the median line within the box is not equidistant from the hinges, then the data is skewed.

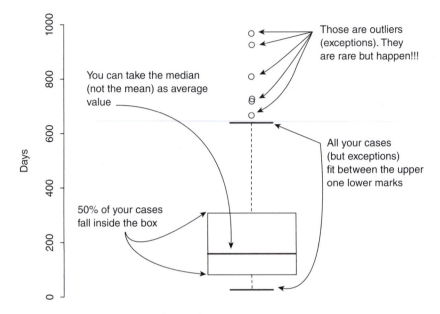

Figure 5.2   Interpreting a box plot

(Copyright © 2012 Franco Graziosi. Reproduced with permission. Source: www.
cbsolution.net/pba/2012/box_plots_clearly_explained.html)

- The ends of the vertical lines or "whiskers" indicate the minimum and maximum data values, unless outliers are present, in which case the whiskers extend to a maximum of 1.5 times the inter-quartile range.

- The points outside the ends of the whiskers are outliers or suspected outliers.

Advantages of Box Plots

Box plots have the following strengths:

- They graphically display a variable's location and spread at a glance.

- They provide some indication of the data's symmetry and skewness.

- Unlike many other methods of data display, they show outliers.

- By using a box plot for each categorical variable side-by-side on the same graph, one quickly can compare data sets.

One drawback of box plots is that, in a sense as the opposite of the normal distribution assumption, they tend to emphasise the tails of a distribution, which are the least certain points in the data set. They also can still hide many of the important details of the distribution.

Understanding Outliers

Grubbs (1969) provides a common if rather tautological definition of an outlier as, "An outlying observation, or outlier, is one that appears to deviate markedly from other members of the sample in which it occurs". Beyond this we must be more specific about the nature and meaning of the outlier values for any particular variable or set of variables.

In a strict sense outliers are just that – outliers. Of course to identify an outlier within a population in the first place we require some agreement about the likely distribution in the population. A number of popular examples, for instance, suggest we may be treating certain observations as outliers only because we have assumed a "normal" rather than a "fat-tailed" distribution. For many purposes in statistical analysis the major intention is to avoid outliers significantly influencing the specific results.

However, management researchers and even more management practitioners are often specifically interested in outliers and particularly where they are interpreted as exceptional performers mainly because they are indeed outliers. Malcolm Gladwell (2008) particularly emphasises both the importance of dedication – the 10,000 hours "rule" – as well as very specific "structural" conditions, that mean exceptional performance emerges amongst a particular population. He starts with the observation that almost all the top Canadian hockey players have been born in the first three months of the year and develops a rationale around the effect of birth dates. His analysis is that since youth hockey leagues determine eligibility by calendar year, children born on 1 January play in the same league as those born on 31 December in the same year. Because children born earlier in the year are bigger and more mature than their younger competitors, they are often identified as better athletes, leading to extra coaching and a higher likelihood of being selected for elite hockey leagues. Malcolm Keating (2009) in the *Guardian*, however, commenting after Gladwell's book was published, wished to suggest that generalising this conclusion to a wide range of other competitive sports can be quite problematic:

- Amongst a list of Britain's 100 best footballers only 17 out of 100 had birthdays between January and March.

- Amongst a list of England's top 10 cricketers only one was born in the first quarter.

- All 12 of Britain's fastest sprinters were born between April and September.

But:

- eleven of the 13 fastest-ever British 10,000 metre runners were born in the winter (and even four out of the top six in the four weeks between 30 December and 25 January).

- Of the 34 men's singles Wimbledon champions 18 were born between January and March. On the other hand 25 women champions were summer born compared with seven winter born.

So he concludes finding explanations for all of these might involve rather a lot of working "backwards from the answer". We might note this is also a process rather like Rudyard Kipling's *Just So* stories!

Further, as other reviewers have noted, in much of what Gladwell has to say about the more general questions of influences of society, networks and individuals, he presents common knowledge as new insight:

> Gladwell wants his readers to take away from this book 'the idea that the values of the world we inhabit and the people we surround ourselves with have a profound effect on who we are'. But I don't know anyone who would dispute this.

> The world for Gladwell is a text that he reads as closely as he can in seeking to decode and interpret it. He is adept at identifying underlying trends from which he extrapolates to form hypotheses, presenting them as if they were general laws of social behaviour. But his work has little philosophical rigour. He's not an epistemologist; his interest is in what we think, rather than in the how and why of knowledge itself. (Tonkin, 2008)

On top of this he shows scant regard for the rigours of basic research design and interpretation, and is satisfied with no more than plausible claims:

> Gladwell scuttles around his chosen field like a distracted crab on speed. We begin, bizarrely, with the long, healthy lives of migrant Italians in a Pennsylvania town – proof of the protective strength of close community, but

a study of longevity more than of success. Then we learn how given circumstances may make or break individual talent. Arbitrary birth-date rules for each cohort decide whether young Canadians become ice hockey stars or also-rans (also-slids?). In a flash, we're growing up with young Bill Gates, sharing his nine crucial early advantages – from the future Microsoft mogul's access to real-time computing aged just 13 to his long nights programing for free at the University of Washington. They illustrate the point that every virtuoso needs roughly 10,000 hours of practice to excel. (Tonkin 2008)

Fundamentally, maybe Gladwell is trying to do the impossible. Outliers are only similar to the extent that they all in their own specific ways are to be seen as distinct from their reference group. They are in no way a group in their own right. The philosopher Gilbert Ryle might well have dismissed Gladwell's book on the simple grounds that in the very title he makes a fundamental category error![1]

We certainly can benefit from studying and trying to understand individual outliers but it's a case of each one on its own. Equally, to advance from interest to understanding, let alone managerial and organisational action, we need to also know more about three aspects in any particular situation: whether they are sustainable outliers, how they have become outliers and the degree to which the development route that they followed is itself open to subsequent imitation.

Significance, Correlation and Causality: What's Significance Got to Do with It?

There are two critical but often misused concepts in statistical analysis: one is significance and the other correlation. Statistical significance normally means that we can be 95 per cent confident that the particular relationship which we have found in our sample of observations will also exist in the population from which the sample is drawn. Common sense suggests that if we make the sample large enough then we are very likely to find that any relationship found in the sample is significant in this sense. What many do not realise is how quickly this effect kicks in: in general, any sample size over 100 to 200 observations will make most relationships significant. Figure 5.3 illustrates this effect based on the most common standard test of significance ($p < .05$).

---

[1] A category mistake (or category error) is a term coined by philosopher Gilbert Ryle, meaning a type of informal fallacy where things that belong to one grouping are mistakenly placed in another.

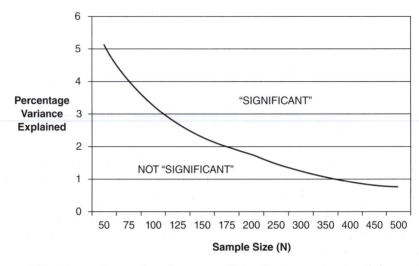

Figure 5.3   Percentage of variance explained vs sample size (N)

© Robin Wensley

We therefore need to at least consider this sort of measure alongside giving more weight to the so-called power or size effect: what proportion of the variation in the values of the key variable is "explained" by the particular factor? In particular we should perhaps try and always avoid shortening "statistical significance" to "significance"!

Perhaps even more fundamental has been the common use of statistical testing in the particular form of the Null Hypothesis Statistical Test (NHST). Cohen (1994), in his amusingly titled "The Earth is Round (p < .05)", reminds us of the severe limitations and heroic assumptions involved in using such an approach. We will return to this issue later in the chapter when looking at the ways in which we estimate and interpret more complex statistical models, but we should always recall that we also need to be clear when talking about "significance" that the question "compared with what other plausible effects?" is also important.

Overall, as Starbuck sees it:

> There are many more combinations of symptoms than there are diagnoses, so translating symptoms into diagnoses discards information. Moreover, there are many more treatments than diagnoses, so basing treatments on diagnoses injects random errors. Doctors can make more dependable links between symptoms and treatments if they leave diagnoses out of the chain. (2006: 108–109)

He continues:

> Academic research is trying to follow a model like that taught in medical schools. Scientists are translating data into theories, and promising to develop prescriptions from the theories. Data are like symptoms, theories are like diagnoses, and prescriptions like treatments ... Theories do not capture all the information in data, and they do not determine prescriptions uniquely. ... The systems social scientists are trying to understand are very complex and flexible, perhaps too complex and flexible for traditional research methods that rely on spontaneous data and static analyses. (Ibid.: 113)

Or, as Andy Van de Ven suggests in the lament of the doctoral researcher:

> You educated me terribly for this buzzing, blooming, confusing world!
>
> You trained me in the static linear model of variables, causal modeling, and experimental design. But organizations are dynamic, nonlinear, complex, and pluralistic. They cannot be explained with your unitary theories and linear methods.
>
> You forced me to read all those studies that explain no more than 2–10% of the variance in the real world. You didn't tell me the difference between statistical significance and practical significance. (2007: 262)

Perhaps an even more critical set of comments are to be found in the writing of Deirdre McCloskey who as an economist has not only been highly critical of the (mis)use of statistical significance but more broadly the whole thrust and nature of empirical research in economics:

> The progress of economic science has been seriously damaged. You can't believe anything that comes out of [it]. Not a word. It is all nonsense, which future generations of economists are going to have to do all over again. Most of what appears in the best journals of economics is unscientific rubbish. I find this unspeakably sad. All my friends, my dear, dear friends in economics, have been wasting their time. ...They are vigorous, difficult, demanding activities, like hard chess problems. But they are worthless as science.
>
> The physicist Richard Feynman called such activities Cargo Cult Science. ... By "cargo cult" he meant that they looked like science, had all that hard math and statistics, plenty of long words; but actual science, actual inquiry into the world, was not going on. I am afraid that my science of economics has come to the same point. (McCloskey 2002: 55)

Perhaps unexpectedly Richard Feynman's own suggestion is that rather than pretending researchers are doing real experimental science in activities such as statistics or econometrics a much wider range of knowledge claims should be admitted:

> Now whether the scientific method would work in these fields (education, criminology) if we knew how to use it, I don't know. It's particularly weak in this way. There may be some other method. For example, to listen to the ideas of the past and the experiences of people for a long time might be a good idea. (1985: 243)

Type I and Type II Errors

In statistical test theory the notion of statistical error is an integral part of hypothesis testing. The test requires an unambiguous statement of a null hypothesis, which usually corresponds to a default "state of nature", for example "this person is healthy", "this accused is not guilty" or "this product is not broken". An alternative hypothesis is the negation of null hypothesis, for example "this person is not healthy", "this accused is guilty" or "this product is broken". The result of the test may be negative, relative to null hypothesis (not healthy, guilty, broken) or positive (healthy, not guilty, not broken). If the result of the test corresponds with reality, then a correct decision has been made. However, if the result of the test does not correspond with reality, then an error has occurred. Due to the statistical nature of a test, the result is never, except in very rare cases, free of error. Two types of error are distinguished: type I error and type II error. Figure 5.4 helps illustrate this state of affairs.

In certain scientific fields the quantification is pretty severe: note for instance the rule applied in the analysis of the Hadron Collider traces and the attempt to prove the existence of the Higgs Boson. Here, the critical value for certainty is conventionally regarded as "five sigma" which based on a normal distribution actually implies 99.9999426697% confidence!

However, the more general notion of such errors allows us to relax some of the technical details attached to specific probabilities and indeed the very particular nature of a null hypothesis. Often we are more interested in both:

- a relationship which has a positive or negative tendency (see for instance the section below on the "rule of 10 per cent") rather than just an absolute effect/no effect choice; and

- a broader less quantitative notion of error: say, large, medium or small.

	Null hypothesis (H_0) is true	Null hypothesis (H_0) is false
Reject null hypothesis	Type I error False positive	Correct outcome True positive
Fail to reject null hypothesis	Correct outcome True negative	Type II error False negative

Figure 5.4 Type I and Type II errors

(Copyright © 2010 Richard Beck (modified). Reproduced with permission. Source: experimentaltheology.blogspot.co.uk/2010/09/theology-of-type-1-type-2-errors.html)

On a somewhat unusual blog Richard Beck (2010) notes:

> I use the following illustration to help my students get the logic of Type 1 and Type 2 errors. Imagine, I say, a guy who has just started dating a girl. He remembers that on their first date she mentioned that her birthday was coming up this week. But the guy can't remember the exact day. It might be today. Or maybe not. Embarrassed to admit to her that he didn't remember he decides to make a guess. He has two choices. When he sees her today he can say "Happy Birthday!" Or he can say nothing, hoping that today isn't her birthday. The reality behind the situation is pretty simple: Either today is her birthday or it isn't.

The four possible outcomes – guesses plotted against reality – are given in Figure 5.5.

	It's not her Birthday	It's her birthday
"Happy Birthday"	Type I error False positive	Correct outcome True positive
Say Nothing	Correct outcome True negative	Type II error False negative

Figure 5.5 The "Happy Birthday" outcomes

(Copyright © 2010 Richard Beck. Reproduced with permission. Source: experimentaltheology.blogspot.co.uk/2010/09/theology-of-type-1-type-2-errors.html)

Saying "Happy Birthday!" when it is not her birthday is like a Type 1 error. It is a false positive: I'm saying it is your birthday when, in fact, it isn't. Conversely, staying quiet when today is her birthday is like a Type 2 error. It is a false negative: Today is my birthday and you said nothing to me, you missed it.

This example helps to identify some of the broad issues which develop in what might be termed an error analysis, such as the fact that there are potentially significant differences in the costs attached to false negatives compared with false positives. Differing probabilities for what is often called the "states of nature" (her birthday in this case) and, finally, often other action choices as well such as admitting the uncertainty!

Other contributors have also extended in various ways the taxonomy or error types. However, it should be noted that these are not universally accepted. Types I and II have been standard for nearly a century, but various people have extended the series in various directions since then; so there is no real convention for what Types III and IV are. In the context of the basic thrust of this book and our specific attention to interrogative approaches I wish to highlight those that focus particularly on questions and answers.

Type III Error: Answering the Wrong Question

A Type III error is when you answer the wrong question; and how this usually comes around is when you base some assumption upon a faulty or unproven premise, and so you jump one step ahead and solve a problem that isn't yet the question at hand. The ghost hunters in the haunted house make a Type III error when they start with the assumption that a ghost makes a cold spot in the room, and so they walk around the haunted house with all sorts of fancy thermometers and collect detailed temperature readings throughout the building. This is great; they've done fine work, and documented it all very nicely, and they correctly reported temperatures. However, it is a Type III error, because the question of temperatures has not yet been shown to be relevant, since it has never been established that ghosts affect temperatures.

The vitamin salesman commits a Type III error every time he answers a customer's question about what vitamin is best to take to treat or prevent cancer. He'll no doubt give some such answer and recommend a particular supplement, and perhaps recommend a dosage. This is a Type III error because he's ignoring and skipping the precedent question, which is whether the vitamin in question will treat or prevent the particular cancer in question at all. (Dunning 2012)

Type IV Error: Asking the Wrong Question

While the Type III error is usually committed innocently and with good intentions, the Type IV error—asking the wrong question—often suggests a deliberate deception. By selecting the wrong question to investigate, it's possible to have greater control over the results. Selecting the wrong question is a great way of diverting attention away from the right question.

Conspiracy theorists of all flavors love the Type IV error, as it is one of the most effective tools to build arguments in support of nonexistent phenomena. If the conspiracy theorist wants to convince us that the government is building prison camps to enslave American citizens, it's not necessary to actually ask that question. Instead, ask a whole assortment of related questions that are guaranteed to have positive answers. Are there examples of government corruption? Has the government imprisoned people in the past? Are there laws that permit the government broader powers during times of emergencies? Are there plots of land for which there is no obvious purpose? These questions are all great Type IV errors for the conspiracy theorist.

Similarly, alternative medicine proponents can ask Type IV error questions to suggest that their central claims, which are unevidenced, are actually true. Are there examples of corruption in Big Pharma? Do any natural compounds have therapeutic value? Do scientists rely on grant money? Is medical science big business? Again, these questions are easily answered positively and appear to justify the use of vitamins to treat cancer; when in fact, none of them have any direct relevance to that. (Dunning 2012)

However, we should recognise that in Dunning's examples, he also under-estimates the extent to which in many situations the sequence of questions and answers are about moving from possibility to probability, much as the process in a court of law particularly maybe in the case of jury trials.

The Rule of 10 Per Cent

One way of developing our appreciation of the underlying analytical problems in understanding such "very complex and flexible" systems is to look at the problem of the so-called "rule of 10 per cent". The rule suggests that in such situations we can do no better than explain 10 per cent of the variance in our dependent variable (say performance) by any particular independent variable of interest (say market share) and that even if we develop a regression equation with a number of "independent" variables, we rarely achieve an adjusted R^2 in excess of 0.15 or 15 per cent.

What does this mean? Well, for a start a single variable which only "explains" 10 per cent of the variance means there is still a great deal of unexplained variance or scatter. We can illustrate this by using some simulated data which displays some of the same aggregate statistical properties as the empirical data for the relationship between profitability and market share, first widely reported by Bob Buzzell, Brad Gale and Ralph Sultan in the *Harvard Business Review* in 1965, as shown in Figure 5.6.

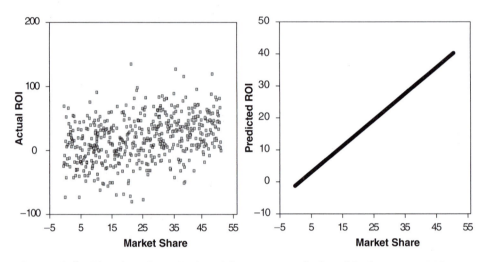

Figure 5.6   Simulated analysis with correct relationship between MS and ROI

© Robin Wensley

However, this relationship was represented in the original *Harvard Business Review* article by a plot of cohort (decile) means;[2] this inevitably focused attention in the explained 10 per cent rather than the 90 per cent as shown in Figure 5.7. It gave a much clearer picture of the "relationship" of course but possibly at the cost of distorting the essential empirical evidence.

How and why was it therefore that the initial article – and indeed its many subsequent representations in countless strategy and marketing textbooks – failed to reflect on the fact that around 90 per cent of variation in performance was still "unexplained"? Over time cohort means have of course become a rather outdated way of representing the data but they have nearly always been replaced by other equally misleading forms.

---

[2]In other words, the averages for each of the respective market share cohorts: 0–10, 10–20, 20–30 and so on.

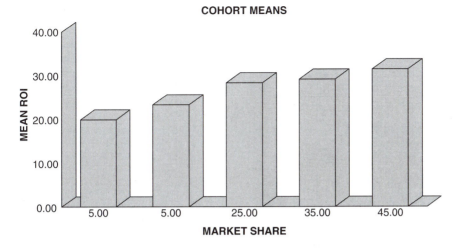

COHORT MEANS

Figure 5.7   **ROI/Market share plotted as cohort means**

© Robin Wensley

So what was going on? One form of explanation was that this was a laudable attempt to communicate widely the actual results of a major piece of statistical analysis. Taking the cue from an editor of the *Harvard Business Review*, who in an unguarded moment noted that most executives did not like statistics, the authors chose to focus attention on a "useful" result rather than focusing on the larger proportion of "unexplained" variance where the only solution is to recognise the randomness and trust to luck to ensure the desired outcome!

A more recent example which illustrates many of the same problems but in a field which has a strong reputation for practising an evidence-based approach comes from the *British Medical Journal*, which has made it a policy to provide a succinct summary of its articles for busy professionals (Perneger 2004: 546).

In this case, whilst the scatter in the data is not "disguised", the text box still focuses on the single relationship (see Figure 5.8). Although the scatter diagram is provided in the article in fact the relevant basic relationship only accounts for about 33 per cent of the variance in the citation rate but no such figure is given in the summary.

Mediators and Moderators

I will now consider how statistical analysis is used and interpreted when trying to unravel a bit further "very complex and flexible" systems. As Starbuck indicates, these systems are both complex and dynamic but to avoid near impossible analytical complexity we tend to approach these two aspects in rather different ways.

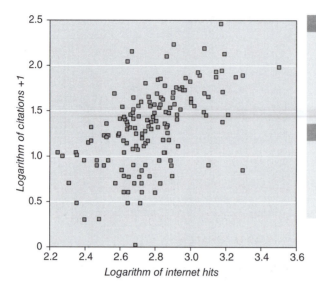

Figure 5.8 **Scatter diagram and description of citations VS hits**

(Copyright © 2012 BMJ Publishing Group 2012. Reproduced with permission)

To deal with static (or at least cross-sectional) complexity in our model we introduce the notion of a chain of links between our independent and dependent variables where any direct effects are complemented or indeed replaced by the effect of mediator variables, which lie direct in the path of the relevant link, and moderator variables, which themselves effect the scale of the effect of one variable on another. Whilst these distinctions relatively easily in diagrammatic forms (as in Figure 5.9), unravelling them statistically can be a much more laborious task although well-established analytical protocols do exist.

Even when the protocols are applied correctly there is still the difficult task to identify which particular version of the more complex model is "correct". Many of the straight statistical tests are comparisons with the so-called null hypothesis which is really a very weak test as well as subject to all the problems previously identified about any form of "statistical" significance. A rather more appropriate approach is analysis based on the so-called "Goodness of Fit". This gives us a measure of the improvement in overall fit by adding in particular new independent variables or changing the interaction pattern between the variables in the model.

In the general field of structural equation modelling (SEM) it is argued that a more strict comparison would be with a so-called equivalence model: "An equivalent model is an alternative model that fits the data equally well, thus

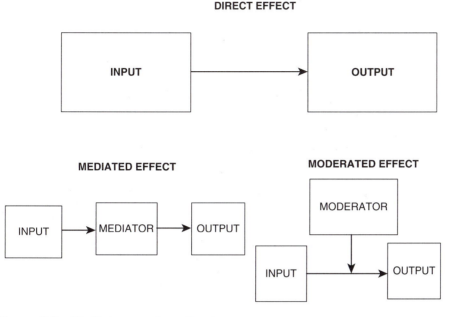

Figure 5.9   Mediators and moderators

© Robin Wensley

producing the same covariance or correlation matrix but often differing sig-nificantly in theoretical interpretation" (Henley et al. 2006: 516). Such an approach forces the analyst to do their best to produce an alternative model which matches the empirical data just as well but contradicts some of the conclusions that might otherwise be drawn. Some will recognise that this reflects the principles of hypothesis testing (or more correctly conjecture test-ing), enunciated by Karl Popper, in encouraging a serious and sustained effort to refute the conjecture rather than merely look for confirmatory evi-dence. A useful example is given in Henley et al. (2006), in which they re-analyse the empirical work done by Stimpert and Duhaime (1997). They set up two additional models (B and C) to test against the one used in the initial paper (A). As illustrated in Figure 5.10, they conclude that:

> As expected, the three models returned identical fit indices ... the standard-ized path estimates were similar but not identical across the three models. The most striking difference is the standardized path estimate representing the extent of diversification's effect on capital investment. The original model exhibited a non-significant value of −.07 for this relationship. In the two alternative models, the standardized path estimate for this relationship increased in strength to −.16 (p <.05). In sum, an important substantive insight is different for the alternative models; diversification influences

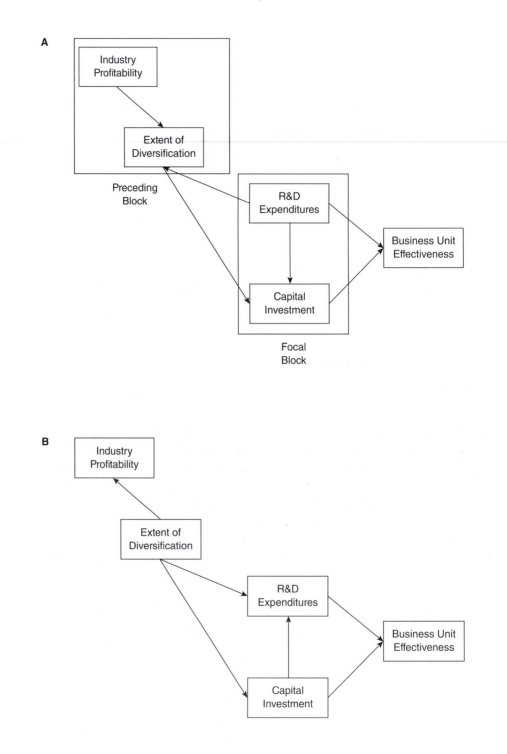

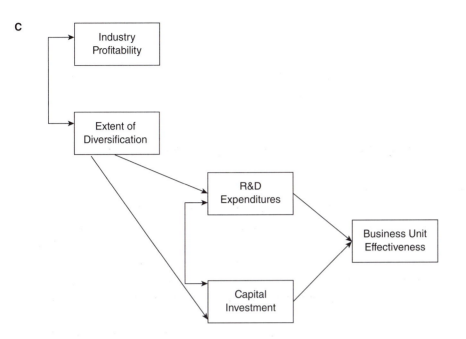

Figure 5.10   Alternative SEM diagrams

(Copyright © 2006 Sage Publications Ltd. Reproduced with permission)

capital investment in a statistically significant negative way in the alternative models, whereas this relationship was not demonstrated in the original model. (p. 523)

As they also note, one of the most common problems in the interpretation of an SEM analysis is that with cross-sectional data it is very difficult to infer let alone prove causality. Pearl (2000) notes that it is somewhat confusing when an SEM approach often claims to provide a facility for causal modelling:

Caution should always be taken when making claims of causality even when experimentation or time-ordered studies have been done. The term "causal model" must be understood to mean "a model that conveys causal assumptions", not necessarily a model that produces validated causal conclusions. Collecting data at multiple time points and using an experimental or quasi-experimental design can help rule out certain rival hypotheses but even a randomized experiment cannot rule out all such threats to causal inference. Good fit by a model consistent with one causal hypothesis invariably entails equally good fit by another model consistent with an opposing causal hypothesis. No research design, no matter how clever, can help distinguish such rival hypotheses, save for interventional experiments. As in any science, subsequent replication and perhaps modification will proceed from the initial finding. (Dwyer et al. 2012: 97)

Time Series Datasets: Lead and Lag Structures

Whilst the availability of time-series data enables us in principle to address more directly the questions of causality, it also creates further statistical issues for us to consider in our analysis, because we must incorporate a way of modelling potential, let alone actual, dynamic behaviour. In understanding, let alone modelling, such behaviour we need to recognise two basic mechanisms, both of which might exert a significant effect on outcomes and therefore our interpretations. The two basic issues are that:

- The system may take time, and therefore depending on the periodicity of our actual measurement of variable values, a number of "periods" are needed to settle to a stable state even if there are no subsequent changes in what might be termed the "input" variables.

- Even if the system were to adjust relatively instantaneously, the impact of particular variables might be more related to the cumulative measure of the input variable, reflecting some form of lagged weighting structure of the previous and current values for the variable rather than just its most recent value.

In economics terminology the first issue relates to assumptions about partial – as opposed to general – equilibrium whilst the latter is a version of the well known "stock and flow" problem. The underlying assumption about partial equilibrium is particularly fraught with problems – from the very general issue of its underlying theoretical underpinnings (see Loasby 1971) to the basic issues illustrated by, say, trying to derive a demand curve from a sequence of price/volume measures at particular time points. Of course in real situations it is very likely that both effects will be present but this only makes the analytical problem more complex.

In general, we have to assume certain forms for, say, the lag structure (one such example is assuming the lag structure effect follows a pattern known as the Koyck distribution which reduces a complex lag structure to two parameters) before the estimation of a particular model but with more sophisticated statistical estimation and modern computer power we can estimate for a whole range of forms or weights and then choose the best fit. Of course, as with the relatively simpler case of SEM with cross-sectional data there is still the question of the analogous equivalent model which could raise important issues about our interpretation of the overall results, in that a range of different specific models which have different theoretical and practical implications could be found to fit the data pretty much equally well.

Casual Causality

The truth that "correlation is solely about association not causality" is probably the most often repeated and equally often ignored statement in statistical analysis. "Proving" causality is actually a difficult analytical task when confronted with data from a natural experiment. For instance, the basic test to establish Granger causality is: A series x may be said to cause a series y if and only if the expectation of y given the history of x is different from the unconditional expectation of y.

There are two ways of dealing with this continuing and ubiquitous problem. One is to require a self-denying ordinance amongst any researchers presenting results based on cross-sectional data when it comes to questions about causes; the only acceptable answer is that the results tell us nothing about causes. The second is to require the use of the rather contorted phrase "causes or is caused by" in such explanations. A variant of the second is to require any paper to present the best arguments why we might assume A causes B, or B causes A or indeed C causes A and B and leave the reader to decide!

In the end it may make more sense, for a world in which there are many interacting variables and many paths, and where any of our models however complex tend to only explain a small proportion of the variance, to try and avoid any attribution of causality and stick merely to correlation. Just as certain authors (see Shugan 2002) have suggested that introducing complex models around competitors intentions and anticipations may be a step too far, so it may often be true that attempting to go from correlation to causality may also be not worth the effort, particularly in terms of the resultant practical insight.

Indeed, in a wry commentary on the earlier discussion on the issue of translation, it is perhaps noteworthy that the Google multi-language translation engine that is currently being developed is apparently based primarily on word correlation data distilled from almost unimaginable large amounts of text.

There is one further caution to consider, at least in management research: it is often the case that the raw data comes from surveys filled in by key informants. Often the variables being measured are, however, represented more as facts than opinions – items such as corporate performance, the extent of particular management practices, strategic objectives and so on.

Overall, however, there is a much more fundamental reason why I have entitled this sub-section "casual causality". It has already been noted in the previous chapter that Alicia Juarrero, from a dynamic systems perspective, argued that in such situations "the meaning of individual events can be fully understood only in context", which means that any valid causal interpretation has to in one way or another include the particular context. Someone whose writings also develop on analogous lines is Nancy Cartwright, who describes rather colourfully in *The Dappled World* that:

> as appearances suggest, we live in a dappled world, a world rich in different things, different natures, behaving in different ways. The rules that describe this world are a patchwork, not a pyramid. They do not take after the simple, elegant and abstract structure of a system of axioms and theorems. Rather they look like—and steadfastly stick to looking like— science as we know it apportioned into disciplines, apparently arbitrarily grown-up, governing different sets of properties at different levels of abstraction; pockets of great precision; large parcels of qualitative maxims resisting precise formulation; erratic overlaps; here and there, once in a while, corners that line up, but mostly ragged edges; and always the cover of law just loosely attached to the jumbled world of material things. For all we know, most of what occurs in nature occurs by happenstance, subject to no law at all. What happens is more like an outcome of negotiation between domains than the logical consequence of a system of order. The dappled world is what, for the most part, comes naturally: regimented behavior results from good engineering. (1999: 1)

Her more recent work is to be found in a book suggestively titled *Hunting Causes and Using Them*. In a generally critical review Hoover notes:

> The distinction gets its bite in Cartwright's belief that the strategies that successfully allow the identification of casual mechanisms frequently serve policy applications ill. Building on a longstanding theme of her work, real world processes are seen as the complex composition of a variety of deeper tendencies. The function of scientific experiments is to isolate those tendencies through stringent controls so that they can be exhibited in pure form. The application of scientific knowledge in practice is frequently complicated – if not thwarted altogether – because the real world is open and, unlike in the laboratory, the complicating tendencies are uncontrolled. In such cases, it is not necessarily reliable to infer that effects found under stringent controls will play out similarly in the world. (2009: 4)

A more far-reaching and at least as critical set of concerns has been expressed in various writings by Andrew Abbott, who challenges not only the very notion of event A causing event B but also the underlying assumptions in the general linear model (GLM) which provides the basis for pretty much any of the statistical estimation techniques:

> to use a [GLM] model to actually represent social reality one must map the processes of social life on to the algebra of linear transformation. This connection makes assumptions about social life: not statistical assumptions required to estimate the equation, but philosophical assumptions about how the social world works. Such representational use assumes that the social world consists of fixed entities (the units of analysis) that have attributes (the variables). These attributes interact, in causal or actual time, to create outcomes, themselves measurable as attributes of the fixed entities. The variable attributes have only one causal meaning (one pattern of effects) in a given study, although of course different studies make similar attributes mean different things. An attributes causal meaning cannot depend on the entity's location in the attributes space (its context) since the linear transformation is the same throughout the space. For similar reason the past path of an entity through the attribute space (its history) can have no influence on its future path nor can the causal importance of an action change from one entity to the next. All must be the same transformation. (2001a: 39)

One can also detect some links between the issues that Abbott develops and the way Byrne (2002) is keen to refer not to variables themselves but as "variate" traces.

Early in my career as a junior brand manager at RHM Foods, I still recall the bimonthly meetings to receive and discuss the Nielsen Store data. Novices at the meeting were often exposed to the "wit" of our Marketing Manager, Frank Tapling, when we encountered an unexplained anomaly in the data. Frank would almost always say, "It's due to the bread strike", and one of the poor unfortunates would ask Frank to expand. "The bread strike of 1932" would be the explanation. I was never at all sure there was a bread strike in 1932 anyway!

Overall, whatever one's personal philosophical take on these issues it does seem as if in practical terms we should be very wary of a specified general cause unless it is pretty much a tautology.

Conclusion: Half a Statistical Loaf may be Better than the Whole

I conclude that the biggest danger with more and more sophisticated statistical analysis is that we become seduced by the equivalent of the theory of everything. It seems that the more of the complexity we try and explain statistically the more likely we are to either misinterpret the results or be misled into false actions. Surely it is better to look for robust, reliable but essentially partial explanations than somehow believe that with better and more statistical analysis we can explain everything.

This is particularly true for those who are primarily interested in understanding a single or limited range of specific instances. Hence, as always this also depends somewhat on context; different criteria apply in considering policy type situations in which we are indeed interested in the net result of a whole portfolio of individual actions, where a consistent "small" effect can still be very important. It is perhaps no surprise that policy makers, or at least some of their civil servants, are more interested in sophisticated econometrics than most if not all business women and men!

As for the wider search for the "Theory of Everything", an intriguing recent development is one essentially based on the second law of thermodynamics. As Vlatko Vedral (2012) comments:

> The physicist David Deutsch thinks we should take things much further. Not only should any future physics conform to thermodynamics, but the whole of physics should be constructed in its image. The idea is to generalise the logic of the second law as it was stringently formulated by the mathematician Constantin Carathéodory in 1909: that in the vicinity of any state of a physical system, there are other states that cannot physically be reached if we forbid any exchange of heat with the environment.

> James Joule's 19th century experiments with beer can be used to illustrate this idea. The English brewer, whose name lives on in the standard unit of energy, sealed beer in a thermally isolated tub containing a paddle wheel that was connected to weights falling under gravity outside. The wheel's rotation warmed the beer, increasing the disorder of its molecules and therefore its entropy. But hard as we might try, we simply cannot use Joule's set-up to decrease the beer's temperature, even by a fraction of a millikelvin. Cooler beer is, in this instance, a state regrettably beyond the reach of physics.

Indeed James Joule, who was known as a great experimenter, had his fair share of "failed" experiments, including Cascade de Sallanches in 1847 that I mentioned in Chapter 1, but overall he laid the foundation for the theory of conservation of energy and maybe in the future even more.

6   Returning to Practical Wisdom: The Frameworks for Analysis

Common sense is the collection of prejudices acquired by age eighteen. (attributed to Albert Einstein in Bell, 1951)

Do not imagine that mathematics is hard and crabbed, and repulsive to common sense. It is merely the etherealization of common sense. (Quoted in *Life of Lord Kelvin* (1910, 1976) by Silvanus Phillips Thompson)

When it comes to what the French call "the human sciences", the quote from Einstein above is both right and wrong. Recall that the great initial insight that Einstein developed – that time was relative but the speed of light was constant – contradicted pretty much all of our own experience of the physical world; hence quite understandably Einstein's scepticism about the extent to which common sense can provide a basis for understanding phenomena which are way outside our normal domain of experience.

As discussed previously, however, within our normal domain of experience and particularly those where human agency and interpretations are critical elements, the role of "common sense" is much more ambiguous. The issue becomes much more one of critical questioning about the degree to which multiple experiences are reduced to statements of meaning. Such questioning would involve issues of possible selection bias and the extent to which the particular claimed insight has been tested against contradictory or solely confirmatory evidence.

Practical Wisdom: Reasoned Analysis and Deliberate Action

When it comes to linking judgement to action, a number of writers have espoused "practical wisdom" as the way forward to developing an appropriate set of management skills. This approach is often linked to Aristotle's original notion of "phronesis". So what did Aristotle have to say about practical wisdom? Well, quite a lot and indeed since his views were written down in the *Nicomachean Ethics* many others have too!

The Aristotelian approach is well summarised in the *Stanford Encyclopaedia of Philosophy* (2001):

> [Aristotle] rejects Plato's idea that a training in the sciences and metaphysics is a necessary prerequisite for a full understanding ... What we need, in order to live well, is a proper appreciation of the way in which such goods as friendship, pleasure, virtue, honor and wealth fit together as a whole. In order to apply that general understanding to particular cases, we must acquire, through proper upbringing and habits, the ability to see, on each occasion, which course of action is best supported by reasons. Therefore practical wisdom, as he conceives it, cannot be acquired solely by learning general rules. We must also acquire, through practice, those deliberative, emotional, and social skills that enable us to put our general understanding of well-being into practice in ways that are suitable to each occasion.

I could, at perhaps a little bit of a stretch, argue that this description of Aristotle's notion of practical wisdom is rather close to the underlying argument in this book that we have to achieve a balance between appropriate analysis and a wider sensitivity to values and context along with a clear but considered commitment to intervention and action.

Much the same argument for what may be seen as an appropriate balance between analytical approaches and a more general context defined by ethics and morals can, surprisingly to some, be found in the fact that Adam Smith emphasised very clearly a relationship between the workings of markets and the importance of a broader context. He wrote two major books: *A Theory of Moral Sentiments* being the first and *The Wealth of Nations* being the second.

Aristotle also emphasised the importance of a commitment to considered rather than hasty action as part of practical wisdom, in emphasising the need to avoid what has often been translated as "incontinence" but might be better seen as an "absence of restraint":

> Nor can the same man have practical wisdom and be incontinent; for it has been shown that a man is at the same time practically wise, and good in respect of character. Further, a man has practical wisdom not by knowing only but by being able to act; but the incontinent man is unable to act – there is, however, nothing to prevent a clever man from being incontinent; this is why it is sometimes actually thought that some people have practical wisdom but are incontinent, viz. because cleverness and practical wisdom differ in the way we have described in our first discussions, and are near together in respect of their reasoning, but differ in respect of their purpose-nor yet is the incontinent man like the man who knows and is contemplating a truth, but like the man who is asleep or drunk. And he acts

willingly (for he acts in a sense with knowledge both of what he does and of the end to which he does it), but is not wicked, since his purpose is good; so that he is half-wicked. And he is not a criminal; for he does not act of malice aforethought; of the two types of incontinent man the one does not abide by the conclusions of his deliberation, while the excitable man does not deliberate at all. And thus the incontinent man like a city which passes all the right decrees and has good laws, but makes no use of them. (*Ethics*, Book VII: Chapter X)

As already discussed earlier, this could be seen as directly linked to more recent discussions about the benefits and costs of a "bias for action". We will also note later on in this book that this is similar to Daniel Kahneman's (2011) notion of the importance of what he calls System 2 thinking.

In more current popular management parlance we might note that such concerns for deliberation and reasoned analysis before action do not chime well with the current enthusiasm in some quarters for "active" leadership rather than "bureaucratic" management. However, some of the enthusiasm for leadership which is itself not grounded on reasoned analysis and evidence may be rather misplaced: visionaries may be more often wrong than right. I will take a closer look at some of the current issues in leadership later in this book. At the moment it is worth noting that some of the critique of bureaucracy itself often comes from a misrepresentation of both the purpose and the equity inherent in well-designed bureaucratic processes and organisations (Du Gay 2000). This is particularly important when we consider a range of management issues in the public sector.

Watching Out for Boxes, Linear Diagrams and Other Simplifying Tools

I have already discussed the various issues with applying forms of statistical analysis to empirical data in order to provide an evidence base for decisions and action, but there is a much wider repertoire of approaches designed to a greater or lesser extent to provide some form of empirically based framework in making action choices. Each of these approaches, however, also achieves its impact and usefulness by some form or other of simplification and it is important to remain aware in any particular situation as to the likely validity of the simplifying assumptions inherent in a specific approach. I have already considered in general terms some of the implicit assumptions in various commonly used representations. I will now delve a bit further into the analytical issues involved.

Broadly speaking, the simplifications concerned can relate to one or more of the dimensionality of the problem space, the orthogonality of the categorising variables or vectors and the linearity of the time dimension.

The Dimensionality of the Problem Space

The issue of the overall number of dimensions we should consider in the analysis of particular problem choice is often under-played or even ignored in particular representations. To take an obvious example, consider the marketing strategy issues to consider in the interaction between a range of competitive offerings on the supply side which can be differentiated in a number of dimensions – indeed in the extreme case this number of dimensions is the same as the number of offerings – and on the demand side the number of dimensions that adequately reflect the preference space of the relevant heterogeneous customers.

We might have expected that there would have been a significant amount of empirical research on what might be termed the appropriate level for a reduced form dimensional model in such situations but in fact there has been little such work. Over the years there have been some interesting developments on the basic Hotelling model of spatial competition but this has effectively been with respect to a one-dimensional or at best two-dimensional space.

Factor analytic studies of consumer preferences have also tended to produce results that are most robust with three or four dimensions or factors which also cautions against analysis which is merely one or two dimensional. In a recent and fairly typical example, Abdullah and Asngari (2011) identify four factors: brand, price, taste and appearance.

However, there is some tentative evidence that simplification to a reduced form may be appropriate, particularly if the dominant interest is how we represent what happens from a strategic perspective in terms of actual purchase behaviour in a competitive market through time. There have been a number of attempts to apply space-segmentation analysis to behavioural data with no information as to consumer attitudes or competitive intentions. In one of the more detailed of such studies, Chintagunta (1994) focuses on the degree to which the data analysis reveals interesting differences in terms of brand position as revealed by individual purchase patterns through time. He suggested that the dimensionality of the revealed competitive space was two dimensional but even this might be really an over-estimate; it can probably be reduced to one.

The Orthogonality of the Categorising Variables or Factors

As already noted, when performing statistical analysis, factors that affect a particular result are said to be orthogonal if they are uncorrelated. That is to say that one can model the effect of each separately, and then combine these models (adding no extra information) to give a model which predicts the combined effect of varying them jointly. In practice, in the contexts in which we are interested correlation between the initial variables is almost always present to some degree and hence we have to rely on the estimation algorithm to force the combined factors to become orthogonal. This often means that the analytical result provides a complex arrangement of the loadings of individual variables across multiple factors which means severe difficulties in interpretation.

We do have statistical techniques to help resolve this problem but they sometimes bring with them certain further interpretational problems. For instance, in factor analysis we can transform the relevant factors, using approaches such as Varimax rotation, so that new factors are created which have a parsimonious loading matrix in terms of the original variables. However, there is still the problem of labelling these factors in an appropriate manner and at least assuming that they represent meaningful latent variables. Sometimes latent variables correspond to aspects of physical reality, which could in principle be measured, but may not be for practical reasons. In this situation, the term hidden variables is commonly used (reflecting the fact that the variables are "really there", but hidden). Other times, latent variables correspond to abstract concepts, like categories, behavioural or mental states, or data structures. The terms hypothetical variables or hypothetical constructs may be used in these situations.

On top of this there is the question of the reliability of the composite factors which result; the common practice in statistical analysis is to measure the Cronbach alpha which roughly measures how well each individual item in a scale correlates with the sum of the remaining items. The normally applied minimum cut-off particularly in empirical analysis in areas such as strategy and marketing is 0.7 with no upper limit nearer to 1.0, but over an extended period there have been those who warn against such an uncritical single criterion. For instance, as far back as 1989:

> It is nearly impossible these days to see a scale development paper that has not used alpha, and the implication is usually made that the higher the coefficient, the better. However, there are problems in uncritically accepting high values of alpha (or KR-20), and especially in interpreting them as reflecting simply internal consistency. The first problem is that alpha is dependent not only on the magnitude of the correlations among items, but also on the number of items in the scale. A scale can be made to look more 'homogenous' simply by

doubling the number of items, even though the average correlation remains the same. This leads directly to the second problem. If we have two scales which each measure a distinct construct, and combine them to form one long scale, alpha would probably be high, although the merged scale is obviously tapping two different attributes. Third, if alpha is too high, then it may suggest a high level of item redundancy; that is, a number of items asking the same question in slightly different ways. (Streiner and Norman 1989: 64–65)

Revisiting the Two-by-Two Box

As already discussed, perhaps the most common medium used to translate management research into descriptions and prescriptions for management practice is the two-by-two matrix or similar device. I noted in Chapter 1, that as a basic form of representation it implicitly but crucially assumes that the two axes concerned are orthogonal and that the individual elements are fully distributed within the boundaries defined by the box.

When we shift the focus to the question of managerial prescription then we encounter some further critical assumptions, most obviously that one of the axes represents an aspect where a degree of managerial discretion is available whereas the other represents an outcome state. In modelling terms this is roughly equivalent to treating the first variable as exogenous and the second as endogenous.

Many of these interpretational and analytical problems in the case of arguably the most famous of the two-by-two matrix tools; the Boston Consulting Group (BCG) market share/market growth matrix or the "Boston Box". Amongst other things it was originally intended to represent the "fact" that any corporation needed to have a portfolio of real investments in its businesses or units to ensure both short- and long-term performance, in other words balance rather than privilege any one of the four quadrants. However, it often became used as a device to justify an almost exclusive managerial focus on increasing market share. The basic argument was that market share could be treated as a managerial choice whilst market growth was endogenous to the relevant market/industry.

Hence, even in some presentations the market growth/market share diagram is overlaid with two different possible development paths, one labelled success and the other failure, as shown in Figure 6.1.

The basic additional assumptions underlying this prescription was that either or both:

- The cost of gaining market share in high-growth markets was relatively lower than in low-growth markets; this assumption was justified on the grounds that competitors focused on volume rather than share and were

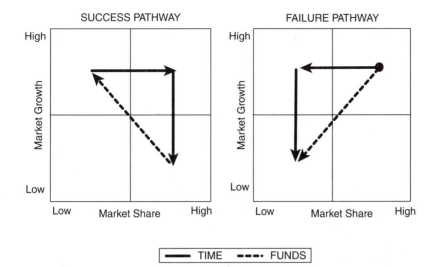

Figure 6.1 Success and failure "pathways" in the BCG matrix

© Robin Wensley

therefore less liable to react in high-growth markets as long as they saw their own volumes increasing.

- The cash flows that could be generated from high-growth market shares at a later date in more slowly growing markets were greater than in fast-growing ones; this assumption was justified on the basis that as markets slow and mature, market share becomes a good indicator of sustainable advantages.

In fact both these assumptions are contested, and particularly so in the case when the particular form of analysis is widely known and followed. It may well be true that market share broadly represents the economy of scale effect (based on both current and past cumulative volumes) in a way which is relatively dimensionless for cross-industry and market comparisons, but the costs of market share gains are directly linked to competitive behaviour and competitive expectations. The more competitors take market share as a critical indicator the more the cost of market-share gains reflects the value they attach to market share itself. This will mean that any perceived value of market share is more likely merely to reflect economies of scale effects combined with a risk premium attached to the riskier nature of an investment in rapidly evolving rather than mature markets. Of course the combined effect of these two economic facts is that after the event we can indeed expect to see a positive relationship between the market share of those firms which have survived and prospered, and economic performance.

For a further discussion on this and many other issues relating to the development and subsequent teaching of the BCG matrix, see Morrison and Wensley (1991).

Introducing Dynamics into a Static Representation

The focus has now shifted to what is the essence of most management choices and action in that they take place in a dynamic and interactive context rather than one which is static and non-interactive. On top of the more specific concerns and limitations above, most box presentations are also based on positional and generally cross-sectional data. This creates further confusions when they are used as a basis for discussing managerial actions.

Being positional they represent outcomes not processes: a common mistake in interpreting the boxes is to assume that one can move around the "board" relatively easily; just because they are 2D does not mean the world is that simple nor that there are not "hidden" constraints, which we might term valleys and hills in a 3D world. An historical but rather illuminating commentary on some of the issues in a 2D interpretation of a 3D world is to be found in Abbott's Victorian novella *Flatland, a Romance of Many Dimensions* (1884). Indeed, even the valleys and hills analogy may be misleading in that they suggest the competitive space in which the firm operates itself is a relatively static "backcloth". It may often be nothing like this, as already hinted earlier during the discussion of the role of intention and anticipation. In some cases the so-called backcloth may be changing as fast if not faster than the actions and strategies of any particular firm.

The role of the physical landscape can be seen very clearly in what might be termed traditional military strategy, before we entered the world of virtual information spaces and the like. Perhaps most useful from the point of view of competitive strategy is the focus on the balance between clarity and confusion in one's intentions and the general notion of signalling. It is important to avoid becoming over-committed to a particular approach because one's intentions can be read unambiguously by the enemy; on the other hand, a sense of direction is required to maintain internal cohesion and morale. The military perspective also reinforces the multiple time periods perspective. In most military conflicts it is assumed that the problems can be overcome with enough resources and effort but then this degree of commitment could prove too much from a wider perspective, and hence the old adage of winning the battle but not the war. The physical terrain often occupies a critical role in the analysis of competitive dispositions and there is equal focus on the nature of external factors, as opposed to internal organisation and control, and supply logistics. However, military analogies inevitably emphasise conflict, and again, often in their most popular manifestations, direct and immediate conflict. This all suggests we might gain from analytical perspective which is more grounded in a co-evolutionary process between the firm, its competitors and its customers.

There have indeed been some interesting developments in empirical studies of co-evolution but unfortunately most of these have so far been focused solely on the competitive and co-operative processes between organisations. It is also noteworthy that even those few studies which attempt to model the nature of market evolution specifically, rather than treat it more as a backcloth upon which other sociological and economic processes take place, tend to represent the actual process in very limited ways. Only in the resource partitioning approach (Carroll and Swaminathan 1992) do we perhaps see the direct opportunities for a more complex model of market development which represents both its continuity, in the sense that one can reasonably expect cycles of competitive imitation followed by the emergence of new forms and market positions for competition, and its indeterminacy, in that various new "realised niches" could emerge. Even here, however, the implicit emphasis is on the individual firms as the motivating force rather than the collective of customers in the various markets.

Advances in agent-based modelling promise new ways of simulating more complex interactive processes of spatial competition (Tesfatsion 2001 and Ishibuchi et al. 2001). Agent-based modelling essentially depends on allowing a simulation to evolve with individual "agents" making choices within an undetermining but defined rule structure. It may well provide us with a better understanding of the patterns of market-based evolution and the nature of some of the key contingencies. However, again it is proving difficult to adequately reflect the evolving behaviour of customers in the market place. Chang and Harrington (2003) did include a process of consumer research in their model but their focus remained on the potential advantages of centralisation for what were in effect multi-unit retailers.

A focus on position also has major implications as to how one tends to view competitive strategy; in particular it emphasises strategy as position rather than as flow. This is often combined with sports game analogies but the ones in most common currency tend to be games of position, such as American football, rather than games of flow such as soccer, and the focus on a simple territorial logic and a well-defined and unchanging set of rules (Kierstead 1972). A wider perspective on the sports game approach recognises the complexity of the:

- relationship between prior planning and the action in the game itself

- degree of co-ordination between the various individual players

- interaction between competitive response within different time periods (play, game, season)

- multiple routes to success

- general evidence that it is necessary to compete on more than one dimension

- inevitability that success rapidly encourages imitation.

Within the sports game analogy, we recognise the key role of "rules" and particularly changes in rules as a means of influencing competitive strategies but also tend to presume a high degree of control over the activities of individual players.

Finally, as discussed earlier in the book, there is often a theoretical confusion as to whether we are observing at least on average a picture of partial equilibrium or one which is pretty much always in transition. The general notion of partial equilibrium was an apparently convenient way of recognising that economic adjustment processes are rarely if ever instantaneous. But, as Loasby noted, this convenience is notional rather than real in theoretical terms: it solely implies that when we have a particular observation it represents an unknown mixture of a transition process and an equilibrium outcome. Indeed, perhaps rather unusually for an economist, Loasby suggests a stronger focus on cognition rather than rationality:

> Rather than bounded rationality, which (as already noted) is usually interpreted as a particular limitation in processing knowledge, it is better to begin with bounded cognition. In the early stages of evolution, standard behaviours were genetically programmed; later creatures were genetically endowed with some capacity to vary behaviour; and in the pre-conscious stage of evolution towards homo sapiens, individuals formed classification systems and linkages between sensory perceptions and actions which proved sufficient for the survival of the species. ... However, the emergence of consciousness introduced the important novel possibility of creating ideas about the future by making conjectures about new categories and relationships as yet unrecognised, leading to the possibility of taking novel actions with the intention of producing novel effects. The scope for variation between individuals was correspondingly increased, and with it the rate at which knowledge could grow. (2001: 7–8)

Dr Who and the Time Dimension

The ongoing popularity of the *Dr Who* TV series suggests that there is something about the notion of time travel which catches the imagination of many of us. Perhaps this is because the time dimension is one that in most circumstances we are unable to alter compared with our capabilities when it comes to the spatial dimension.

However, the fact that most, if not all, the time we are subject to the constraint of time's arrow and its irreversibility should not mean we do not recognise that individually time is rarely experienced as strictly chronological let alone the fact that collectively there seems to be as much circularity as linearity in the evolution of human experience both individual and collective. At the individual level we might note the poignancy and circularity in Shakespeare's "Seven Ages of Man" and, more broadly, it is worth recalling Hegel's observation "that nations and governments have never learned anything from history, or acted upon any lessons they might have drawn from it" and trying to avoid this error in both our own and our organisation's practice let along fall foul of Karl Marx's rider to the original quotation, referring first to Napoleon I and then Napoleon III: "He forgot to add: the first time as tragedy, the second as farce."

This suggests we should be particularly cautious of representations which take the linearity of time as self-evident. We may not be able to go back in time to change the starting conditions that we face now in making choices for the future but we should look critically at some of the ways used to represent our future choices. Indeed, the determinacy of starting conditions is itself a contested issue which has produced some challenging story-lines in *Dr Who* and also in many other examples of science fiction. Some will argue that founding conditions are critical in understanding the later pattern of events but others will place more emphasis on the evolutionary processes and the options therein after the initial starting conditions.

Loasby, in the paper referred to above, concluded:

> Imagination and the assignment of possibility require the making of new connections, and often the discarding of old connections, a process that is easier to understand in retrospect than it is in prospect. Since the number of connected networks that are conceivable is unimaginably greater than the number that can be handled by any human brain – or indeed by any organisation that depends on manageable interactions between human brains – it is not surprising that there will be a great variety of opinions about what will work, and what will be profitable. There will be a high rate of failure; economic dynamics requires both ex-ante and ex-post selection. This variety, and its potential, justify concluding this sketch of industrial dynamics by invoking George Richardson's (1975, p. 359) principle: 'Surely it is of the essence of competition that the participants hold uncertain and divergent beliefs about their chances of success'. This is competition between different ways of thinking; and the co-ordination problem within an economy is that of achieving the necessary compatibility between different ways of thinking while preserving the differences. (2001: 12)

Others will be more convinced of the open systems notion of equifinality. The idea of equifinality suggests that similar results may be achieved with different initial conditions and in many different ways: there are multiple routes through time which may lead to quite similar if not the same outcomes.

Specific Representations and Implicit Assumptions

This particular concern should also be seen as part of the wider issue that many of the ways we represent choices and situations carry certain unspoken assumptions, as illustrated by some common forms of representation shown in Figure 6.2. Of course such problems do not only arise with diagram-based representations. The most commonly used analytical technique – SWOT analysis – often gets reduced to seeing which quadrant has the longest list of issues!

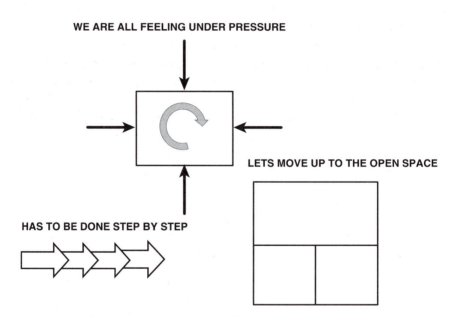

Figure 6.2 Particular analytical representations

© Robin Wensley

Contradictory Common Sense

This brings us back to where the chapter started: is practical wisdom much the same as common sense? As noted earlier, it is certainly often asserted that many of the conclusions from management research are "merely common sense".

However, this statement tends to underplay the extent to which in practical situations, "common sense" can be both contradictory and ambiguous – and indeed very much in the eye of the individual beholder. Table 6.1 gives some examples of commonly used but contradictory aphorisms.

Table 6.1   A selection of contradictory aphorisms

The pen is mightier than the sword	Actions speak louder than words
Don't judge a book by its cover	The clothes maketh the man
Look before you leap	Strike while the iron is hot
Too many cooks spoil the broth	Many hands make light work
Half a loaf is better than none	A miss is as good as a mile
All that glitters is not gold	Where there's smoke there's fire
Better safe than sorry	Nothing ventured, nothing gained
What's good for the goose is good for the gander	One man's meat is another man's poison
The best things in life are free	There's no such thing as a free lunch
Slow and steady wins the race	Time waits for no man
You are never too old to learn	You can't teach an old dog new tricks
Never look a gift horse in the mouth	Beware of Greeks bearing gifts
Birds of a feather flock together	Opposites attract
Seek and ye shall find	Curiosity killed the cat

(Edited from http://everything2.com/title/Contradictory+proverbs: accessed 29/04/10)
© 2010 Nick Kapur

A good test might be to reframe the particular practical situation into a different but related context and ask what common sense says we should do.

However, let us treat this as a thought experiment. Actually reframing a particular type of choice raises difficult questions in many experiments both in cognitive psychology and in education. Already mentioned is the translation of a simple but abstract mathematical reasoning test into an example grounded in everyday experience (Nunes et al. 1993) but this is only one example of a very general problem:

> The process of transadapting (translation and adaptation) psychological and educational tests embraces two objectives which are potentially conflicting. The first is to obtain maximal accuracy in translation while ensuring that the difficulty of the transadapted item approximates the difficulty in the source language as closely as possible. The second is to have the transadapted items read as fluently and naturally as they do in the source language. (Cohen et al. 2007: 17)

We also need to recognise that in many cases the most honest "common sense" answer is probably going to be "it all depends" but this inevitably leads to the supplementary question on the nature of the dependencies.

Maybe one should reverse at least to some extent the old canard that management research is "one half common sense and one half nonsense" and, following Lord Leverhulme on advertising, refine the assertion to "common sense is half right and half wrong; the trouble is often which half is which".

Conclusion: Common and Uncommon Sense

Einstein was indeed right if we "hide" behind the justification of common sense and avoid both critically examining the basis on which our judgements are made and also the nature of the empirical evidence that we access to support our action choices. This is particularly true when we try and apply "common sense" in a domain which is far removed – in either or both space and time – from the context in which we – individually or collectively – developed our understanding. However, for many of us, particularly maybe those with considerable managerial experience, it may well be that the codification of our learning and experience into "common sense" provides useful guidance in future choices and interventions. In such circumstances common sense does indeed also become practical wisdom.

However, particularly in competitive market situations there is a further wrinkle on this analysis. As Goddard and Eccles (2012) note, in such situations there are few winners and many losers. One way in which we can overcome this challenge is, to use their term, to actually rely on uncommon sense: to be different and contrarian. Of course there are also major risks in following their advice, since in a particular instance "common sense" may also be seen to embody the central and important notion that our analysis and interpretation needs to be grounded in a robust sense and experience of the practical.

7   The Central Role of Stories

It takes a thousand voices to tell a single story. (Native American saying)

Storytelling is the most powerful way to put ideas into the world today. (Robert McAfee Brown, American theologian)

There can be little doubt that stories can be one of the most powerful ways of communicating ideas and concepts to others. Recently, when doing some background research for this book on what is termed the phenomenon of unconscious thought effect (UTE), I came across what appeared to be a neat example. On his BBC Radio 4 programme *Start the Week* of 30 April 2012, Andrew Marr discussed creativity with the writer Jonah Lehrer. In his latest book, *Imagine*, Lehrer unpicked the creative process in both science and art, to ask where inventiveness and imagination spring from, and how they can be harnessed. (For those who wish to hear the interview itself, it can still be accessed at www.bbc.co.uk/programmes/b01gnq8y.)

The interview focused on a particular incident described in some detail in the book. Lehrer encapsulated the story under the sub-title "Bob Dylan's Brain":

"Bob Dylan looks bored. It's May 1965 and he's slumped in an armchair at the Savoy hotel in London. … For the previous four months, Dylan had been struggling to maintain a gruelling performance schedule. At times, Dylan lost his temper and became obstinate with reporters. "I've got nothing to say about these things I write," he insisted. "There's no great message. *Stop asking me to explain.*"

In London at a sold-out Royal Albert Hall, Dylan told his manager he was quitting the music business. He was finished with singing and songwriting and was going to move to a tiny cabin in Woodstock, New York …

It took a few days to adjust to the quiet of Woodstock. Dylan was suddenly alone with nothing but an empty notebook. And there was no need to fill this notebook – Dylan had been relieved of his creative burden. But then, just when Dylan was most determined to stop creating music, he was overcome with a strange feeling. "*It's a hard thing to describe,*" Dylan would later remember. "*It's just this sense that you got something to say.*" What he felt was the itch of an imminent insight, the tickle of lyrics that needed to be written down. "I found myself writing this song, this story, this long piece of vomit," Dylan said. "I'd never written anything like that before and it suddenly came to me that this is what I should do." Vomit is the essential word here. Dylan was describing, with characteristic vividness, the uncontrollable rush of a creative insight. "I don't know where my songs come from," Dylan said. "It's like a ghost is writing a song." This was the thrilling discovery that saved Dylan's career: he could write vivid lines filled with possibility without knowing exactly what those possibilities were. He didn't need to know. He just needed to trust the ghost…

He would later say that Like A Rolling Stone was his first *"completely free song … the one that opened it up for me"*. Those six minutes of raw music would revolutionise rock'n'roll." (Edited version from www.guardian.co.uk/music/2012/apr/06/neuroscience-bob-dylan-genius-creativity)

This is in many ways an appealing story which seems to illustrate a rather common truth: the sense of frustration that precedes the spark of creativity or imagination. There is just one problem: some of the Dylan quotes – the ones in italics – are apparently fakes. How important is this?

Well, pretty important at least for Mr Lehrer: on Monday 30 July 2012, he released a statement through his publisher, Houghton Mifflin Harcourt, saying that some Dylan quotes appearing in "Imagine: How Creativity Works" did "not exist", while others were "unintentional misquotations, or represented improper combinations of previously existing quotes". Lehrer said he acknowledged his actions after being contacted by Michael Moynihan of the online publication *Tablet Magazine*, which released an in-depth story on the Dylan passages in *Imagine*.

Lehrer wrote in his statement:

> I told Mr. Moynihan that they (the quotes in question) were from archival interview footage provided to me by Dylan's representatives. This was a lie spoken in a moment of panic. When Mr. Moynihan followed up, I continued to lie, and say things I should not have said.
>
> The lies are over now. I understand the gravity of my position. I want to apologize to everyone I have let down, especially my editors and readers.

Houghton Mifflin said in a statement that Lehrer had committed a "serious misuse". Listings for the e-book edition of *Imagine* were removed and shipments of the physical book stopped. *Imagine*, published in March, had sold more than 200,000 copies, according to Houghton Mifflin. It spent 16 weeks on the *New York Times'* hardcover non-fiction bestseller list (see www.csmonitor.com/Books/Latest-News-Wires/2012/0731/How-Jonah-Lehrer-was-caught-inventing-Bob-Dylan-quotes).

Herein perhaps does lie a cautionary tale, but what is the central message beside the rather prosaic one that when claiming to quote high-profile living individuals it is a good idea to check one's sources? It is worth considering, as earlier on in this book, the degree to which certain objects be they maps or stories can serve useful purposes even when their strict truth value may be rather limited. Indeed, in this section of the book what are the more colourful quotes that remain: in particular, "vomit" and "ghosts". In a different context one might expect a riposte from Jonah Lehrer along the lines of Whistler's reply to Oscar Wilde when the latter reputedly commented "I wish I had said that": "You will, Oscar, you will".

The chapters of this book have so far moved from how we understand the particular nature of any managerial knowledge, through the analysis of empirical and numerical data, to the use and application of particular frameworks. I will now move to the least codified but perhaps most common approach, that based on individual stories and the presentation of arguments that convince others; what in academe we often refer to as the development of a "plausible narrative" and a convincing rationale for a particular course of action.

Much of the recent research and commentary on the nature of plausible narratives in organisational life has focused on the use of narrative by elite groups in organisations to legitimise actions. Partly because of data-access problems there has been much less attention to the process of constructing the narrative but Abolafia provides a very interesting example. He also notes: "Narrative helps organizational actors make sense of their successes or failures because it contains indicators of who and what are causing the observed outcomes" (2010: 350).

I will also consider how the issues around the nature of such narratives are also reflected in a form of teaching that most encounter at various times in their MBA or equivalent studies: the case study.

Organisational Success and Failure: The Perils of "Learning from the Past"

I was never properly trained in sociology but it did seem that one of the key insights it provided was that events unfolded as a mixture of continuity and change. Hence, an understanding of history is important but there is a Janus-like character to these two perspectives which means that we should never privilege one to the exclusion of the other. Studying history should not be seen as an attempt to produce a singular and unambiguous causal conclusion let alone one which is generalisable to different time periods and different contexts. The old adage about those who do not learn the lessons of history being condemned to repeat the mistakes has already been discussed, but just as often quoted is Henry Ford's "History is more or less bunk. It's tradition. We don't want tradition. We want to live in the present and the only history that is worth a tinker's dam is the history we made today",[1] and we are caught with the knowledge that in our economic and political environment, context is critical and almost inevitably context changes over time.

Indeed, it is argued that in the wider context of Henry Ford's interview, this was actually pretty much what he was saying also:

> A few years ago, in an essay called "Doing History," [Eugen] Weber analyzed Henry Ford's famous remark, "History is bunk". Since Ford was a bigot and a tyrant, that's usually quoted as an example of ignorance. But Weber used it to demonstrate that we can understand nothing except through context. Ford actually said "History is more or less bunk", which is slightly different, and he said it in 1916, in the middle of the First World War.
>
> Ford thought that devotion to the past prevents us from grappling with the present and may encourage us to make war out of historical grievance. In 1914 all the European leaders knew their history, Ford said, yet they blundered into the worst war ever.
>
> On another occasion Ford recalled looking in American history books "to learn how our forefathers harrowed the land"; he discovered that historians barely mentioned harrows, the iron-toothed rakes essential to modern farming. Harrows, Ford argued, meant more in history than guns and speeches. When history "excludes harrows, and all the rest of daily life," then history is bunk.
>
> Maybe Ford felt strongly about harrows because he manufactured them, Weber says; even so, he was right when he argued that history should tell how ordinary people lived. And Ford won. The rise of social history began in the 1920s with the Annales movement in France, and has spread ever since. As Weber says, "The sort of history that Ford wanted is pretty much the history that we do today." (Fulford 1999)

We might also slightly alter the (in)famous Keynes dictum that "in the long run we are all dead"[2] to an equally valid "in the long run pretty much every human organisation will fail". Of course this seems to be less

---

[1] Henry Ford, interview in *Chicago Tribune*, 25 May 1916.

[2] The extended quote is "The long run is a misleading guide to current affairs. In the long run we are all dead. Economists set themselves too easy, too useless a task if in tempestuous seasons they can only tell us that when the storm is past the ocean is flat again" (*A Tract on Monetary Reform* (1923: Ch. 3). Many have thought this meant Keynes supported short-term gains against long-term economic performance, but he was actually criticising the belief that inflation would acceptably control itself without government intervention.

true of non-commercial organisations such as the church – and maybe even many universities – so perhaps we should focus our concerns on the long-run survival rates for commercial organisations.

The Shell Study

In an interesting study initiated by Arie de Geus at Shell, a study group was formed to look for inspiration in companies that were:

- older than the Shell Group (then almost 100 years of age)

- relatively as important in their industry as Shell was in theirs

- still existing with their corporate identity intact.

> One of the first findings of the group was that so few companies can be found that meet the three criteria. Of the tens of thousands of companies that existed around the turn of the century, only a handful of (major) ones are still alive today. In the end, out of some thirty companies found, twenty-seven were studied in detail. Amongst those were Booker McConnell and British American Tobacco from this country, Mitsui and Sumitomo from Japan, Siemens and the Société Générale from continental Europe, and Kodak and Dupont from the States. (1997: 1)

He does, however, believe we can learn something even from this small sample:

> So, history has something to teach us. Successful, long-lasting companies require a patient build-up of their human community – a thoughtful caring for the relationship between its human members to reach the required levels of trust. Only trust allows the mobilisation of the internal brain capacity that the company needs for renewal and survival. (1997: 5)

The Success or Failure of Mergers

Vaara, in discussing the narratives used to explain success or failure in specific post-merger integration projects, noted that:

> "The 'rationalistic' discourse proved to be the dominant discourse of these narratives, while the other discourses – 'cultural', 'role-bound' and 'individualistic' – could be seen as alternative discursive frameworks. This is not an unexpected finding in the sense that the existing literature on

mergers and acquisitions is largely dominated by 'rationalistic' discourse. (2002: 237–238)

He then, however, notes that there are two particular features of the "rationalistic" discourse. The "rationalistic" discourse offers few possibilities for "plurivocal or critical interpretations" and, within it, there is a tendency to hide internal political differences among the decision makers.

He also notices the importance of constructing the "other" – to use a psychoanalytical term – although he chooses to use the term "adversary" in discursive approaches in both credit and blame situations:

> As could be expected, the narrators frequently emphasized their **own** responsibility in success accounts and the role of **others** in failures. This analysis particularly points to the central role of the 'adversary', both in credit-taking and blame-avoiding accounts; a discursive feature that has received little attention in prior research on attributions in organizations. The 'adversary' was needed for the heroification or glorification of one's own actions in success accounts, but it was even more central in the failure accounts where the narrators wished to avoid responsibility. (Ibid.: 238–239)

In the failure accounts, he noted that the narrators could exploit two strategies when avoiding blame. First, they could try to limit their own responsibility by, for example, representing themselves as being not too central a decision maker. Second, they could attach blame to others by using different strategies such as "scapegoating" or "conspiracy-theory" building. As a result he noted that:

> success accounts were often rather straightforward narratives highlighting particular actions performed by collective management as causes of success, while failure accounts were usually more complex narratives. This can be taken as further evidence of failure accounts being more detailed descriptions than success accounts (see also Brown 1998). However, one can go further and argue that, while success narratives often manifested a linear logic of successive temporal events, the failure stories were characterized by more complex logics, as these accounts could include many kinds of interconnected explanatory elements (see also Burrell 1992). (Ibid.: 239)

It is worth noting that Kaplan who has undertaken a different sort of empirical research in this area, comments:

> Perhaps the best single paper on announcement returns (and the economics of acquisitions, in general) is Andrade, Mitchell and Stafford (2001). They look at all acquirers and targets in the merger and acquisition database of the University of Chicago Center for Research in Security Prices database over a 25-year period.

They first look at a three-day period around the announcement. They find that the combined announcement returns over that period are economically and statistically significant and positive. The combined values of the acquirer and target increase by 2% of the total initial value of the acquirer and target. This is equivalent to an increase that is roughly 10% of the initial value of the target alone.

This result is consistent across all three decades, the '70s, the '80s and the '90s. Bruner (2004) surveys a number of other papers and reaches the same conclusion. The returns to the targets are clearly positive. The returns to acquirers are slightly negative, but not statistically different from zero. The combined returns are positive. If one were to judge acquisition success only by the acquirer return, one would conclude mistakenly that acquisitions did not create value on average.

When Andrade et al. use a period that's longer and noisier – 20 days before the announcement until the acquisition closes – the combined returns are positive and of the same magnitude, but no longer statistically significant. Again, they are roughly 2 percent of the combined value, but because of the extra time (particularly after the announcement), there is more noise. And again, the returns to targets are positive; the returns to acquirers, slightly negative, but not significant. (2006: 5–6)

Given this broad evidential basis that mergers and acquisitions do show net economic benefits, but they tend to flow purely to the acquired organisation, maybe a merger (or indeed more generally a change) bias should be added to the previous comments about the evidence for "action bias"!

The Honda Case: Interpreting Success

One of the best-known examples of a case history which has been interpreted to generate a number of contradictory strategy lessons is the case of Honda and their entry into the American motor-cycle market. The various interpretations and comparative commentaries can be found in a series of articles in the *Californian Management Review* (Pascale et al. 1996).

In summary, the original consultancy study conducted for the UK government by Boston Consulting Group (BCG) interpreted the success that Honda enjoyed in the USA particularly at the expense of the UK imports as the result of substantial economies of scale for their small bikes based on the Cub model along with a market-entry strategy to identify and exploit a new segment and set of customers. Richard Pascale, on the other hand, later interviewed a number of the key executives who had worked for American Honda at the time and they told a story which suggested the whole operation was very much on a shoestring and the final success was down to a

number of lucky breaks including a buyer from Sears persuading them to let
him sell their small-model bikes when they were really trying, and failing,
to break into the big-bike market.

The debate recorded in the *Californian Management Review* certainly illustrated how the same story can be interpreted in very different ways. It also
emphasises the problem that learning from the undoubted final success that
Honda achieved can be very problematic; even perhaps for Honda itself. It
would seem that in many ways one of the underlying dilemmas for Honda,
as indeed for any new market entrant, was that if they took the existing
market structure as fixed and given then the possibilities for them were
remote; on the other hand, the current market knowledge could only really
hint at possibilities for new market structures.

In the end, Michael Goold, who worked for BCG at the time, concludes that:

> The [BCG] report does not dwell on how the Honda strategy was evolved
> and on the learning that took place. However, the report was commis-
> sioned for industry in crisis, with a brief of identifying commercially viable
> alternatives. The perspective required was managerial, not historical. And
> for most executives concerned with strategic management the primary
> interest will always be what should we do now?
>
> Presumably the [Mintzberg] recommendation would be "try something, see if
> it works and learn from your experience"; indeed there is some suggestion
> that one should specifically try probable non-starters. For the manager such
> advice would be unhelpful even irritating. "Of course we should learn from
> experience" he will say, "But we have neither the time nor the money to
> experiment with endless fruitless non-starters". Where the manager needs
> help is in what he should try to make work. This surely is exactly where strate-
> gic management thinking should endeavour to be useful. (1996: 169–170)

Whilst Mintzberg comments:

> How then did BCG's clients actually learn from this report? And what
> lessons did BCG itself take from this particular bit of history? Did it take a
> good look at its own performance – do some analysis about the impact of
> its own analysis?
>
> The British motorcycle and parts exports to the United States collapsed to
> 10 million dollars in 1976, the year after the report was published. So
> much for the result of this practical managerial perspective. I believe that
> managers who have neither the time nor the money to experiment are
> destined to go to the road of the British motorcycle industry. How in the
> world can anyone identified those endless, fruitless non-starters in
> advance? To assume such an ability is simply arrogance, and would, in
> fact, have eliminated many, if not most of really innovative products we
> have come to know. (1996: 96–97)

In the terms of our previous analysis we could argue that Goold is focusing attention on the 10 per cent that can be explained analytically whilst Mintzberg is arguing not only that the 90 per cent is much more important but, even more significantly, that a realisation of specific causes of success can be achieved more effectively through processes such as learning. This is in practice a strong assertion about the efficacy of leaning processes in organisations that others might dispute.

In a further and somewhat more recent commentary on the whole debate about the Honda study, Mair argues that:

> There is considerable evidence to suggest that a significant characteristic of management thinking at Honda is a focus on the reconciliation of apparently contradictory conceptual dichotomies, and that this is a specific route to innovation. ... Elsewhere this capacity to manage apparently contradictory concepts and practices has been called Honda's dichotomy-reconciling strategic capability. What is therefore required is an investigation of strategic management at Honda Motors from a theoretical perspective which admits the possibility that strategic thinking at Honda is not constrained by a dualist philosophy requiring choice between learning and design, industry analysis and resource-based strategy, core capabilities and core competencies.

> Indeed it might be speculated that Honda in particular has become embroiled in the strategy debates not simply because of its undoubted commercial successes in recent decades, but precisely because, with a dichotomy – reconciling approach to management thinking in which both poles are retained (albeit in new ways), the company does in fact offer evidence which permits 'each side' of the arguments to feel justified in clinging to their position (so long as they are blind to the other side). (1999: 39)

Fads and Fashions

Isaiah Berlin, in commenting on the prospects for so-called scientific history, noted:

> Even if such symbols of inference as 'because', 'therefore' or 'hence' were omitted a piece of reasoning in mathematics or physics or any other developed natural science (if it were clearly set out) should be able to exhibit its inner logical structure by the sheer meaning and order of its component propositions ... This is very far from being the case in even the best, most convincing, most rigorously argued works of history. No student of the subject can, I think, fail to note the abundance in works of history of such phrases as 'small wonder if', 'it was therefore hardly surprising when', 'the inevitable consequences swiftly followed', 'events took their inexorable course', 'in the circumstances', 'from this it was a short step to', and most often of all the indispensable, scarcely noticeable, and deeply treacherous,

'thus', 'whereupon, 'finally', and the like. If these bridges from one set of facts or statements to the another were suddenly withdrawn from our textbooks, it is I think not too much to say that the transition from to the other would become a great deal less smooth. (1980: 117)

There are certainly analogous problems in much management research and indeed the expression "a great deal less smooth" might itself be seen as rather an understatement.

Finally, there are certain words or concepts which seem to be used so widely and indiscriminately that they lose any real meaning. Much as many years ago Aaron Wildavsky entitled a paper on public policy "If Planning is Everything, Perhaps it is Nothing", so on an annual basis the same fate befalls the next crop of new ideas in management. A simple approach might be labelled the Dilbert test: if the concept/approach has featured three or more times in Scott Adam's excellent cartoon strip then it is certainly over-used and maybe already past its sell-by date. Figure 7.1 reproduces two such cartoon strips. Many of us might pause to think about much that is written let alone actually practised in the field of management strategy.

A (slightly) more sophisticated version of this test might be to compare the frequency of mentions in Dilbert cartoons with the equivalent popularity as revealed by the annual Bain survey of specific management techniques (see Table 7.1).

Figure 7.1   Dilbert on strategic management

Table 7.1 Expected change in technique use

	Actual 2008 usage	Actual 2010 usage	Projected increase 10 to 11	Projected 2011 usage
Strategic planning	67	65	21	86
Benchmarking	76	67	16	83
Customer relationship management	63	58	24	82
Mission and vision statements	65	63	15	78
Strategic alliances	44	45	28	73
Core competencies	48	46	27	73
Customer segmentation	53	42	29	71
Knowledge management	41	38	31	69
Change management programmes	–	46	23	69
Outsourcing	63	55	13	68
Business process re-engineering	50	38	29	67
Scenario and contingency planning	42	30	35	65
Satisfaction and loyalty management	17	32	32	64
Balanced scorecard	53	47	16	63
Total quality management	34	38	24	62
Supply chain management	43	39	21	60
Open innovation	24	21	36	57
Enterprise risk management	–	30	27	57
Social media programs	26	29	27	56
Price optimisation models	–	21	34	55
Shared services centers	41	28	25	53
Mergers & acquisitions	46	35	18	53
Decision rights tools	10	17	29	46
Rapid prototyping	–	11	21	32
Downsizing	34	25	6	31

Source: Darrell Rigby and Barbara Bilodeau, Management Tools & Trends 2011, Bain and Company [available at: http://www.bain.com/Images/BAIN_BRIEF_Management_Tools.pdf]

Most of the specific techniques are widely understood except perhaps the term "decision rights tools" which are designed to help companies organise their decision making and execution by setting clear roles and accountabilities and by giving all those involved a sense of ownership of decisions: when to provide input, who should follow through and what is beyond their scope. They are reasonably synonymous with the notions of procedural rationality discussed in Chapter 1.

Overall, however, we should perhaps be a little cautious with the projected percentage points increases for 2011; it does seem a little unlikely that they will all be positive and an average of 24 percentage points, particularly given that on comparable items there was an overall 4 percentage points drop between 2008 and 2010!

We should also recognise that Bain and Company are just one of a number of substantial strategy consultancies and therefore perhaps have an interest in encouraging senior managers to adopt more "sophisticated" management tools which themselves often are seen to require the assistance of the consultancies. I will return to a wider discussion on the role of management consultants later in the book.

Revisiting the Onus of Proof Issue

Earlier in this book I looked quite closely at statistical approaches to the issue of some form of proof of an assertion, but of course in making collective decision and action choices this is only one way to convince others to agree on the most appropriate option. Indeed, as noted earlier, Deidre McCluskey for one would argue that it is only an effective approach when the oft-confused recipient is convinced not through understanding but by the appeal to notions of the higher level (unchallengeable nature) of the analytical approach. The wider perspective considers both the most appropriate form of argumentation and the extent to which the suggested choice has to be seen as proven to the others.

In the terminology we are more used to in courts of law this means we need to pay attention particularly to what would be termed the "onus of proof" question but also to the general issue of the admissibility of evidence. In legal situations we have two different types of judgement which affect the nature of the "onus of proof" criterion. In criminal cases we are concerned with "beyond reasonable doubt", whereas in civil cases we are concerned with the "balance of probabilities". Some have argued that one of the key analytical and practical problems in the analysis of action options is that we are often obliged to represent a balance of probabilities as something much more certain – moving much more towards the beyond reasonable doubt criterion. This inevitably means the analytical representation often relies on a combination of analysis and rhetoric to achieve the desired certainty.

When and How Does the Decision Get Made?

In a brief commentary in a 1990 paper, Mintzberg and Waters asked "Does Decision Get in the Way?" They noted the common difficulty in tracing actual decisions in observing organisational practice: "If a decision is really a commitment to action, then the trace it leaves behind in an organization can range from a clear statement of intent – as in the recorded minute of a meeting – to nothing" (1990: 2). And they quoted with approval an earlier commentary by Nicolaides:

> It is evident on the basis of [my] analysis that an organizational decision is in reality a constellation or a galaxy of numerous individual decisions. Some of these decisions are "registered" in the book of the organizational activities, while others remain hidden in the inner sanctum of the human psyche. When and where a decision begins and ends is not always clear. (1960: 173)

In passing, with a fine sense of unconscious irony, they refer to this thesis as "rarely cited" and then fail to give the citation in their own references!

In research that Kathryn Thomas, Paddy Barwise, Paul Marsh and I undertook on strategic investment decisions (see Marsh et al 1988) many years ago, we noted two types of problem if one adopted a "decision-making" perspective. The first was the one to which Mintzberg and Waters referred in that, certainly ex post, it was much easier to trace actions rather than decisions but it was also true that we were observing, in real time, a process as much or more than an event.

This meant, for instance, that the actual identification of decision was almost always at a rather different point in time from the official "bureaucratic" decision-making schedule. A combination of the previous discussion about the rather continuous nature of the time dimension and the more complex optional nature of most choices helps to explain this analytically but alongside this there is also the ongoing process of building support and negating objections.

The more continuous nature of the time dimension means that individual decisions tend to evolve and undergo at least some degree of metamorphosis before they finally emerge as "a decision". Their optional nature is reflected in the fact that most important decisions are in fact more or less a sequence of individual decisions which both open up and close down future choices from a range of options.

So do "decisions" get in the way either or both in research and/or practice? As both Pettigrew and Butler in their separate commentaries on the Mintzberg–Waters note recognise, it is rather a matter of what we are trying to do. If we are studying strategy and adopt a definition that strategy is a pattern in a sequence of actions then the notion of one or more decisions is of very limited additional value. Pettigrew's response to this is broadly to focus on change and context and downplay both a pure decision and also a pure action focus. Butlers approach is rather more trenchant, and also rather more in line with the approach adopted in this book.

He argues that:

> strategy must surely involve a degree of intention to act, a kind of plan which is to be put into effect. The word strategy belongs, after all, to a language borrowed from the study of military campaigns translated into the business arena. A military commander who, when asked to describe his strategy, had to say 'I can only tell you after the battle' could not really be said to have a strategy. Certainly, one can attempt to retrospectively reconstruct a strategy by looking at the kinds of decisions made and the actions taken by a general over time. If one did this, decision processes cease to be dependent variables and now become independent variables, that is, one might use a description of decision processes to attempt to work out whether there was a plan, or an intention, worked out beforehand; process would become an explanation of strategy. (1990: 15)

I have already considered in Chapter 4 how the more flexible nature of the military hierarchy provides for both the control of and autonomy for local units and more generally the application of the writings of military strategists, particularly von Molkte. I will return later in Chapter 10 to consider how such writings also provide useful insights in the more current debates, in particular the change in emphasis from both strategy and decisions to the notion and application of leadership.

It is also worth noting that the extent to which we privilege a decision, action or change perspective very much depends on pragmatic as well as more fundamental ontological[3] and epistemological[4] questions. If, for

---

[3]Ontology (from the Greek onto-, meaning "being; that which is", and -logia: science, study, theory) is the philosophical study of the nature of being, existence, or reality, as well as the basic categories of being and their relations.

[4]Epistemology (from Greek epistēmē, meaning "knowledge, understanding", and logos, meaning "study of") is the branch of philosophy concerned with the nature and scope (limitations) of knowledge.

instance, we are focusing attention around intervention to influence particular action choices there are good reasons to do so in the name of the decision process even if the context means that other processes and structures are at work. If, on the other hand, we wish researchers and observers to understand "what is going on around here" we may well find that a focus more on processes and structures is more enlightening.

To give two particular and relatively simple examples. First, when we were undertaking our study of strategic investment decision making, Kathryn Thomas, who was observing a long and detailed meeting between the focal firm and one of its key suppliers, was rather taken aback that the whole atmosphere of the meeting seemed to deteriorate after a short "comfort break". In discussing this with one of the participants afterwards he told her of a quick discussion with his colleague in the gent's toilets: they had both realised one of the people they were negotiating with was previously known to both of them and was not to be trusted!

Second, a PhD student of mine – Alex Faria – was doing field research amongst first-tier suppliers to the auto industry in both Brazil and UK. It just happened that the main auto companies were at the time German owned: VW in Brazil and Austin–Rover in the UK. He was discussing with the chief executive of the Brazilian supplier the background to a major shift in their suppliers and asked, "What actually happened?" Somewhat to his surprise the CEO responded with the question, "Which story do you want: the Brazilian or the German one?" In the end Alex got both stories (see Faria and Wensley 2002) and they were very distinct: the German one was all economics and costs, the Brazilian one about the bad relationships with and behaviours of the relevant supplier.

Insights from Stories

This brings us to the role of empirically informed stories, which in one sense are always about one particular case. The old adage that "empirical data is not just the plural of anecdote" may in fact be fundamentally wrong; we could alternatively argue that such data is no more than the collection of anecdotes! From this perspective "stories" which are reduced to a single series of numbers are perhaps to be seen as one end of the spectrum with rich in-depth case descriptions at the other.

Indeed, it is worth recalling that a critical realist perspective on much of statistical analysis discourages us from treating the constructed variables in any data-set as strictly real. Byrne (2002), while continuing to endorse measurement, has argued that the products of measurement should be understood not as variables possessing independent causal powers but rather as 'variate traces' which help us to understand the state of a system.

But what of stories as a basis for management insight? The genre that might be termed the "case study" or "case example" is an interesting one for management academics both researching and teaching yet it has been subjected to relatively little critical scrutiny. From a research perspective we might perhaps focus attention on a text which allows a range of interpretations and is also rich enough to allow critical scrutiny of what might be termed the surface narrative(s). From a teaching perspective we are often more concerned with engaging the interest of the key audience.

In most situations the "research case" is seen as distinct from the "teaching case" and indeed the latter is often reduced to a potentially interesting "case example". The most obvious and high-profile alternative approach is to be found within the research and teaching tradition of the Harvard Business School, where over the years since the first book of cases was published in 1918, there has been a consistent if intermittent attempt to argue that producing and using case studies is also itself a legitimate and valuable form of management research. The most recent example of an attempt to make such an argument is to be found in Christensen and Carlile (2009).

Alternative approaches see the case as a generally extended often multi-vocal text which can be anything from 4000 words to a whole book at one extreme and a 300–500-word illustrative story at the other extreme. Although it is quite common to refer to any of this wide range of objects just as case studies, this is often misleading. Consider, for instance, the nature of a research case study, where it is common to have only one to three detailed cases in a whole book and compare this with the advice on writing a persuasive short "case study" that it should be "short, candid and revealing" and that it should "build suspense, have a satisfying conclusion and solve a generalizable business problem" (Weil 2004).

I will return to the more detailed issues in using the case study as a teaching method in the next chapter.

Numbers as Stories

We can indeed consider what might be termed a statistical case study, encompassing many of the issues considered in Chapter 5, as a particular form of story-telling. One is reminded of the old joke told in various forms about the comic who merely speaks numbers to indicate a particular joke and an ingénue who attempts to imitate his performance but gets no laughter. Following his puzzlement, the explanation is that it is not the joke itself but the way the comic tells it. Maybe there is a lesson here on interpreting much statistical data.

The statistical version of the story in principle represents one extreme in which what we might call the grammar and language is highly restricted and stylised. Beyond this there are other important differences, as described by Paulos (2010) in comparing statistical stories with narrative ones:

> there is a tension between stories and statistics, and one under-appreciated contrast between them is simply the mindset with which we approach them. In listening to stories we tend to suspend disbelief in order to be entertained, whereas in evaluating statistics we generally have an opposite inclination to suspend belief in order not to be beguiled. ... we have different error thresholds in different endeavours, but the type of error people feel more comfortable may be telling. It gives some indication of their intellectual personality type, on which side of the two cultures ... divide they're most comfortable.

> People who love to be entertained and beguiled ... might be more apt to prefer stories to statistics. Those who don't particularly like being entertained or beguiled ... might be more apt to prefer statistics to stories. The distinction is not unrelated to that between those (61.389% of us) who view numbers in a story as providing rhetorical decoration and those who view them as providing clarifying information.

> The so-called "conjunction fallacy" suggests another difference between stories and statistics. After reading a novel, it can sometimes seem odd to say that the characters in it don't exist. The more details there are about them in a story, the more plausible the account often seems. More plausible, but less probable. In fact, the more details there are in a story, the less likely it is that the conjunction of all of them is true. Congressman Smith is known to be cash-strapped and lecherous. Which is more likely? Smith took a bribe from a lobbyist or Smith took a bribe from a lobbyist, has taken money before, and spends it on luxurious "fact-finding" trips with various pretty young interns. Despite the coherent story the second alternative begins to flesh out, the first alternative is more likely.

Maybe this is part of the explanation for Jonah Lehrer's additions to the Bob Dylan quotes discussed at the start of this chapter. Not only did the additional "quotes" add weight to his interpretation but they also might be seen to add to the credibility of the story itself.

One of the advantages of a statistical story is that, in principle at least even if not in practice, we can apply refined testing of the specific nature of the set of relationships. However, many academic articles in management research adopt rather less rigorous processes. For instance, as already seen in Chapter 5, in the case of more complex statistical models, often generated by a structural equation modelling (SEM) approach, we should apply a more strict comparison based on a so-called equivalence model but often fail to do so.

The Narrative Approach

In the case of the story as narrative we encounter two challenges. First, as already alluded to, there is a tendency for the reader to regard the greater amount of detail about specific context as a sign of authenticity. On top of this there are at least some ways in which researcher's stories about organisational narratives reflect if not repeat the nature of the dominant stories passed on throughout the organisation.

One influential analysis concentrated on the so-called "uniqueness" paradox. Stories which embody the unique nature of the organisation are themselves based on far from unique scripts (Martin et al. 1983). The seven "scripts" are summarised as themselves linked to three enduring dualities for individuals within organisations in Table 7.2. There are "negative" and "positive" versions of each story but this is only to be expected given the enduring nature of the dualities.

Table 7.2   **Dualities underlying common concerns in organisational stories**

Dualities	Concerns
Equality vs. Inequality	What do I do when a higher status person breaks a rule?
	Is the big boss human?
	Can the little person rise to the top?
Security vs. Insecurity	Will I be fired?
	Will the organisation help me if I have to move?
	How will the boss react to mistakes?
Control vs. Lack of Control	How will the organisation deal with obstacles?

(Copyright © 1983 Sage Publications Ltd. Reproduced with permission)

If we wish to go further in our analysis of stories, then we need to recognise, as Pentland observes, that:

> In process theory typical patterns of events, such as variation and selective retention, are core theoretical constructs (Van de Ven & Poole, 1995). These archetypal stories are used to explain surface patterns that we observe in our data. In narrative theory these underlying narrative structures are stories (Chatman, 1978; Rimmon-Kenan, 1983) or fabula (Bal, 1985). They reflect the deep structure of a narrative, and they are used to explain and interpret the surface structure, which is the text or the discourse (Rimmon-Kenan, 1983).

Usage of the term construct has been honed by years of training and experience with variance-based research (Mohr, 1982), so some readers may find
this claim surprising. Nonetheless, to say that stories are constructs is not
just a play on words. In narrative theory stories are abstract conceptual
models used in explanations of observed data. (1999: 711)

But, as he recognises, when it comes to questions of action and intervention
informed by previous evidence represented in various schema we still face
major issues:

We want to know how changing X will affect Y. Our literature is filled
with statements about relationships between constructs that claim to offer
an explanation (e.g., "this regression model explains 30 percent of the
variance in Y"). But the explanation lies in the story that connects X and Y
not the regression model itself. Knowing that the relationship between X
and Y is mediated by a complex, generative process that we cannot
directly observe is an interesting and humbling insight. I think this insight
is especially valuable when one is considering interventions to change or
improve a process. If one conceptualizes a process as a fixed sequence,
like a piece of videotape that gets played over and over, one might be
tempted to try splicing in a new segment. This is also a kind of "surface-
only" perspective. If one conceptualizes a process as a set of interacting
roles and subplots that just happen to produce a typical pattern in their
current configuration, then there is no tape into which one can splice.
(Ibid.: 722)

There are perhaps analogies here with the changing nature of our understanding in the mapping and interpretation of the human genome. It was
recently reported that:

The Encyclopedia of DNA Elements project has discovered that 80 percent
of the human genome has a biochemical function, debunking the theory
that non-coding genes are simply "junk DNA".

When the Human Genome Project revealed that only around two percent
of the genome is made up of protein-coding genes, it was suggested that
the rest was made up of "junk DNA".

The new research instead shows that 80 percent of the 98 unaccounted for
has some kind of biochemical function, with 10,000 genes tasked with
regulating the DNA responsible for coding proteins—these 10,000 are
responsible for building single-strand RNA molecules that regulate the
20,000 protein-coding genes. The mass of otherwise unaccounted for DNA
actually represents a series of around four million "switches" that regulate
other genes, and around nine percent of DNA helps code these switches
(the figure could end up being nearer 20 percent, however) …

It is only down to the accurate function of these millions of switches that our bodies can function, suggesting mutations among these control hub genes could be the cause of diseases. (Edited from www.wired.co.uk/news/archive/2012-09/06/encode-human-genome)

Conclusion: an Effective Role for Analysis in Management Practice

Based on this and previous chapters in the book, I suggest that when it comes to the specifics of a decision or intervention we can derive seven simple rules to ensure that analysis is effective in assisting choices within any organisation:

1 Most importantly, use any of your analysis to frame a better question not to provide the universal answer.

2 Test the boundaries of the justification: in what ways might the proposed action have so far unanticipated costs or indeed benefits?

3 Make sure that the risks have as far as possible been factored into the analysis.

4 Make sure that inevitable increase in uncertainties over time has been properly considered; action later is sometimes more advantageous than action now.

5 Test out the commitment and understanding of those who will be essential to the success of the action proposed.

6 Never look for certainty but focus on the balance of the evidence and analysis.

7 Encourage others to take a different perspective on the overall issue and to introduce both stories and numbers as they wish to illustrate this.

8   Linking the Classroom to the Workplace

"I want to say that I dread very much the effect of a committee of the faculty. It is not easy to make a success of the thing by making it an academic instead of a professional school, as has been the case, I believe, in other institutions … we are trying a great, but I think, delicate experiment". (Letter from Lawrence Lowell to President of Harvard Charles Elliot in August 1907 about plans for a Business School at Harvard)

Learning from Case Studies

Most participants on MBA and similar programmes have their share of case studies. Such case studies provide a good starting point to understanding and developing our skills at learning to learn in a way which is useful in the context of management practice. For those who can get hold of a copy it is worth looking at Geoff Easton's book *Learning from Case Studies* (1992), which gives a very good step-by-step introduction as to how one can get the best out of case studies, be they found in courses or indeed in one's own experience. The basic structure of the book is around what he calls the "seven steps process" of a case analysis:

- step one: understanding the situation;

- step two: diagnosing the problem areas;

- step three: generating alternative solutions;

- step four: predicting outcomes;

- step five: evaluating alternatives;

- step six: rounding out the analysis;

- step seven: communicating the results.

Overall the book remains an excellent and comprehensive but succinct book which is informative for both learners and instructors. However, if you cannot get hold of a copy, a shorter introduction is available from Harvard itself. It is biased towards the public sector but the guidance really applies to cases in any sector and it has the benefit of being only five pages long. It is entitled "Learning by the case method" (available at www.case.hks.harvard.edu/images/other/1136_0.pdf).

A rather different but equally instructive perspective on the methods of case teaching and its specific application to a number of key issues in strategic management is to be found in Richard Rumelt's book *Good Strategy/Bad Strategy*, which is also a useful book for both learners and instructors by someone who was fully schooled in the orthodoxy of Harvard case teaching but has spent most of his academic career outside Harvard Business School (HBS).

It is also perhaps worth emphasising that in the context of case-study teaching at least to some extent we are actually all learners anyway. My own rude awakening to this truism was as a young lecturer teaching marketing management on the MBA programme at London Business School. There was one very bright member of the class who seemed to make rather a habit of turning up about 15 minutes late. On the day in question we were working on a very traditional and at the time well-used case: the Avon Company (HBS ref 9-590-022), which confusingly was a firm not in the cosmetics business but in the industrial fractional horse-power electric motor market. X as was his wont came in around 15 minutes late and sat listening to the discussion for about ten minutes. He then joined in and started by suggesting that we had all got it wrong and proceeded with an analysis and argument which was certainly not to be found in the instructor's crib sheet – otherwise known as the teaching note. My only claim to any level of wisdom was that I let him develop his argument. It turned out he had a novel and much more convincing analysis than any other that had been developed!

"Learning to Learn", both in the context of an MBA programme itself but also more broadly, is inevitably a combination of the application of particular theoretical approaches to specific situations and also a process of what might be called forensic analysis of the case or situation itself. In this book I emphasise the development and application of a number of analytical tools and approaches to aid this process of "forensic analysis". However, we also need to understand the extent to which the assumptions embodied in any particular framework or tool are to be seen as valid in a particular decision context; after all one of the central messages of rich case studies, as opposed to those which we might call case examples, which are merely used to demonstrate the application of a theory or analytical framework, is that the particular context matters crucially.

In research methodology there is broadly a distinction between approaching issues deductively (i.e. starting with a more general theory and deriving specific hypotheses to the tested against the empirical data) and alternatively inductively, where we consider the more detailed specific empirical context and then attempt to establish some more general conjectures which could be applied more widely. In most MBA programmes what is taught overall is a rather uncomfortable mix between an inductive and a deductive process except when the curriculum is almost exclusively at one end of the spectrum, as for instance in the design of the Harvard MBA which since really the 1920s has been dominated by the case-method approach.

It may not be much of a surprise that, particularly for more experienced managers, the inductive approach is often found to be more congenial, as indeed more generally where Birkinshaw et al. (2012) find that "on average, inductive [academic] papers are more likely to be cited in managerially-oriented publications, relative to deductive papers". However, it still requires considerable effort and understanding to avoid a feeling at the end of a case-study session that it was "just another case study" or that implicitly or explicitly the conclusion is "anything you want it to be". Particularly in the latter case we need to be aware that the effective learning approach to a case study is not at all the same as a case presentation where the evidence, as discussed earlier, suggested a generally rather episodic series of vignettes from the presenter are individually reconfigured into different and often contradictory meaningful narratives by most members of the audience (Sims et al. 2009).

What are Case Studies for?

I now return to the issue of how we might teach and indeed learn from a focus on the practice, rather than just the theory, of management. This brings us back to some of the issues raised at the start of this book and in particular the espousal of case teaching in both of the original 1959 US Foundation Reports. Much of the underlying pedagogy for case teaching in management has been misrepresented both in what is written about and also taught in the name of "case teaching". Broadly speaking the case method, as practised particularly at HBS, was an attempt to help individuals develop the analytical but also communication skills to be able to make effective decisions in management situations and at the same time to convince others of the correctness of their particular action choice. The case study itself represented a particular organisational context and the discussion is the process of refining the argument with one's peers in favour of a particular course of action. It is also worth noting in the context of the discussion in the previous section that the key emphasis was on the choice of action to be followed rather than a decision per se. Indeed, within the orthodoxy of this pedagogic approach it was recognised that in some particular situations it could be appropriate to conclude that no action was the best course to be followed.

Whilst there was inevitably some link between the way in which cases were used for teaching in the Harvard Law School there were important differences as well. Many legal cases were accompanied by a detailed legal judgement which in a sense provided an answer to the problem proposed by the case itself. In such cases the learning exercise was more linked to appreciating the legal basis on which the "correct" decision had been made. In the Business School there was in principle no correct or right answer to the case study – it was open ended even to the extent that some professors would argue that what in fact happened after the case study was totally irrelevant.

Of course, in practice, life was not quite as simple as this. In Harvard practice, as I have already indicated above, each case study was accompanied by a teaching note which provided some guidance not only on the teaching process but also the issues that might be covered and the forms of analysis that might be encouraged. Equally, it was not unusual to have the CEO or someone else senior in the organisation concerned also observing the class discussion and commenting at the end.

The twin effects of a process of critical questioning which was often initiated by the participants but also guided by the instructor, who would have previously studied the teaching note and the frequent focus on the issues and choices as seen from the perspective of a senior executive, was to emphasise analytical thinking – much as espoused in this book as well – but also often to avoid contentious issues of power, expertise and authority. Another PhD student of mine – Ianna Contardo – spent some time doing her research at HBS and found that at least some of the faculty recognised the extent to which in practice the claim that the case study and the teaching was of an open-ended nature was often not borne out in practice: there was a clear agenda and some topics were effectively ruled in and others ruled out (Contardo and Wensley 2004).

This observation may also help to explain why many case studies are not particularly, or maybe even at all, good stories. In general, the formula for a good case study is distinctly different from that for a good story. The intention of course is still to engage the interest of the reader/participant, but in the case study there is a clear focus as well as agenda for discussion. In this sense at least a case study discussion is almost always constrained rather than open-ended. But at least in many cases, novels are themselves rather less open-ended than life; we might recall E.M. Forster (1927: 95) in *Aspects of the Novel*:

> Nearly all novels are feeble at the end. This is because the plot requires to be wound up. Why is this necessary? Why is there not a convention which allows a novelist to stop as soon as he feels muddled or bored? ... Incidents and people that occurred at first for their own sake now have to contribute to the dénouement ... most novels do fail here – there is this disastrous standstill while logic takes over the command from flesh and blood. If it was not for death and marriage I do not know how the average novelist would conclude.

Differences between Case Study Learners: Novices and Experts

Easton and Ormerod (2001) in a detailed study of both novice and expert learners considered the differences in their approach to case studies. It should, however, be noted that their definitions of expert and novices refer solely to experience with learning and teaching from case studies.

They concluded that:

> Although the time spent on analyses did not differ reliably between experts and novices, large qualitative differences were found between the groups. Experts generated more alternative recommendations, identified more critical issues and used more evaluative criteria than novices. The outcomes of their analyses were generally qualitatively better than those of novices and were more likely to bring in issues not specifically referred to in the case statement. Novices also tended to reach a firm viewpoint or recommendation early often during the first reading of the case statement while some experts deferred reaching a recommendation until later in the analysis, were more likely to change their stance during the analysis, and in some cases did not reach a specific recommendation at all. Novice analyses focused more upon outcome while expert analyses were more likely to focus on process issues.

> Novice analyses tended to be disappointingly shallow, and constrained by the content and order of the case statement. Perhaps the most important general finding is that the final output of the analyses often seems to be a poor summary of the richness of the process that has gone before. This contrasted with expert analyses, which became more focused yet did not lose the richer issues generated earlier in the analysis.

> Comparisons between novice analyses before and after training revealed
> evidence, both of an improvement in the quality of analyses, and changes in the
> process of analysis. In particular that, the depth of analysis increase, and
> solution development tended to be deferred until later in the analysis. (2001: 2)

A number of differences between case analysis and other creative problem-
solving domains were identified. While phases of problem understanding,
solution development, evaluation and review are common across domains
there was relatively little evidence in the expert protocols of the control
activities specifically scheduling and monitoring that dominate protocols in
domains such as designing problem-solving.

Although in the majority of expertise domains increased expertise typically leads to a convergence of process and outcome across individuals, they
found the opposite effect in their study. Some experts claimed to avoid early
note taking deliberately, as it encouraged the reification of bad ideas. Indeed,
there was some evidence that early documentation by some novices inhibited
the quality of their subsequent analyses they tended to collate documentation
in place of a properly structured analyses output.

In returning to the nature of the case itself, they note:

> The kinds of outcomes generated by both expert and novice groups are, at
> least in part, a function of the nature of the case itself. Where case state-
> ments represented the analysis is a choice between alternatives, this
> highly constrained the nature of the analyses while cases that were open-
> ended typically elicited richer analyses, especially with the expert and
> post training novice protocols. In the pre-training novice protocols,
> however, there is evidence that open-ended cases gave rise to large
> individual difference while some participants produced richer analyses
> then with more constrained cases others produced highly superficial and
> truncated analyses. (Ibid.: 40–41)

The Challenge of Simulating and Learning from Management Practice

The balance between some degree of structured learning and the wish to
import the lived nature of management practice into the "classroom" is ever
present and almost always somewhat problematic.

Amongst other major concerns, there is the whole question of the nature
of lived management practice anyway. Most management teachers are all
well aware of the old canard about doing and teaching but as any seasoned
business school academic knows, the best thing to do when challenged with
some assertion about the real nature of anything is to ask the challenger to

identify what they see as the essential characteristics of the said reality. With any luck within ten minutes one has a raging debate between the participants about what is and is not reality!

Of course, at least to some extent this stratagem is a bit of a cop-out but no more so that the opposite claim that only individual experience can be the basis for systematic knowledge and understanding in fields such as management. Indeed, we should be equally wary of collusion between academe and practice. A long time ago when I first really got involved in executive education one of my mentors, Dennis Pym, used to argue that when it came to senior executive teaching there was often an implicit collusion between the participants and the instructor: they would treat the instructor as if s/he had useful knowledge to impart and the instructor would treat the participants as if they were persons of major influence. Indeed, it is perhaps arguable that the only management domain in which academic knowledge has become fully privileged by practitioners is in the field of financial economics and we now know how dangerous and misleading this can be on a truly major scale.

So how do I define a mid-way position between these two unsustainable extremes? Those who have read this far through this book will be hardly surprised by the answer: multi-method. I would argue that even the "great" HBS case, valuable as a teaching method as it is, cannot achieve a real synthesis on its own. There has to be room for simulations, video material, self-directed activities and also indeed some theoretical and research input.

Video Material

I would still wish to argue that the *Decision* series of fly-on-the wall documentaries produced in 1978 by Roger Graef remain one of the best video materials for discussing many aspects of actual management decision making.[1] This is particularly true of *Decision: Steel*[2] and *Decision: Oil*.

Despite some element of "playing to camera", the videos overall provided rich and engaging material that allowed the instructor to design a session which could investigate the interaction between analysis, process and personalities in a practical context which had a ring of authenticity

---

[1] The three documentaries and their airing dates on Granada TV were: *Steel: The Korf Contract* (27 January 1976); *Rates: The Search For Cuts* (03 February 1976); *Oil: The Claymore Field* (10 February 1976).

[2] It is now difficult to obtain a library copy of *Decision: Steel*. The only DVD listed on the web is held at Charles Darwin University in Australia (see www.cdu.edu.au/library/).

about it. Not surprisingly it was adopted by HBS and turned into what we might call more an orthodox case study with the attendant teaching note (Kotter and Stengrevics 1985; Sasser 1986). The teaching note encouraged the instructor to require participants to watch the whole video beforehand (although the teaching note rather gnomically observes that "Ninety minutes of tape is quite long for the attention span of many AMP[3] executives"). It is also suggested that participants be given two study questions to consider about their own evaluation of the way in which the decision was made and their thoughts about Sir "Monty" Finniston as Chief Executive Officer. As the teaching note recognises, handling the initial case discussion of these two study questions in this way means that the discussion will move towards a view that "the process used at BSC [should] be characterised as the typical economic justification of a decision made viscerally by the chairman", and that the verdict at the end of the session will be that "Finniston is a loser and the process used in making the decision … was a farce".

The instructor is encouraged to get the class to consider issues of process and power but with a basic assumption that the extent to which any changes in the subsequent economic analysis are not analytically well grounded.

Paddy Barwise at LBS particularly worked at developing the teaching material in a rather different way. The video itself was split into a number of chronological stages and the class was encouraged both collectively and individually to comment on their own evolving position as more facts and opinions are revealed. This approach with the central notion of an evolving understanding incorporating both facts and opinions is itself a very important characteristic of the collective decision-making process.

The debrief inevitably leads to a discussion which is not only about the analytics of the choice but also the role of both process and personalities. Of particular interest is the way in which individuals are seen as more or less convincing on the basis of their role, expertise and presentation. On top of this it was also possible to return to some of the key analytical questions and recognise that some of the changes in the process had at least some legitimacy in terms of their analytical equivalents; for instance, the extent to which one should or should not anticipate future commitments in areas such as investment when considering a current investment decision which is related or linked.

There is some similarity between this approach and the more common one with a set of case studies which are in a chronological sequence (generally labelled (A), (B), (C) …) with a class discussion between each one but the

---

[3]Advanced Management Programme: the title of the main HBS Executive Programme.

process is different – in particular only a short personal recording of one position and interpretation after each section – and the unit of basic analysis remains the one decision.

However, the biggest problem with the BSC and similar video material is that it perhaps reveals too much: in getting access, albeit with some concern about narrative structure and impact, to video material which reveals clearly personalities and senior individuals struggling with conflicting options and considerable uncertainties particularly when the individuals are in no way disguised meant there was a significant public impact of the programme itself. Indeed, the synopsis of the programme included the rather value-laden – but perhaps correct – comment that it was the "first of three films in a series about the decision-making process operated by the faceless men at the top whose decisions affect all our lives". Not very face-less, however, after the airing of the programme! It is difficult to image many corporations being willing to put their senior executives through such a process in the future.

We have therefore often had to revert to a rather different way of using video material to bring the real world into the classroom, most commonly in the form of an interview with a senior executive. Indeed, in the HBS treatment of the British Steel video, Alice Sapienza recorded an interview with Sir "Monty" Finniston in 1980 which was subsequently edited by John Kotter and Jay Lorsch to be aired as part of the second class discus-sion (Kotter 1982) in the treatment of the case. In this particular context the interview facilitates a further discussion around the wider perspective of Finniston's role including the broader stakeholder groups or constituen-cies he needs to consider and the extent to which, to quote the final conclu-sion in the teaching note, "the work of corporate management requires complex decisions, not always subject to neat economic analysis and often requiring subjective judgement, including ethical and value judgements" (1986: 7). To those of us inclined to a more analytical view of management, however, the overall teaching note fails to reflect on the extent to which such additional considerations can also be incorporated into the so-called economic analysis!

However, this example is probably better than many other video inter-views as a way of bringing the corporate world into the classroom. In the BSC case it allows the instructor to move the class discussion away from the rather facile conclusion that Finniston is a "loser" and therefore it adds value. In many other video interviews their more hagiographic nature can mean the interview is used more to create some form of closure in a way which maybe an anathema to the view of orthodox Harvard case teachers that even "what happened" is not relevant.

Experiential Exercises: Simulations and Projects

There are other generic pedagogic tools which provide ways in which we might attempt to introduce what is termed a "real-world perspective" into the way we teach. For instance, Navarro, in a survey of the top 50 US business schools and the information provided on their respective websites, noted that:

> Experiential exercises range from real-world business and consulting projects to management game simulations and business plan competitions. Together, as discussed earlier, multidisciplinary integration coupled with experiential learning methods are said to better reflect the real-word business environment where teams and integrated processes are typically used to solve problems, develop new products and processes, and strategically manage the firm and thereby better prepare MBA students for the future. (2008: 114)

I will focus on the two most important options which are either those that attempt to simulate the external world in the classroom as broadly defined (simulations) and those which attempt to take the classroom out to the external world (projects).

Of course neither of these are themselves unproblematic nor are they likely to fully achieve the objective of real-world relevance. In the case of business simulations, it seems to be generally agreed that the prime focus of the learning should be to assess the group dynamics and decision-making processes of the players. For instance, Gentry asserts that process feedback is much more valuable than outcome feedback. As games are less-than-perfect representations of the real world, it should be the decision process used that needs to be applauded or critiqued, not the gaming outcome. However, this principle often creates some problems both in teaching practice and also in relating the simulation lessons to wider experience:

> In simulation games, we do not weight the entire game grade on the game results, but rather place quite a bit of emphasis on the students' discussion of their game strategies and their justifications for the specific decisions. On the other hand, it is simpler to observe their game-end profit or their recommended case solution than it is to delineate the process used to bring about these outcomes. Further, far less effort is required to critique the outcomes than to critique the process ...

> Students are not alone in finding the distinction between good/bad decisions and good/bad outcomes to be counter intuitive. Most people do. After all, we have a lifetime of experience in learning from outcomes. Outcomes are visible, available, and often unambiguous; the process, however, often must be inferred on the part of the instructor. (1990: 16)

The issues with project-based learning approaches are somewhat different and in terms of the core curriculum of many MBA programmes they remain a minor component if at all. As Navarro notes:

> in the experiential learning tradition of Revans (1983), we can see that the Action Learning Project at Rice involves the creation of a project, the gathering of data, conducting interviews, and performing analyses, all with the goal of presenting results to the senior management of the company in question. Similarly, at MIT, students work with management at a Fortune-500 company on a multidisciplinary business problem. Incorporating a "contest element" common to many of these types of exercises, the project culminates with a presentation to company executives and MIT faculty, with the winning team moving on to present to the entire school. ... The picture that emerges from this analysis is that a relatively small number of top-ranked schools require multidisciplinary and experiential exercises as part of the core. (2008: 115)

Anecdotal evidence suggests that particularly the project element is more common in European business schools but there remain a set of issues to contend with. In particular, in reviewing a more recent example of the implementation of a Revans action-learning sets approach to an executive MBA, Johnson and Spicer comment that:

> The lack of extant research considering the effectiveness of action learning should be recognised. The conception of the approach is straightforward and action learning is certainly intuitively appealing, yet wider uptake of action learning is limited. This may be a result of the fact that the evidence of its application remains relatively limited. Our experience and existing uptake of action learning by individuals and organisations suggest face validity for the theory only, and wider consideration is required. Competent and rigorous research into the process and effectiveness of action learning is likely to help its diffusion and adoption. Such research needs to address a range of issues, not least of all the obstacles and constraints limiting its adoption and acceptance by individuals and organisations, and further evidence for its effectiveness in both demonstrating the, and impacting on, the workplace. (2006: 50)

We might well conclude therefore that in many ways at least when it comes to pedagogy and method the very notion of "real-world relevance" is itself problematic despite being espoused by such august accrediting bodies as AACSB (Association to Advance Collegiate Schools of Business). We might indeed rather misquote Harold Wilson in suggesting that one person's reality is another's fantasy! This is not to deny the value of the various suggested individual methods but merely that no one of them is an adequate solution to the overall problem. More importantly the impact and effect is more about how the specific method is used itself.

As others have suggested, this shifts the focus more to adopting a more critical approach in our style of teaching whatever specific method or methods are used. For instance, I was part of a teaching team at Warwick University that in the nineties designed and then delivered a new core course for our third-year undergraduates entitled, intentionally ambiguously, "Critical Issues in Management". The background and detail of this particular activity is well covered by John Mingers (2000), who was also a full member of the team.

Of course this particular instance refers to the design and execution of a course for third-year undergraduates but is interesting to compare this with the experiences reported by Hay and Hodgkinson with respect to an Executive MBA. They note that:

> The manager's interaction with diverse others may be seen to prompt a critique of authority (to again borrow from Mingers, 2000). The manager's introduction to difference seemingly challenges his assumption of one right or dominant view and encourages an acceptance of a plurality of divergent, but equally valid, perspectives. As Mezirow (1991) suggests, the individual is seen to learn to 'negotiate meanings, purposes and values critically … instead of passively accepting the social realities defined by others'. Moreover, the manager's account suggests that his changed perspective in turn provides a confidence to further challenge his management practice. The earlier examples serve to illustrate the potential of experience in facilitating critical learning within MBA programmes. We suggest that the experience that is brought to and lived in the MBA programme appears to crucially introduce difference which can be seen to reveal aspects of managing that remain taken for granted in day-to-day practice. Difference potentially makes accepted understandings problematic, thus adding complexity to the manager's ways of knowing. The doubts and dilemmas that follow provide opportunity for alternative ways of thinking and acting. The critical learning which is seen to be evident here is a questioning in terms of practice and self rather than concepts and ideologies. (2008: 36)

Conclusion: Learning through Questioning

Since the essential role of questioning has been repeated throughout the text it is no surprise that it is also the critical element in any approach that is recommended for linking the classroom to the workplace. The processes involved should not only espouse forms of critical questioning but also enact them in the teaching itself.

In so doing, we must ensure that we also encourage questioning outside the virtual box of the teaching method we adopt. In the relatively ubiquitous world of case studies in particular this means also considering for instance those categories of issues which are relatively suppressed in most studies: the contentious issues of power, expertise and authority. Another such contentious issue, which will be considered further in Chapter 10, links to the role of management consultants and the extent to which they may collude with senior management to dis-empower rather than empower less senior managers.

9 An Ongoing Decision Process of Questioning and Dissonance

"It is easier to judge the mind of a man by his questions rather than his answers." (Frequently misattributed to Voltaire)

Thinking, Seeing and Doing

How should decisions be made? Easy, we figured that out long ago. First define the problem, then diagnose its causes, next design possible solutions, and finally decide which is best. And, of course, implement the choice. But do people always make decisions that way? We propose that this rational, or "thinking first," model of decision making should be supplemented with two very different models—a "seeing first" and a "doing first" model. When practicing managers use all three models, they can improve the quality of their decisions. Healthy organizations, like healthy people, have the capacity for all three." (Mintzberg and Westley 2001: 89)

This book is unashamedly biased towards the "thinking first" perspective but this is in no way to deny the value of the tripartite approach advocated by Mintzberg and Westley. The main purpose of this book is to use analytics as a lens rather than just a set of techniques: we can also be analytic to at least some degree about the other modes of behaviour and also look more closely at what is really going on in these other modes.

Both "seeing first" and "doing first" perspectives are seen above as non-cognitive processes, but this can include both elements of what we call intuition and also habit/reflex. As noted much earlier in the book, in the sixties there seemed to be little analytic interest in the intuitive aspects of management. Even Herbert Simon, who did appreciate a role for intuition, described it as "just recognition". More recently, however, intuition has come much more centre stage.

One of the popular contributors to this development is Malcolm Gladwell and his book *Blink: The Power of Thinking Without Thinking* (2006). He argues that not only do we often make decisions on an unconscious and rapid basis but that in many circumstances this resultant decision is more appropriate than the one arrived at by a more deliberative and analytic approach. This is very much to privilege a "seeing first" perspective in the terms used by Mintzberg and Westley (2001).

Gladwell's book provides some interesting examples to illustrate his point such as his initial story of the J. Paul Getty Museum and the kouros statue supposedly dating from the sixth-century BC, where a number of experts on first sight thought it "didn't look right". The Getty convened a special symposium in Greece but it hardly resolved the issue. As Gladwell records:

> by the time the symposium was over, the consensus among many of the attendees appeared to be that the kouros was not at all what it was supposed to be. The Getty, with its lawyers and scientists and months of painstaking investigation had come to one conclusion, and some of the world's foremost experts in Greek sculpture – just by looking at the statue and sensing their own "intuitive repulsion" – had come to another. (2006: 7)

He then argues that afterwards "bit by bit, the Getty case began to fall apart" and for Gladwell at least there is a clear conclusion.

Personally, I rather prefer the case of the remaining uncertainties about the authenticity of the so-called Vinland map. In the early 1960s, the "Vinland map" was uncovered. It seemed to be a map of the North Atlantic as drawn from Scandinavian discoveries between 800 and 1100 AD, well before western Europe's great Age of Exploration that began around 1400. It was announced by Yale University, receiving much fanfare and much scepticism.

However, the issue of whether it is a fake or genuine remains unresolved despite many tests, so much so indeed that there is an interactive exhibit on the web set up to allow individuals to make their own assessment on the basis of the evidence available (see www.webexhibits.org/vinland/).

Overall, Gladwell is exploring what is now known more widely as the phenomenon of unconscious thought effects (UTE) and more recent work seems to support his general assertion that there are advantages to a decision-making process which combines the rational and what Gladwell calls the judgemental. Indeed, he quotes with approval Sigmund Freud:

> When making a decision of minor importance, I have always found it advantageous to consider all the pros and cons. In vital matters, however, such as the choice of a mate or a profession, the decision should come from the unconscious, from somewhere within ourselves. In the important decisions of personal life, we should be governed, I think, by the deep inner needs of our nature. (2006: 268)

And he notes that in one of the examples he uses involving the treatment of potential heart failure in a hospital emergency room:

> In this particular instance, the best decision-making came from using rational computer analysis to do what rational analysis does best – find statistical patterns in mountains of data – and using human clinical judgement to do what they call judgement does best – apply general statistical lessons to the particulars of a situation and a person. (Ibid.: 269)

So far maybe so good but it can become rather confused. Gladwell himself notes: "I think that the task of figuring out how to combine the best of conscious deliberation and instinctive judgement is one of the great challenges of our time" (ibid.: 269). But he seems to conflate at least three different strands of theory: UTE, a range of specific judgement biases and some key insights from military strategy. At the end of his book he puts considerable weight on the Battle of Chancellorsville (1863) in the American Civil War, in which Lee overcame a much larger force under the command of Hooker. He asserts:

> Chancellorsville came down to some ineffable, magical decision-making ability that Lee possessed and Hooker did not. What was that magical thing? It's the kind of wisdom someone acquires after a lifetime of learning and watching and doing. It's judgement and what Blink is – what all stories and studies and arguments add up to – is an attempt to understand this magical and mysterious thing called judgement. (Ibid.: 260)

As already noted earlier in this book, any sound military strategy has to be agile and adaptable in the moments of battle but this seems a rather different issue from the notion of unconscious thought. His description of the battle also involves important elements of confusing the enemy as well as recognising the often false assumption that there is always a net gain to further information in complex and messy situations. Sun Tsu would have fully appreciated the former stratagem and in illustrating the latter challenge Donald Schön once memorably in his Reith Lectures suggested that during the Troubles the only way of being certain about what was going on in Northern Ireland was to ask one person–after that it got more and more confusing.

However, there is little doubt that UTE is here to stay even if it is only part of the rather disparate approach adopted by Gladwell. What can be said from more recent research in the area?

Gladwell references some of the work done by Ap Dijksterhuis and his co-researchers. More recently they have conducted a thorough meta-analysis on UTE empirical research and concluded:

> Across a total of 92 studies, [the] result provides strong support for the existence of the UTE. However, as estimated from a random-effects model,

about 66% of the variance in effect sizes was attributable to systematic differences between studies. This result indicates that although the UTE is a real effect, it does not always occur. (Strick et al. 2011: 738)

On the more thorny question of the "optimum" mix between conscious and unconscious decision making, their further work resulted in a conclusion that:

> both modes of thinking have particular advantages: conscious thought can follow strict rules, whereas unconscious thought is better suited for integrating numerous decision attributes. Because most complex decisions require both adherence to precise rules and the aggregation of information, we hypothesized that complex decisions can best be made by engaging in periods of both conscious and unconscious thought. In both studies we found that the sequential integration of conscious and unconscious thought solved complex choices better than conscious or unconscious thought alone. In Study 2 we examined whether the sequential order of the integration condition matters. In line with our prediction, we found that integration worked best when unconscious thought followed conscious thought. (Nordgren et al. 2011: 509)

To this we should add the conclusions from a recent review article in the area of UTE and unconscious thought theory (UTT) by Bargh:

> It is unfortunate but understandable that there remains such resistance to even the idea of unconscious processes operating in judgment and decision making … but from personal experience I can vouch that this was true of each and every previous research domain where the concept of automatic or unconscious processes was introduced. Especially when a broader evolutionary perspective is taken, the notion of unconscious influences is unproblematic, and not nearly as controversial as it was 20 or 30 years ago. The findings by UTT and other researchers of superior decisions made unconsciously rather than consciously, at least in some judgmental domains, are less surprising when it is remembered that unconscious systems producing adaptive behavioral responses to the environment (i.e., behavioral decisions) existed long before the relatively recent advent of conscious modes of thought. Thus, newer (i.e., conscious) mental processes built on or made use of preexisting (i.e., unconscious) processes, instead of emerging de novo as isolated and independent processes. There are domains in which conscious processes produce better decisions than unconscious processes, and those in which unconscious processes produce better decisions than conscious processes; it is not a matter of one processing mode being "dumb" and the other one superior in every way. Above all, nearly all higher mental processing is complex enough to be a combination and interaction of conscious and unconscious processes. (2011: 643)

There remains a further important question about UTT approaches: some would claim that encouraging the unconscious processes also encourages more innovative solutions as well; however, the empirical evidence for this is rather mixed (see Zhong et al. 2008).

The Case for Slow Thinking and Procrastination

The other relevant strand of empirical and theoretical work in this area seems at least superficially to go in the opposite direction: Gladwell was of course well aware that the title of his book implied favouring relatively instant intuitive judgements even if the actual content is both more compli-cated and more multi-dimensional. Other writers have either looked for a rather different balance between the fast and the slow or even apparently espoused delay rather than either thought or action.

Clearly in the latter category is the book authored by Frank Partnoy (2012) with the rather arresting title *Wait*. However, just as with Gladwell's *Blink* the implications in the title can be taken as rather more extreme than the detailed text implies. Rather, Partnoy argues that even in what he calls super-fast sports, baseball, tennis and, as he notes with some surprise, cricket, where the central event(s) involves two focal play-ers and reaction times are very limited, the empirical evidence suggests that the superior players take longer to assess and analyse the situation before actually making their response: one could say they wait longer but not too long!

The key elements in Partnoy's analysis is the assumption that the increased delay will result in the availability of further useful information as well as the ability to process more of it. In his two key examples – super-fast sports and high-frequency financial trading – the assumption is that the additional information that is obtained will be both useful and relatively unambiguous. With the delay we acquire respectively more reli-able information on the trajectory of the ball or the response of other market traders.

As discussed earlier, however, there are many other more "complex" situ-ations where the value of the further information may be much more ambig-uous. So we can often assume, as with many things, that we will more commonly find ourselves "in the middle" between a situation in which additional information will resolve outstanding uncertainties at one extreme and actually increase confusions at the other.

In decision analysis, the notion of the "expected value of perfect informa-tion" (EVPI) was developed to provide an upper bound on what we should be willing to pay for additional information when it completely reduced any uncertainties to point figures for the probabilities of the future states:

> In defining EVPI, 'Perfect' information means perfectly accurate knowledge, or absolute certainty, about the values of some or all of the unknown parameters. This can be thought of as obtaining an infinite sample size, producing a posterior probability distribution that is a single point, or alternatively, as 'clairvoyance' – suddenly learning the true values of the parameters. Perfect information on all parameters implies no uncertainty about the optimal adoption decision. For some values of the parameters the adoption decision would be revised, for others we would stick with our baseline adoption decision policy. By investigating the pay-offs associated with different possible parameter values, and averaging these results, the *'expected'* value of perfect information is quantified. (Brennan et al. 2007: 3)

This all sounds very technical but in essence we are trying to estimate the value of additional information but also recognise the remaining inevitability of various outcome states with different pay-off consequences.

In practice, therefore, an EVPI approach may lead us to conclude that in many complex and real situations the improved knowledge advantages of delay may actually be rather small. Why then does Partnoy still argue for delay? In essence, he argues for additional time so as to:

- reasonably quickly review the situation using empirically validated simple checklists;

- experiment and learn before making final choices – this mainly refers to identifying the unexpected rather than refining the expected outcomes.

Both of these activities clearly have merit and, in particular, we might note that at least in the public policy field so-called pilot programmes are more about fine tuning the intended intervention rather than trying to recognise and estimate unintended consequences. Equally, in the private sector it is often in practice the case that so-called test marketing is more about testing the proposed launch programme rather than a broader test of the efficacy of the overall proposal.

Thinking Fast, Thinking Slow

Overall, neither Gladwell nor Partnoy are in fact quite as extreme in their actual prescriptions than their titles and positioning might suggest. Gladwell does not really advocate making all decisions in the blink of an eye and equally Partnoy certainly does not advocate what might be termed pathological procrastination as described and discussed so effectively by Rowan Pelling in her BBC radio documentary (see www.bbc.co.uk/news/magazine-19389707).

Despite their rhetoric they actually rather converge "in the middle" and on an overall position not far from Nobel laureate Daniel Kahneman. Kahneman (2011). In his book *Thinking, Fast and Slow* he elaborates on what he terms the two systems which together drive the way we think and make choices. One system (System 1) is fast, intuitive and emotional; the other (System 2) is slower, more deliberative and more logical.

In a book which is wide ranging and, as one would expect, well grounded in research evidence, Kahneman is careful to avoid stereotyping either one of the two systems or indeed their efficacy in daily life. As he himself notes:

> System 1 is indeed the origin of much that we do wrong, but it is also the origin of most of what we do right—which is most of what we do. Our thoughts and actions are routinely guided by System 1 and generally are on the mark. One of the marvels is the rich and detailed model of our world that is maintained in associative memory; it distinguishes surprising from normal events in a fraction of a second, immediately generates an idea of what was expected instead of a surprise, and automatically searches for some causal interpretation of surprises and of events as they take place.

> System 1 registers the cognitive ease with which it processes information, but it does not generate a warning signal when it becomes unreliable. Intuitive answers come to mind quickly and confidently, whether they originate from skills or from heuristics. There is no simple way for System 2 to distinguish between a skilled and a heuristic response. Its only recourse is to slow down and attempt to construct an answer on its own, which it is reluctant to do because it is indolent. Many suggestions of System 1 are casually endorsed with minimal checking. (2011: 416)

Kahneman himself has been in the forefront of experimental work on decision-making biases, which seem to get longer and longer – Wikipedia now lists over 80 decision-making, belief and behavioural biases, although to be accurate it is not clear all of them are strictly biases (see http://en.wikipedia.org/wiki/List_of_biases_in_judgment_and_decision_making).

Kahneman asks rhetorically what we can do to improve decision making, but in general he feels there is little that can be done without considerable effort despite the fact that:

> the way to block errors that originate in System 1 is simple in principle: recognize the signs that you are in a cognitive minefield, slow down, and ask for reinforcement from System 2 ...

The voice of reason may be much fainter than the loud and clear voice of an erroneous intuition, … The upshot is that it is much easier to identify a minefield when you observe others wandering into it than when you are about to do so. Observers are less cognitively busy and more open to information than actors. That was my reason for writing a book that is oriented to critics and gossipers rather than to decision makers. (Ibid.: 417)

I am reminded of the critical role of the "Fool" in many Shakespeare plays:

"They [the Fools] are these strange characters that show up and make witty observations and very often become very central to the action," says Dr Jacquelyn Bessell, a lecturer at the University of Birmingham's Shakespeare Institute.

"They do share a sort of capacity to stir things up, to say things that other characters in their social bracket couldn't possibly get away with saying. In that respect, they're a really useful vehicle driving your moral and argumentative point home if you're a dramatist. They deflate pompous, socially superior characters. They're able to criticise kings." (www.bbc.co.uk/news/magazine-17476117)

Also, in a rather analogous manner, Kahneman argues that "a richer language is essential to the skill of constructive criticism" (2011: 418).

In Praise of Dissonance

In 2009, David Stark, a sociologist at Columbia University, published a book with, depending on your taste, either an arresting or a perplexing title: *The Sense of Dissonance*. To be honest, it hardly made the best-seller lists compared with Gladwell, Kahneman and even Partnoy – and it got just two reader reviews on Amazon, compared with, respectively, 1391, 380 and 30 (figures from amazon.com website, 3 January 2013), yet to quote one of the two reviews:

You might not get it from the title, but this book is about the conditions that lead to creativity, innovation, and entrepreneurship in organizations. According to Stark, the presence of competing notions of value within an organization, or what he calls "dissonance," is one such fundamental condition. (Jonathan Hall, 10 February 2010, available at www.amazon.com/Sense-Dissonance-Accounts-Worth-Economic/dp/0691152489/)

I have already discussed the somewhat similar developments in trying to encourage a more dialectical approach to strategic choices mainly developed by Dick Mason and Ion Mitroff (1981). The approach proposed by Mason and Mitroff involved procedures within the strategic choice processes in the organisation: it would therefore be both routine and transparent. Stark's more recent notion of dissonance emphasises a longer-term sustained situation in which two or more regimes of value which are strictly inconsistent with each other co-exist within the organisation concerned. This could be described as cognitive dissonance: the term used in modern psychology to describe the state of holding two or more conflicting cognitions (e.g. ideas, beliefs, values, emotional reactions) simultaneously. However this is not quite up to the level of the White Queen in *Alice Through the Looking Glass*, who claimed that sometimes she had "believed as many as six impossible things before breakfast"!

In general, the term is most applied to individual cognition and hence there is a major unit of analysis difference between this and the way in which Stark is applying it to the organisation as a whole.

Already noted is the paper by Johnson et al. (2012), which argued that encouragement of contestation was a critical element in the long-term successful development of the organisation and had its roots in the individual histories:

> The first thing to recognize is the importance of valuing history and building on it. In the cases of Tesco and Smith & Nephew, the contestation we saw was built on conflict, even emotional conflict, decades ago. Over time, consciously or not, the skirmishing evolved into a more respectful tug of war. In the case of Cadbury, a tradition rooted in the company's Quaker past was reinforced by a clash of cultures that followed the merger with Schweppes. Building on history requires managers to reflect on the evolution of their organization and the legacy they can draw on. (2012: 30)

But, of course, there are also times when a choice has to be made and all parties have to get behind the decision:

> Essential though constructive confrontation, contestation and experimentation are, there needs to be a point when leadership makes decisions and the different parties fall in line. This requires what we call "corporate maturity": having the confidence to see the value of dissent while accepting the need to move forward for the wider good. Taking this position is not an argument for suppressing dissent. Rather, it's an argument for appreciating the value of diversity and recognizing that there are times when top management needs to take charge. In our research, we found that failures occurred not so much when top management avoided making decisions but when management mishandled the internal debate, by stifling it, cutting it short or failing to build management teams with enough confidence to overcome doubts. (Ibid.: 31)

Debates, Dialectics and Dissonance

I have thus described three rather different but related notions of what might be desirable in a strategic choice process within the organisation. Each in its own way reflects the inevitability that any choice of significance is also to a lesser or greater extent contentious. That commonly used expression a "no-brainer" would often seem to need a further qualifying phrase so it becomes "a no-brainer if you look at the issues this way". One even might go as far as to say if the choice is really a no-brainer under all circumstances then it is certainly not a strategic one! We are in many ways returning to the Kahneman's distinction between "system 1" and "system 2". The "no-brainer" assertion is a system 1 type response which requires no cognitive effort, whereas a system 2 response would require further effort in analysis.

As discussed above, if a decision is, on the other hand, a "brainer", then we need to consider the extent to which the appropriate process becomes a mixture of the "three Ds". On top of this there is the common time sequence in any decision process (while recalling that there is an important distinction between what can be termed the formal decision process – as often docu-mented and minuted – and the more informal activities of persuasion and building support for a particular position). On the basis of the definitions I started with it may be no surprise that the actual process we tend to find is almost always a mixture of all these three. Indeed, it is often a rather confusing mixture since at almost all times in the process we find different orders of assumption which we could represent as:

Debate (D1): we should ask critical questions of Plan A to ensure it is sound although we do not expect the proposers to make any substantial changes.

Dialectics (D2): we should challenge certain general assumptions in the proposal so we can come up with a better Plan A +.

Dissonance (D3): we should articulate and develop a different Plan B.

To be fair I have somewhat stretched the word definitions so as to clarify the expected outcome of the process in terms of Plan A, Plan A+ and Plan B. However, it is possible now to refine and perhaps partly explain the misunderstanding that arose in one of the debriefing interviews during the field work for the strategic investments decisions research considered much earlier in the book. To ask about the process of scrutiny of any major proposal in terms more related to Parliamentary Questions (PQ), is to imply the D1 motivation underlies what is going on: it may encourage the proposers to make further and bolder claims and assertions but they are unlikely to significantly alter the plan (after all it would then become a U-turn). Although much of this does happen in practice I suspect that the process participants would often implicitly believe that they were engaging in a D2 process to produce a Plan A+, so the comparison with PQs would be seen to be misleading.

So what about a D3 approach? The best personal example I can think of goes far back to work I did with Marks & Spencer on management development in the mid-seventies. M&S were developing their food business at the time but also going through a wide-ranging debate as to the strategic legitimacy of such moves. Of course they did not use this expression: within M&S it was framed in terms of following or ignoring the founding principles – a statement of which was provided to any employee who attended a management development programme as an elaboration of the basic espoused principles of the company values, quality, value, service, innovation and trust.

The group we might reasonably call the traditionalist argued that any major move into food retailing was inconsistent with the then current customer expectations and trust, whilst the radicals argued that not only was there no inconsistency but that at the same time a major development into food represented just the sort of innovation embodied in the principles!

Both groups were therefore arguing that to remain consistent with the founding principles one should take diametrically opposite moves in the situation. Long after the whole issue had been resolved – by M&S moving strongly into food retailing – the outcome in terms of the relative growth and profitability of their food business compared with non-food would appear to vindicate the radicals. In 2012 M&S reported a 6.8 per cent decline in clothing and general merchandise sales in the 13 weeks to 30 June – the worst since December 2008 – and things did not get much better later in the year. But as always counter-factuals (what would have happened if they had not made a sustained strategic move into retailing) are difficult to evaluate. Additionally, the traditionalists might wish to argue that the overall way in which the move was made particularly towards high-quality ready-prepared chilled meals meant that the core principles were actually upheld.

Making Some Sense of Innovation

There is much written nowadays about the importance of innovation in the management of organisations. Sometimes indeed there seems to be so much focus on it that one might suspect that there was no other strategic priority but innovation.

In a rather similar manner the notion of modernisation has come to dominate much political discourse. In both cases, be it innovation or modernisation, it is important to realise that there are pretty inevitably both winners and losers so the advocacy of any particular change also requires us to recognise the particular reasons why such a change is likely to be advantageous for the organisation itself. Of course such an advantage can sometimes be framed almost exclusively in terms of the least worse outcome encapsulated in the notion of "cannibalisation" – better that we successfully compete with ourselves rather than losing out to others.

From an analytical perspective, it is useful to look more closely at the broad distinction between incremental and disruptive innovation but at the same time recognise that whether a particular innovation is incremental or disruptive depends a great deal on the point of view one adopts. Nick Woodward, a long-established colleague of mine, neatly encapsulated this in the working title of a paper he wrote many years ago: "Turbulence is Frozen Peas". He was making the point that in that original Emery and Trist (1965) study on the ways in which organisations coped with turbulent environments one of the case studies used was a manufacturer of canned peas. Frozen peas create market turbulence for canned peas manufacturers, but perhaps from a wider customer perspective they may be seen more as a significant but hardly dramatic improvement in product quality! He later published the paper under a perhaps more acceptable academic title: "The Myth of Turbulence" (Woodward 1982).

The oft-quoted injunction to "Think outside the box", just like the earlier espousal of double-loop learning by Argyris and Schön (1978) clearly links in some way towards encouraging further analysis of possible disruptive innovations and we might also surmise that an organisation that encourages dissonance and/or debate would find it easier to encourage such behaviour.

Indeed, rather like the world of frozen peas, academic publishing currently face a major and potentially disruptive innovation in the impact of so-called open-access journals.

Much that is going on in the overall field of scientific journal publications is dominated by the impact of what is happening in experimental science and medicine. However, rather like the pea canners, it also has substantial possible implications for those involved in the social sciences such as business and management.

In general, it is not difficult to see why the overall issue should have arisen recently, most obviously given the dramatic changes in the costs of publishing and distribution of journals. In many areas the distribution system is now electronic and therefore access is via remote downloading of individual articles rather than accessing hard-copy volumes produced on a quarterly or monthly basis. As the situation has evolved there have been a number of pilot developments along with increased critical analysis of the balance between the costs and values of various stages in the overall supply chain.

One response, currently embodied in UK Government response to the Finch report (2012), is broadly to shift the revenue base in the industry from subscription to submission and beyond this to retain a broadly similar cost structure. However, there are quite strong arguments that this relatively incremental development will not of itself be sustainable unless the submission costs are also reduced by at least a factor of ten.

How might this be achieved? An academic journal depends on a flow of good-quality articles, a peer-review process with active editorial intervention and a publication and distribution system. Let us assume that if the rest of the system is working well there is no reason to believe that the flow of articles will dry up: academics want to publish their ideas and any form of research evaluation must at least partly be based on research output. This leaves the peer-review/editorial and publication/distribution systems where we are likely to see a critical challenge. So far the peer-based system has been severely under-costed, indeed in the case of many journals actually done on a pro bono basis, yet it will remain an essential value-adding element. On the other hand, the costs and indeed rationale of the current publication and distribution system seem to be unsustainable given the nature of the changing technology.

Thinking outside the box can be difficult; it is much more difficult if you are inside the box and have a portfolio of assets attuned to the way the box currently works!

Questions and Answers: The Central Role of "Interrogation"

Much that is written about interrogation is in the context of what we might call adversarial interrogation. The surface nature at least of strategic choice processes within an organisation is more one of collaborative interrogation in most cases although there do seem to have been some robust inquisitors: Harold Geneen in his days at ITT, Jim Olson at Hewlett-Packard. Often it is perhaps only genuinely a mutually co-operative process up to a point; there can for instance be differences around priorities and there is often a negotiating process taking place at the same time.

This more collaborative process means that we need to consider how far we might transpose the generic rules developed in mainstream interrogation practice to a management context but we can argue that just as the assertion "we are all in it together" has more recently run into a rather considerable amount of disbelief, so the notion that any organisation is solely a multiple collaborative entity in all its practices is rather naive about the nature and practice of organisational politics.

One example of potential transfer is to be found in a note on the four rules for interrogators (Annotated from http://changingminds.org/techniques/interrogation/four_rules.htm).

1. Prepare well

The effective interrogator is well prepared. The person being interrogated may well be resistant to your questions, so you need to have many alternatives at your call.

Build a list of core questions plus many other supplementary questions that will nudge them towards critical answers.

2. Promote a path of least effort

The best interrogators never have to raise their voice and the session seems to the other person to be less an interrogation and more a friendly conversation.

Always leave an easy route in the direction you want them to move.

Sun Tzu, the famous Chinese military strategist, said "Build your enemies a golden bridge". If the other side feels cornered, they will fight hard. If, however, there is one easy way out, then they are more likely to take that than fight.

3. Be methodical

Interrogation can be a long and intricate affair in which answers can contradict one another and things be left undiscovered and unsaid.

Ask questions carefully. Record responses. Take time out to cross-check responses for consistency or otherwise. Repeat questions that have not been answered yet.

4. Be patient

When the other side does not want to answer your questions, then they may use all kinds of resistance tactics.

Even when the other person is collaborative, they may not easily remember what you are seeking or even understand what you really want of them.

How much further can we go in drawing a parallel between interrogation and co-operative information gathering? Walton argues that we must take care:

Interrogation is typically portrayed as a type of information-seeking dialogue. The goal of interrogation is to get information from the party being interrogated. The presumption is that he has the information and that it can be gotten from him by questioning, and possibly by using other methods as well. But the questioner's goal is to get the information. Can that be the goal of the dialogue as a whole, as well? The answer is that interrogation is a hybrid type of dialogue that involves a shift from deliberation to information-seeking. The goal of the dialogue as a whole is to take action that may prevent harm of some sort by finding the information needed to carry out this practical goal. The interrogator's goal is not only to get the needed information from the other party, but also, if possible to test it by critically examining the answers given by that party during the interrogation, based on whatever other evidence she has. The other party may be cooperative, and may simply give out the information, but even if he does, the interrogator cannot take it at face value. And in typical cases, as noted above, the other party has very good reasons for being extremely careful about what he says. A "confession" may be the only evidence needed to convict him. Thus, as Megid put it, an interrogation is virtually always deceptive. Deception and coercion are always there, even if they are in the background. (2003: 1797–1798)

10 Putting the Masters Back into Management Education and Development

Whoever cannot seek the unforeseen sees nothing for the known way is an impasse. (Heraclitus, *Fragments*)

It requires a very unusual mind to undertake the analysis of the obvious. (Alfred North Whitehead)

How often have I said to you that when you have eliminated the impossible, whatever remains, however improbable, must be the truth? (Sherlock Holmes in Sir Arthur Conan Doyle, *The Sign of the Four* (1890))

This book started with reviewing amongst others the particular contribution to the development of management education and indeed management research that has been attributed to the two so-called Foundation Reports of 1959. As has been discussed at points throughout the book it would appear that the more recent critical commentators have tended to miss the mark. To criticise the archetypical MBA course or equivalent for being analytical is to fail to recognise its position in a wider context. Overall, a programme of management development aims not only to equip the participants with useful analytical approaches but also provide the opportunity to reflect on the experience of being a manager. Clearly the balance between analytical processes and structured reflection will vary with the individual particularly in terms of age and experience.

The much more critical point is that the process of reflection should be informed by a realistic characterisation of the managerial task itself. It is here that the Foundation Reports unwittingly only saw part of the picture. In their understandable enthusiasm to improve the situation they adopted a highly cognitive and technically biased perspective on the nature of management. When at a later date Henry Mintzberg (1973) conducted with others his path-breaking work on the "real" nature of managerial work, this tended to be characterised by academe and indeed to some extent by Henry himself as "anti-MBA". My argument in this book has been that the critical flaw was not the focus on analysis but the underlying often implicit assumptions about the nature of management itself and in particular that alongside the development of cognitive approaches there must also be a recognition of the importance of the intuitive.

This means there must be proper space for the intuitive in the analysis of management action but I wish also to argue that we can raise a number of important and rather critical questions if we equally recognise that critical analysis can also be brought to bear on the so-called soft skills of managing people. In the particular area of leadership there are some troubling questions which can lead to the relative promotion of a small group of managers who now become identified as leaders and the relative demotion of the role and importance of a much larger group. One might even note for the limited group of "new leaders" this also encourages them to negotiate service contracts, incentive structures and general terms and conditions, particularly in the private sector, that their colleague managers can only dream of!

Administration, Management and Leadership

It is indeed ironic that most business schools have maintained a title for their flagship degree which embodies the central notion of "administration" whilst the dominant focus on what is actually taught has shifted first to "management" and now apparently to "leadership".

More recently, there seem to have been renewed attempts to disassociate the newer leadership from the earlier management. Krantz and Gilmore in an early comment on this development noted that:

> We do not question the need for innovative leadership which is responsive to emerging economic conditions; rather we are concerned with a dysfunctional reaction to these pressures. The social defense we wish to examine has two variants: either a cult of management tools and techniques, or alternatively a cult of the charismatic leader. Idealization of one aspect of the executive process and denigration of the other prevents integration of a vision and the machinery for achieving it that is necessary for effective innovation. We view the elevating of management without leadership as allowing us to not to think about substantive directions that would be disturbing (Miller and Gwynne, 1972). Conversely, the lionization of leadership and denigration of management serves to neutralize the potentially disturbing ideas of genuine leadership by keeping it separated from management, which in the best sense of the term, represents the means for realizing the new ideas. (1990: 184)

And they concluded with what might be seen as a serious warning:

> Even when the roles of leader and manager are held separately, they both need to be respected and need to be integrated. The splitting of them, or dramatic ascendancy of one over the other creates a dangerous situation and puts the organization at risk, though this may not be immediately felt. Yet on a different level, we suggest this splitting is inherently conservative. That by splitting apart leadership and management one is separating the new idea from the means to realize it. We suspect that an unconscious aspect of the split is the encapsulation and containment of the creative innovative ideas.
>
> In sum, the splitting apart of leadership and management, with the concomitant idealization of one and denigration of the other leads to two distinct manifestations. One is managerialism, the magical investment in technique and method. The other is heroic leadership, the magical hope for a savior from fossilized organization. We believe both represent a societal level defense against the anxieties inherent in realizing the need for a deep restructuring of contemporary organizations in the face of emerging post-industrial society and in confronting the different world in which we live. (Ibid.: 202)

In their sceptical if not even cynical view, they were preceded by Robert Reich, who noted in the *New Republic* that:

> To sum up, we are faced with a paradox. Our major corporations are stewards for a sizable chunk of our national wealth. The long-term performance of these corporations is abysmal, and continues to worsen. But at the same time we – the citizens and the shareholders – are willing to grant these companies, and their CEOs ever greater license to act in any way they wish. (1985: 24)

What will come of this?

> A more likely possibility, at least in the short run, is that America will consider the twin problems of poor corporate performance and the privileged position of the CEO as challenges to managerial attitudes and techniques. (As a culture, we tend to prefer pep talks to social criticism – stories about what works to exposes about what doesn't – at least until the underlying problems loom so large that they can no longer be ignored.) Indeed there is evidence that we have already embarked upon this Panglossian path. It comes in the form of a new literary genre that has emerged during the last few years: the CEO success story. (Ibid.: 24–25)

It would seem that we have not made much progress since these warnings nearly 25 years ago. As I will discuss in this chapter, the development of the notion of strategic leadership – management of rather than in the organisation – has allowed the dichotomy to be redefined so that leadership within the organisation is seen more as part of the management role, whereas Leadership (capital "L" intended) is what leaders of organisations do. This distinction of course returns us to the dilemma we previously encountered with management: by implicitly defining Leadership as what leaders actually do we are likely to encounter the major problem, that, just as Mintzberg in his previous research showed in the context of management, what occupants of the actual role spend their time doing relates very poorly to what the textbooks say they should do!

For this reason amongst others, this book, as might be expected, does not espouse heroic leadership but recognises that in relatively rare instances, and learning from the military, there is a need for it. I am more concerned in balancing the requirements for good people management alongside critical thinking and analysis applied to managerial choices. Indeed, I would also argue that a mix of administrative skills have a significant role to play as well.

Stress Testing the Analysis

For the most part therefore, we return to the challenge of balancing management and leadership although we might reasonably argue that in fact we are talking of two aspects of management itself: people and critical analysis.

There are of course a number of high-profile incidents where it seems analysis has totally dominated the people aspects. One of the classic examples quoted was Robert McNamara moving from Ford, where he had held the office of President for a short while, to become the Secretary for Defense, from 1960 to 1968 under both John F. Kennedy and Lyndon B. Johnson. However, a more nuanced view of his time at the Pentagon would be that the US neither lost the war on the ground nor failed to gather extensive and useful information. I still remember coming across in the basement of the UCLA library in 1979 a sheaf of Rand Corporation reports detailing the results of earlier field interviews. Indeed, between August 1964 and December 1968 the Rand Corporation conducted approximately 2400 interviews with Vietnamese who were familiar with the activities of the Viet Cong and North Vietnamese army. A good example of one of these reports is Goure et al. (1985):

> The interviews indicate that the Viet Cong [VC] are facing growing difficulties and that their vulnerabilities may have increased since the spring of 1965. These weaknesses have been offset to some extent by the expansion of the VC

forces and the increased infiltration of PAVN (People's Army of Vietnam) units into the South. Although the effectiveness and morale of some civilian cadres, guerrillas, and Local Forces appear to have declined, the Main Forces, despite some deterioration, seem generally to retain good morale and combat effectiveness. The VC organization is still largely intact and capable of controlling and directing large numbers of soldiers and civilians.

With the considerable advantage of hindsight we can see how prescient these comments were but not perhaps in the way in which the authors intended. It turned out that the bigger problems for the US were the political debate outside Vietnam and in particular in the US itself which led to a loss of US morale and the continued infiltration of the PAVN which was not halted by the later and ineffective aerial bombing of the North. Indeed, this later factor had already been recognised in the Pentagon war gaming conducted in 1964, which was discussed in Chapter 4. It was therefore not so much failure of analysis but a failure to extend this analysis outside the relatively limited framework of a local insurgency in South Vietnam. The lesson would seem to be yet again that the key development should not be to discard the analysis but to test the limits of the assumptions made: stress testing on the boundaries of the box.

Innovation as Hard Work: The 3M Post-it Story

We pretty much all think we know the Post-it story. The 3M version is:

> The Post-it® Note was invented as a solution without a problem: Dr. Spencer Silver developed a unique, repositionable adhesive, but the 3M scientist didn't know what to do with his discovery. Then, six years later, a colleague of Dr. Silver, Art Fry, remembered the light adhesive when he was daydreaming about a bookmark that would stay put in his church hymnal. The rest is history. (www.post-it.com/wps/portal/3M/en_US/Post_It/Global/About/About/)

This has been somewhat elaborated but not significantly altered by others. I have taken a typical example of a more elaborate story (the version to be found at "Ideafinder": www.ideafinder.com/history/inventions/postit.htm) and contrasted it with the rather different version to be found in Partnoy (2012: 211–226, shown in italics):

> No one got the idea and then stayed up nights to invent it. A man named Spencer Silver was working in the 3M research laboratories in 1970 trying to find a strong adhesive.

Silver was interested in sticky stuff: glue, gum, cement, and other adhesives. After two years of experimenting, he discovered that he could make an adhesive out of tiny, indestructible acrylic spheres.

Silver developed a new adhesive, but it was even weaker than what 3M already manufactured. It stuck to objects, but could easily be lifted off. It was super weak instead of super strong.

In 1968, Arthur Fry was playing a round of golf with a 3M colleague. ... [who] said we've got a guy, Spencer Silver, he has come up with these sticky micro-spheres, they're little bitty spheres and they're sticky but they don't know what to stick to. They're real interesting. You can't dissolve them. You can't melt them. It's like sticking to a bunch of marbles.

No one knew what to do with the stuff, but Silver didn't discard it. Then one Sunday four years later, another 3M scientist named Arthur Fry was singing in the church's choir. He used markers to keep his place in the hymnal, but they kept falling out of the book. Remembering Silver's adhesive, Fry used some to coat his markers. Success! With the weak adhesive, the markers stayed in place, yet lifted off without damaging the pages.

For five [more] years the sticky acrylic spheres were just another idea percolating within Minnesota Mining. ... Then, one Sunday in 1973, Fry had a thought: "the little paper marker I had put in to mark a spot from rehearsal ... had fallen out and ... I thought I wish I could have a bookmark that would stick to the paper but wouldn't pull it apart. ... So I thought about the microspheres. I remembered if they are spread apart they will be less sticky. There should be some magic spacing that would be just right for this paper. So I went back to Spencer Silver the next day, got samples of his microspheres and we started experimenting."

... When Fry finally thought they had perfected the sticky bookmark, he pitched the idea to his bosses. They were underwhelmed and sceptical. Bookmarks gener-ally worked fine already. Bookmarks were a small market.

Fry and Silver worked on [the sticky residue] problems for more than a year, but their bosses still didn't think they could sell more than $750,000 of the bookmarks annually. That wasn't enough to get anyone excited about some little sticky pieces of paper. Fry's choir epiphany fell short.

3M began distributing Post-it ® Notes nationwide in 1980 – ten years after Silver developed the super weak adhesive.

It took several more years, but by 1977 Fry had persuaded his bosses that the sticky notes had enough potential to support some market research. They called them "Press 'n' Peel" and tested them with potential customers in four major cities. The results were lukewarm, however, and the idea sputtered again.. .Meanwhile, the staff at Minnesota Mining had become addicted to the sticky notes. They couldn't get enough of Fry's samples ... After yet another year, Fry persuaded his bosses to try one last market research effort. They decided to distribute samples widely in one town, to see if they would catch on in the same way they had caught on within the firm. Within days, the notes were a hit. More than 90 percent of the people in Boise who tried them said they would buy them.

Is it at all surprising that so many innovative ideas and products fail? Some of the more recent general ideas in encouraging innovation certainly link to and reinforce the established notion from the 3M philosophy at the time: the 15 per cent free time to work on one's own projects. They include the notions of "absorptive capacity", "open innovation" and "user-led", which all represent different aspects of what might be termed a systems or network perspective.

The extended Post-it story, however, still tells us that more often than not even in relatively benign conditions the radical innovation is quite likely to fail. One might reasonably suggest that the more disruptive the innovation, the greater the likelihood of failure so we shouldn't give up on incremental innovation anytime soon!

Innovation and Entrepreneurship

One of the current vogue areas in the management curriculum is entrepreneurship and discounting the (in)famous aside by George Bush Jr. to Tony Blair that "The problem with the French is that they don't have a word for entrepreneur", it is still reasonable to ask: "What is Entrepreneurship"?

Entrepreneurship often implies action rather than analysis but given the approach adopted in this book, it is reasonable to suggest that, analytically speaking, it is both an innovation and a business model together – although of course sometimes the innovation may indeed be within the business model itself. Both are required to achieve some form of sustainable economic return from the proposed development, and we can frame our analytical questions around these two elements. I have already considered some of the difficulties of "thinking outside the box" but these are compounded when considering whether the proposed business model is economically sustainable. Additionally, for public-sector organisations, the sustainability issue is embodied in the extent to which adequate resourcing is likely to be available in the future.

Unfortunately general understanding of the key factors in the analysis of such sustainability is rather limited, but at the outset the framework being used considers only what are current economic factors rather than wider notion of sustainability in areas such as development studies. However, even this more restricted definition requires judgements to be made both about the nature of the intended market and, of course, the likely behaviour of others.

In a market economy, the basic principle of such analysis should be no different from the one I proposed in Chapter 3 in the elements of possible isolating mechanisms listed by Rumelt: the need to make an assessment as to how far it is likely such mechanisms will allow the innovator to avoid direct competition and so maintain a genuine rent stream. However, it is inevitably more complex when considering a significant innovation partly because the competition will not only come from incumbents but also new entrants within some cases new business models as well. My short and very abbreviated analysis of what is possibly happening in scientific journal publications with the advent of "Open Access" (see Chapter 9) begins to give some sense of the complexity of the required analysis even in a relatively simple case.

Understanding Strategic Leadership

Boal and Hooijberg (2001) claim that the interest in strategic leadership since the 1980s represents a rejuvenation and metamorphosis of the entire leadership field, said to have become moribund towards the end of the 1970s:

> Since 1980, the study of leadership has undergone both rejuvenation and metamorphosis. Rejuvenation in that the study of leadership seemed like an old friend in which the field of management had lost interest. At the end of the 1970s and beginning of the 1980s, leadership as a field of study had reached an impasse: little new theory was being developed, and serious scholars were asking not where the field should go next but whether leadership even matters. ... By the mid 1980s, however, a metamorphosis. away from the study of "supervisory" leadership toward the study of strategic leadership had begun. With this change in emphasis came a newfound sense of excitement initially centering on Upper Echelon theory and the study of Top Management Teams (TMTs) ...

> Included in these new leadership theories are charismatic theories of leadership, transformational theories of leadership; and visionary theories of leadership. Whereas supervisory theories of leadership focus on task- and person-oriented behaviors of leaders as they attempt to provide guidance, support, and feedback to subordinates, strategic leadership focuses on the creation of meaning and purpose for the organization.

In a sense, supervisory theories of leadership are about leadership "in" organizations. Strategic theories of leadership are concerned with leadership "of" organizations and are "marked by a concern for the evolution of the organization as a whole, including its changing aims and capabilities" (Selznick, 1984, p. 5). Strategic leadership focuses on the people who have overall responsibility for the organization and includes not only the titular head of the organization but also members of what is referred to as the top management team or dominant coalition. (2001: 516; edited version of the original with a large number of individual references removed)

Building on this analysis, Iszatt-White and Saunders note that:

The move away from supervisory leadership to strategic leadership in the 1980s was a reflection of the increasing ambiguity and complexity of the environment within which organisations were called upon to operate and the degree of information overload to which leaders and managers were increasingly subject. In this context, ... [we] see the essence of strategic leadership as being the creation and maintenance of 'absorptive capacity' or the ability to learn, 'adaptive capacity' or the ability to change, and managerial wisdom. ... The extent to which strategic leadership is important in determining the performance of organisations thus becomes a function of the degree of discretion enjoyed by top managers – and hence the potential for their decisions to impact on organisational outcomes – and the timing of their decisions to coincide with strategic inflection points in the organisation's trajectory, such as changes in fundamental industry dynamics or the development of new technologies. ...

Strategic leadership theory can broadly be divided into three separate streams of research, some more directly related to the field of strategy than others. Upper echelon theory deals specifically with the notion of those at the top of the organisational hierarchy being responsible for its strategic direction and considers the question of executive accountability. Evolving over time into strategic leadership theory per se this strand of research treats organisational performance as a dependent variable, and measures it in terms of return on investment, return on equity, etc. The second strand, comprised of the so-called 'new' leadership theories – such as charismatic, transformational and visionary – is less concerned with strategic outcomes and more focused on the practice of leadership by individuals. (2013: 8–9; edited version of the original with a number of individual references removed)

The Power of Small Leadership

Sullivan et al. argue in their paper, under the heading "Stepping Away from Big Leadership", that it is much more appropriate to adopt a more prosaic notion of "small leadership":

In the leadership literature, stories abound about individual heroism—leaders triumphing over the business-as-usual cultures of their organizations. Leadership scholarship has a parallel tendency to focus on traits or styles that place leadership solely "inside" the person. Not surprisingly, most of our cultural narratives about leadership moments tend to create a built-in bias applauding individual heroism. Yet by doing so, these reports often discount the interaction between leader and follower or under-tend to the "ripeness" of the moments that make effective leadership possible. Rather, they tell us, for example, that Jack Welch "barnstormed through GE shutting factories, paring payrolls, and hacking mercilessly at its lackluster old-line units" (Smart, 1996). Popular notions of leadership suggest that leaders possess distinctive personal capacities that have made them extraordinarily effective leaders. We argue that, while these figures, and our ideas about their success, sustain our innate desire to venerate "leadership," they often diminish the power and influence of alternative frames for learning about leadership. Stories of this kind can be discouraging as they suggest a "dare to be great" image of leadership that contradicts the actual experience of daily work. Leaders are unable to reconcile their cultural narratives about leadership with their own personal experiences of organizational reality. We believe that these narratives inhibit many leaders from stepping fully and confidently into the stream of moments in which they can make significant differences. The ideal image is simply too far out of reach. We wish to propose an alternative. In this article, we shift the focus away from heroic deeds to small, subtle leadership actions that can have big impact. (2010: 220–221)

Leaders and Followers

As noted above, we often hear much less about followers than leaders. Keith Grint, a valued colleague of mine at Warwick University to whom I owe a considerable debt in that he first introduced me to the research on the penalty striker–goalkeeper interactions discussed earlier, has focused our attention specifically on this issue:

What is leadership? Well, despite almost three thousand years of ponderings and over a century of 'academic' research into leadership, we appear to be no nearer a consensus as to its basic meaning, let alone whether it can be taught or its effects measured and predicted. This cannot be because of a dearth of interest or material: on 29 October 2003 there were 14,139 books relating to 'Leadership' on Amazon.co.uk for sale. Just over six years later that number had almost quadrupled to 53,121 – and clear evidence that within a short space of time there will be more books about leadership than people to read them. You would be forgiven for thinking that more information equates to greater understanding. Unfortunately we just seem to generate ever-greater disparity in our understandings and seem no nearer 'the truth' about defining leadership than before we began to publish so much material.

When I began reading the leadership literature in about 1986 I had already spent some time in various leadership positions, so at that time I'd read little but I understood everything about it from the University of Life. Then, as I read more material I realized that all my previous 'truths' were built on very dubious foundations so my understanding decreased as my knowledge increased. 2006 was a difficult year: I'd read hundreds, if not thousands, of books and articles and concluded that Socrates was right – wisdom only comes when you realize how ignorant you are. I think I'm now on the road to recovery and have got past base camp with this conclusion: at its most basic the 'essence' of leadership – as an individual leader – leaves out the followers and without followers you cannot be a leader. Indeed, this might be the simplest definition of leadership: 'having followers'. (2011: 1)

In his book Grint recognises that we cannot in most instances do without leaders but that we need to consider how leaders are held accountable for their actions:

Where does this leave leadership? On the one hand, we can do without leaders if we want to organize social life through very small-scale and temporary networks, but anything larger or longer-lived seems to require some form of institutionalized leadership. The good news is that we now need to concentrate on mechanisms for holding such individual and collective leaders accountable and on creating a more responsible citizenship that is more willing to engage in acts of leadership. The bad news is that the assumption that somehow collaborative leadership is not as open to manipulation and corruption as individual leadership is highly suspect, We cannot achieve coordinated responses to collective wicked problems simply by turning our backs upon individual leadership – even collaborative leadership requires individuals to make the first move, to assume responsibility, and to mobilize the collective leadership. In effect, the members of the collective must authorize each other to lead because collectives are notoriously poor at decision-making. Leadership is not, then, the elephant in the room that many would rather not face up to; it is the room itself – which we cannot do without. This, in another world, is what Bauman calls, 'the unbearable silence of responsibility'. And this is our collective and individual challenge. (2010: 126)

An Alternative View on Strategic Leadership

I have already noted in this chapter that the basic premise on which the more recent notion of strategic leadership has been developed may be at best shaky and at worst downright flawed. In these terms the old adage about fox-hunting (the unspeakable in pursuit of the uneatable) can be reframed into something like "the unaccountable in pursuit of excess rewards ably supported by strategic management consultants and head-hunters". Besides having wider socio-political implications this can also encourage a relative denigration of the role of management that denies the fact that many managers have leadership roles that are significantly wider than what is normally meant by supervision. Maybe like the priesthood in a number of previous societies we should offer our new-found priests a choice: real accountability for organisational performance – in which case they lose their jobs if they fail (although probably not also their lives as in some previous societies) – or recognition that their post might be better re-designated as CPRO (Chief Public Relations Officer).

Of course, it must be admitted that business schools and business academics are hardly to be seen as innocent bystanders in this development (Khurana 2007). Khurana's primary challenge revolves around what he sees as necessary to establish management as a "true" profession. But this is only part of the story – although admittedly an important part – since there is also a highly skewed distribution of earnings in professions such as medicine and law, which Khurana uses as exemplars. The more systemic issue is the extent to which the growth of the management consultancy has enabled senior management to marginalise middle and other managers within the organisation and hence to insulate themselves from the pressures suffered by those closer to the coalface (see, for instance, Scarborough and Burrell 1996). This development is particularly ironic given that McKenna (2006) in his aptly titled book *The Newest Profession* reminds us that such consultancy initially arose in the USA out of the regulatory environment, post the Great Crash of 1929.

Despite some recent public cases which raised serious questions about, at the very least, judgements and accountabilities of senior executives in a range of large organisations, especially banks and the media, it would seem we are still a long way from confronting the issues raised by both Richard Reich and Krantz and Gilmore.

Useful Insights from Writings on Military Strategy

Earlier in this book I referred to some of the insights offered by writers and in particular the contribution from von Moltke. Stephen Bungay, a military historian and business writer, in his book *The Art of Action*, shows how to apply much of von Moltke's writings to some of the most pressing organisational problems of the twenty-first century.

As Bungay summarises it, von Moltke's overall approach to the role of central command in a large organisation was to encourage an attitude of mind and action that could be summarised as "directed opportunism". In explaining the radical approach adopted by von Moltke, Bungay considers the responses to what he terms the three critical gaps between Plans–Actions–Outcomes, as shown in Figure 10.1.

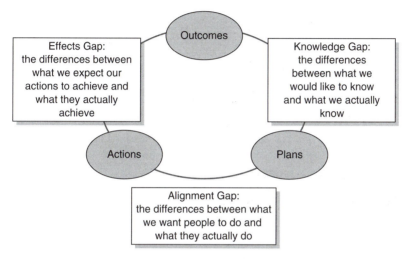

Figure 10.1 **Three critical gaps**

(Copyright © 2011 Stephen Bungay. Reproduced with permission)

He then suggests that what might be termed the common response (in both military and commercial contexts) can be summarised as shown in Figure 10.2.

In contrast, von Moltke's analysis was based on the principle that at one and the same time one required local autonomy and also alignment of action. This is summarised in Figure 10.3.

It seems unlikely that, despite his radical thinking, von Moltke, or indeed Bungay, would, in any way, espouse the distinction that has more recently developed between strategic leadership and supervisory leadership that we discussed above: to von Moltke it seems leadership of any organisation essentially involved leadership both "of" and "in" as well.

Good Management Research as a Means to Useful Insights

It seems entirely reasonable that we might expect any critical analysis to be informed by the results of research conducted in a systematic and

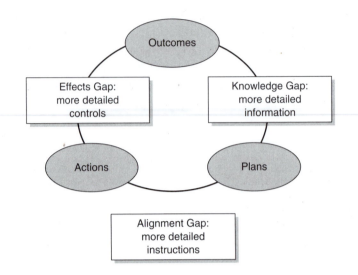

Figure 10.2   Usual reactions

(Copyright © 2011 Stephen Bungay. Reproduced with permission)

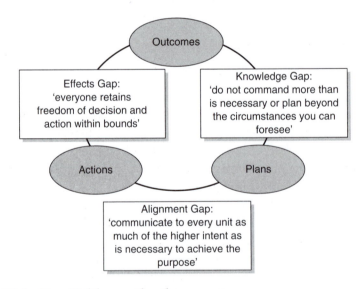

Figure 10.3   Von Moltke on the three gaps

(Copyright © 2011 Stephen Bungay. Reproduced with permission)

consistent manner. I have, however, argued that much of this research is flawed in various ways. In particular in the case of statistics we need to take care when the basic conclusion is framed in terms of 'A [something that can be manipulated by taking action] "causes" B [something that is a desired outcome state]'.

As I have argued earlier in this book, we need to be wary of both interpretations based on significance rather than effect size as well as those based on co-variation rather than causality. Indeed, it would seem that the very notion of a cause is problematic. From a more pragmatic view if there is either a large effect size or strong evidence for causality then there can be reasonable support for taking the relationship seriously but in different ways; in the former case as an element in guiding specific action in a particular instance, but in the latter case as guidance for policy action where there is more concern with the overall behaviour of aggregates rather than individual units.

Being quite often involved in debates around the (ir)relevance of much social sciences research, I sometimes feel that the infamous "angels on a pinhead" jibe should be converted into a more critical question: why was it seen as such an important question itself? However, as I explore further I find I have probably got the "wrong" question:

> How many angels can dance on a pinhead? Even today the question is immediately recognisable – it is emblematic of the unworldliness of medieval discussions of angels and of the foolishness of scholastic theology. It was, however, a Protestant slur on Roman Catholicism coined by 17th-century Englishmen. Its earliest use is by the Protestant clergyman William Chillingworth in 1638. The question then assumed its modern form in 1659 when Henry More mocked those who 'dispute how many of them booted and spur'd may dance on a needle's point at once'.
>
> From the 13th century onwards theologians trying to explain how to understand something beyond man's finite capacities nearly always turned to angels in their interpretations. The pinhead question was absurd to More because medieval philosophers had already decided that spirits were immaterial and therefore had no extension (i.e. physical dimension) in this world. The proposition was therefore a non-question: if angels do not materially exist, then any number could dance on a pinhead without occupying the same space. (Raymond 2010)

In the end this all seems to be a rather good object lesson in adopting a questioning approach to any particular narrative!

Mystery as Method

With case studies or small sample work, we should look more for insights gained from analysis and interpretation which will help us to formulate novel and challenging questions about particular action proposals. It is worth considering some of the advice offered by Mats Alvesson and Dan

Karreman in their book which is intriguingly sub-titled "Mystery as Method". Although their prime audience is researchers, their central message can be directly related to one of the key challenges presented in this book. If the interrogative method is to be used effectively then the key is to identify those elements of any action proposal which seems to be based on ambiguous or problematic interpretation. Then just as a researcher would wish to explore these interpretations further, so should any practitioner.

Finally, they offer clear advice as to the overall approach to research which can also be transposed into the sort of interrogative practice that I am advocating. They refer to the writing of the Swedish sociologist Johan Asplund and the "stimulating idea of social science as involving two elements: the discovery or creation of a breakdown in understanding [of] theoretical interest (the construction of a mystery) and the recovery of this understanding (the resolution of the mystery)" (2011: 16). Perhaps ironically, particularly given the overall emphasis in this book on issues of translation and the notion of audience, it is said that Asplund thinks that the essence of a text gets lost if you translate it, and therefore refuses being published in other languages.

However, I believe we can present the basic interrogative method in very similar terms to his (translated) schema. In the critical analysis of choices we need an initial identification of areas of breakdown in understanding – with practical implications – followed by an interrogative process to recover the understanding. As I am currently learning again from my granddaughter, "why?" is often the most effective form of question to apply in this process! The greater art is how you respond to the answer and develop your own understanding further.

Getting Beyond the False Rhetoric

So what final conclusions should be drawn about the nature of management practice and the role analysis and in particular of theory and research? The first and most obvious conclusion is that we should start from where we are – on the ground – not in the clouds (pun intended about the current vogue for doing everything web based "in the cloud"). We must recognise "the messiness of real life" and the fact that any form of analytic prescription is partial, context dependent and, indeed sometimes, positively misleading.

The second is that we must appreciate both the strengths and the weaknesses of what can be termed broadly the analytical approach to the issues which need some form of action. It is clear that we rely on a combination of intuition and analysis. In the former case we get a quick answer but it cannot easily be scrutinised in terms of our assumptions, in the later case it not only requires more effort but it is inevitably based on a partial perspective because of the unbounded complexity that we face. It was this fundamental characteristic of combination and balance between intuition and analysis that the Foundation Reports failed to recognise.

This book never set out to suggest that there was some sort of analytical "short-cut" to overcome this problem. Analysis in any particular form can only help us develop a particular partial perspective which if it is done properly can be explicit as to assumptions and the evidence base that has been applied.

As long as we accept it's inevitably partial nature, it can be a powerful and challenging approach which helps us compensate for serious biases in a purely intuitive response. What does this mean in practice? If you are in a management role close to the action itself then take heed of Frank Pornoy's advice: ensure you do some thinking but within the time cycle of the need for action itself. If you are more in a role in which you have to consider others' proposals and decide whether or not to endorse them, make sure you subject their proposals to an appropriate level of critical questioning with a clear intention that the outcome is that they improve their proposals.

This may sound rather prosaic advice alongside more dramatic entreaties such as "Innovate or Die" or "Only the Paranoid Survive", and it is certainly rooted in a more everyday and less visionary view of management, but to return to where I started it could mean that we all keep a bit more than just our heads above water, even if we do not quite achieve the sense of balance and poise of the fisherman on the front cover of this book!

Good luck!

Postscript for Management Researchers

As I have gone through re-reading this manuscript I have been struck by not only the relative frailty of the whole notion of causation in empirical social sciences but also the possible benefits of a further move towards research methods which are grounded in some combination of critical realism, hermeneutics and abductive inference; each of these is of course a complex of ideas in its own right and no doubt they may be seen by some as relatively uncomfortable bedfellows. However, from a pragmatic viewpoint there do seem to be common tendencies between them which might well also help us as management researchers to engage more profitably and effectively with management practitioners. In this I side with William Outhwaite, who argued 25 years ago that:

> The revival of Marxism, then, like the eclipse of positivism forms a backdrop to the rise of three traditions discussed in this book. Its impact on them has of course been very different. Hermeneutics has generally developed in opposition to Marxism except where hermeneutics shades off into critical theory. The case of realism is more complicated. A realist philosophy of science does not entail the adoption of a particular variant of social theory ... Furthermore, as a matter of fact, realists concerned with social science have mostly been very sympathetic to Marxist social theory. The three traditions similarly diverge in their critical response to positivism ... I argue that the main initial impact of hermeneutics and critical theory was in stressing the distinctiveness of the social sciences from the sciences of nature. Conversely, the realist critique claimed that positivism had radically misunderstood the natural sciences and suggested that natural and social science may not after all be so radically different in their methods.
>
> My basic message is an ecumenical one. Unlike many representatives of hermeneutics and critical theory within the social sciences, I see these movements as compatible in the last analysis with a broadly realist understanding of both natural and social science. (Outhwaite 1987: 3–4)

In the case of abduction as a research method, it is worth noting its close affinity with the process that critical realists refer to as retroduction, and noting the following commentary from Phil McEvoy and David Richards:

> Although the primary goal for critical realist researchers is explanatory understanding based on the development of retroductive inferences … detailed observations may provide a platform for making retroductive inferences about the causal mechanisms that are active in a given situation. (2006: 73)

In specifically adding abduction to the mix, we recognise that abduction too has potential problems in that there are infinite possible explanations for any of the physical processes we observe, but we are inclined to abduce a single explanation (or a few explanations) for them in the hope that we can better orient ourselves in our surroundings and eliminate some of the possibilities.

A more useful way of putting it is provided by Anna Dubois and Lars-Erik Gadde:

> The abductive approach is to be seen as different from a mixture of deductive and inductive approaches. An abductive approach is fruitful if the researcher's objective is to discover new things – other variables and other relationships. Similar to 'grounded theory', our main concern is related to the generation of new concepts and development of theoretical models, rather than confirmation of existing theory. We stress theory development, rather than theory generation.
>
> Systematic combining builds more on refinement of existing theories than on inventing new ones. One major difference, as compared with both deductive and inductive studies, is the role of the framework. In studies relying on abduction, the original framework is successively modified, partly as a result of unanticipated empirical findings, but also of theoretical insights gained during the process. This approach creates fruitful cross-fertilization where new combinations are developed through a mixture of established theoretical models and new concepts derived from the confrontation with reality. (2002: 559)

Equally, such an approach is indeed well illustrated by Mats Alvesson and Dan Karreman: their emphasis on solving the "mystery" reminds me again of Alex Faria who midway through writing up his thesis came out with the remark that he felt that Sherlock Holmes might be his best role model. Maybe by taking the Alvesson and Karreman approach seriously we should also ask ourselves why it has taken so long for many of us to realise this.

References

Abbott, Andrew (2001a), *Time Matters: On Theory and Method*, Chicago: University of Chicago Press.

Abbott, Andrew (2001b), *Chaos of Disciplines*, Chicago IL: University of Chicago Press.

Abbott, Edwin Abbott (1884), *Flatland, a Romance of Many Dimensions* (available at http://en.wikisource.org/wiki/Flatland_(first_edition)).

Abdullah, L. and H. Asngari (2011), Factor Analysis Evidence in Describing Consumer Preferences for a Soft Drink Product in Malaysia, *Journal of Applied Sciences*, 11: 139–144.

Abolafia, Mitchel Y. (2010), Narrative Construction as Sensemaking: How a Central Bank Thinks, *Organization Studies*, 31: 349–367.

Agarwal, Rajshree and Barry L. Bayus (2004), Creating and Surviving in New Industries, in Joel A. C. Baum and Anita M. McGahan (eds), *Business Strategy over the Industry Lifecycle* (Advances in Strategic Management, Volume 21), Bingley: Emerald Group Publishing Limited, pp. 107–130.

Al-Kuwaiti, M., N. Kyriakopoulos and S. Hussein (2009), Comparative Analysis of Network Dependability, Fault-tolerance, Reliability, Security, and Survivability, *IEEE Communications Surveys & Tutorials*, 11(2), Second Quarter.

Alvesson, Mats and Dan Kärreman (2011), *Qualitative Research and Theory Development: Mystery as Method*, London: Sage.

Andrade, Gregor, Mark Mitchell and Erik Stafford (2001), New Evidence and Perspectives on Mergers, *Journal of Economic Perspectives*, May, 15(2): 103–120.

Argyris, Chris (1985), *Strategy, Change and Defensive Routines*, Southport: Pitman Publishing.

Argyris, Chris and Donald Schön (1978), *Organizational Learning: a Theory of Action Perspective*, Boston: Addison-Wesley.

Aristotle, Nicomachaen, *Ethics*, Book VII (available at http://classics.mit.edu/Aristotle/nicomachaen.7.vii.html).

Aspen Institute, Aspen Ideas Festival: Conversation with Colin Powell, 3–8 July 2007 (www.aspenideas.org/sites/default/files/transcripts/Powell-Lehrer_transcript.pdf).

Bach, George Leland (1959), Managerial Decision Making as an Organizing Concept, in Frank C. Pierson (ed.), *The Education of American Businessmen: A Study of University-College Programs in Business Administration*, New York: McGraw-Hill, pp. 319–354.

Bal, M. (1985), *Narratology: Introduction to the Theory of Narrative*, Toronto: University of Toronto Press.

Bar Eli, Michael, Ofer H. Azar, Ilana Ritov, Yael Keidar-Levin and Galit Schein (2007), Action Bias Among Elite Soccer Goalkeepers: The Case of Penalty Kicks, *Journal of Economic Psychology*, 28(5), October: 606–621.

Bargh, John A. (2011), *Unconscious Thought Theory and Its Discontents: A Critique of the Critiques*, Social Cognition, 29(6): 629–647.

Barnett-Page, E. and J. Thomas, (2009), Methods for the Synthesis of Qualitative Research: a Critical Review, *BMC Medical Research Methodology*, 9(1): 59. Available at: http://dx.doi.org/10.1186/1471-2288-9-59 (accessed 25 April 2013).

Bartram, Söhnke M., Gregory W. Brown and Jennifer Conrad (2011), The Effects of Derivatives on Firm Risk and Value, *Journal of Financial and Quantitative Analysis*, 46(4) 8 September: 967–999.

BBC, Jeremy Paxman's infamous Michael Howard interview, May 1997 (www.youtube.com/watch?v=Uwlsd8RAoqI).

Beck, Richard (2010), Theology-of-type-1-type-2-errors (available at http://experimental theology.blogspot.co.uk/2010/09/theology-of-type-1-type-2-errors.html).

Bell, Eric Temple (1951), *Mathematics, queen and servant of science*. Maidenhead, Berkshire: McGraw-Hill.

Bettman, James R. and Barton A. Weitz (1983), Attributions in the Board Room: Causal Reasoning in Corporate Annual Reports, *Administrative Science Quarterly*, 28(2): 165–183.

Berlin, Isaiah (1980 [1960]), The Concept of Scientific History, in Henry Hardy (ed.), *Concepts and Categories: Philosophical Essays*, Oxford: Oxford University Press, pp. 103–142.

Binmore, K., A. Shaked and J. Sutton, (1989), An Outside Option Experiment, *Quarterly Journal of Economics*, 104: 753–770.

Birkinshaw, Julian, Ramon Lecuona and Patrick Barwise (2012), Which Academic Papers are Cited in Managerially-Oriented Publications?, LBS Working Paper, January.

Blundell-Wignall, Adrian and Paul Atkinson (2011), Global SIFIs, Derivatives and Financial Stability, *OECD Journal: Financial Market Trends*, 2011(1): 167–200. (http://dx.doi.org/10.1787/fmt-2011-5kg55qw0qsbv).

Boal, Kimberly B. and Hooijberg, Robert (2001), Strategic Leadership Research: Moving On, *The Leadership Quarterly*, 11(4): 515–549 (available at www.edu.haifa.ac.il/userfiles/file/lead_files_2/articles2/13.pdf).

Brennan, Alan, Samer Kharroubi, Anthony O'Hagan and Jim Chilcott (2007), Calculating Partial Expected Value of Perfect Information in Cost-Effectiveness Models, *Medical Decision Making*, 27: 448–470.

Brown, A. (2007), Strong Language on Black Swans, *The American Statistician*, 61(3), August: 195–197.

Brown, Andrew D. (1998), Narrative, Politics and Legitimacy in an IT Implementation, *Journal of Management Studies*, 35: 35–58.

Bruner, Robert F. (2004), Where M&A Pays and Where it Strays, *Journal of Applied Corporate Finance*, Fall, 63–76.

Brunsson, Nils (1982), The Irrationality of Action and Action Rationality: Decisions, Ideologies and Organizational Actions, *Journal of Management Studies*, 19(1): 29–44.

Brunsson, Nils (1990), Deciding for Responsibility and Legitimation: Alternative Interpretations of Organizational Decision-Making, *Accounting Organizations and Society*, 15(1/2): 47–59.

Brunsson, Nils (1993), Ideas and Actions: Justification and Hypocrisy as Alternatives to Control, *Accounting, Organizations and Society*, 18(6): 489–506.

Bungay, Stephen (2011), *The Art of Action: How Leaders Close the Gaps between Plans, Actions and Results*. London: Nicholas Brealey.

Burrell, Gibson (1992), Back to the Future: Time and Organization, in M. Reed and M. Hughes (eds), *Rethinking Organization: New Directions in Organization Theory and Analysis*, London: Sage, pp. 165–183.

Butler, Richard (1990), Decision-making Research: Its Uses and Misuses. A Comment on Mintzberg and Waters: "Does Decision Get in the Way?", *Organization Studies*, 11(1): 11–16.

Buzzell, R. D., Gale, B. T., and Sultan, R. G. (1975), Market share - a key to profitability. *Harvard Business Review*, 53(1), 97–106.

Byrne, David (2002), *Interpreting Quantitative Data*, London: Sage.

Caldwell, Raymond (2012), Systems Thinking, Organizational Change and Agency: a Practice Theory Critique of Senge's Learning Organization, *Journal of Change Management*, 12(2): 145–164.

Carroll, Glenn R. and Anand, Swaminathan (1992), The Organizational Ecology of Strategic Groups in the American Brewing Industry from 1975 to 1990, *Industrial and Corporate Change*, 1: 65–97.

Cartwright, Nancy (1999), *The Dappled World: a Study of the Boundaries of Science*, Cambridge: Cambridge University Press.

Cartwright, Nancy (2007), *Hunting Causes and Using Them: Approaches in Philosophy and Economics*. Cambridge: Cambridge University Press.

Castells, M. and Y. Aoyama (1994), Paths towards the Informational Society: Employment Structure in G-7 Countries, 1920–90, *International Labour Review*, 133; (1): 6–33.

Chang Myong-Hun and Joseph E. Harrington Jr. (2003), Multimarket competition, Consumer Search, and the Organizational Structure of Multi-unit Firms, *Management Science*; 49(4), April: 541–552.

Chatman, S. (1978), *Story and Discourse in Fiction and Film*, Ithaca, NY: Cornell University Press.

Chia, R. and R. Holt (2008), The Nature of Knowledge in Business Schools, *Academy of Management Learning and Education*, 7(4), December: 471–486.

Chintagunta, Pradeep K. (1994), Heterogeneous Logit Model Implications for Brand Positioning, *Journal of Marketing Research*, 31(2): 304–311.

Christensen, Clayton M. and Paul R. Carlile (2009), Course Research: Using the Case Method to Build and Teach Management Theory, *Academy of Management Learning & Education*, 8(2): 240–251.

Cochrane Collaboration, About Us (available at www.cochrane.org/about-us).

Cohen, Jacob (1994), The Earth Is Round (p < .05), *American Psychologist*, 49(12): 997–1003.

Cohen, Yoav, Naomi Gafni and Pnina Hanani (2007), Translating and Adapting a Test, yet another Source of Variance; the Standard Error of Translation, IAEA, Baku, Azerbaijan, September (available at www.iaea.info/documents/paper_1162d22ec7.pdf).

Contardo, Ianna and Robin Wensley (2004), The Harvard Business School Story: Avoiding Knowledge by Being Relevant, *Organization*, 11(2): 211–231.

Covey, Stephen R. (1989), The 7 Habits of Highly Effective People: Habit 4: Think Win–Win (available www.stephencovey.com/7habits/7habits-habit4.php).

Covey, Stephen R. (2004), *The 7 Habits of Highly Effective People*, New York NY: Free Press, Revised edition. (available at www.stephencovey.com/7habits/7habits-habit4.php).

Cowan, Nelson (2000), The Magical Number 4 in Short-term Memory: A Reconsideration of Mental Storage Capacity, *Behavioral and Brain Sciences*, 24: 87–185.

Dane, Erik and Michael G. Pratt (2007), Exploring Intuition and Its Role in Managerial Decision Making, *Academy of Management Review*, 32(1): 33–54.

Davis, M.S. (1971), 'That's Interesting! Towards a phenomenology of sociology and sociology of phenomenology', *Philosophy of Social Sciences*, 1: 309–344.

Davis, Philip J. (2002), The Philosophical Poker, Book Review, 7 October (available at www.siam.org/news/news.php?id=478).

De Geus, Arie (1997), Innovation and the Human Contract, *Insurance Specialist*, June (available at www.ariedegeus.com/usr/downloads/publications/insurance_specialist.doc).

de Holan, Pablo Martin and Nelson Phillips (2004), Remembrance of Things Past? The Dynamics of Organizational Forgetting, *Management Science*, 50(11), November: 1603–1613.

Delbridge, Rick, Gratton, Lynda and Gerry Johnson, (2006), *The Exceptional Manager: Making the Difference*. Oxford: OUP.

DiMaggio, Paul J. and Walter W. Powell (1983), The Iron Cage Revisited: Institutional Isomorphism and Collective Rationality in Organizational Fields, *American Sociological Review*, 48(2), April: 147–160.

Dolan, Robert J. (1981), Models of Competition: A Review of Theory and Empirical Findings, in B.M. Enis and K.J. Roering (eds), *Review of Marketing 1981*, Chicago: American Marketing Association, pp. 224–234.

Dubois, Anna and Lars-Erik, Gadde (2002), Systematic Combining: an Abductive Approach to Case Research, *Journal of Business Research* 55(7), July: 553–560.

Du Gay Paul (2000), *In Praise of Bureaucracy: Weber – Organization – Ethics*, London: Sage.

Dunning, Brian (2012), A Magical Journey through the Land of Reasoning Errors, Skeptoid #297, 14 February 2012 (accessed at http://skeptoid.com/episodes/4297).

Dwyer, Larry, Alison Gill and Neelu Seetaram (2012), *Handbook of Research Methods in Tourism: Quantitative and Qualitative Approaches*, London: Edward Elgar.

Easterby-Smith, M.P.V., D. Nicolini, and M. Crossan, (2000), Organizational Learning: Debates Past, Present and Future, *Journal of Management Studies*, 37(6): 783–796.

Easterby-Smith, Mark (2012), Research Collaboration in Management: Exploring the Academic–Practitioner Divide, Working Paper, Department of Management Learning and Leadership, Lancaster University.

Easton, Geoff (1992), *Learning from Case Studies*, London: Financial Times/Prentice Hall.

Easton, G. and T. C. Ormerod (2001), *Experts/Novices Differences in Case Analysis, Final Report to the European case clearing house, February*, (available at www.ecch.com/files/downloads/research/RP0303M.pdf).

Edmonds, David and John Eidenow (2001), *Wittgenstein's Poker*. London: Faber and Faber.

Eijkman, Henk (2011), The learning organization as concept and journal in the neo-millennial era: A plea for critical engagement, *Learning Organization*, 18(3): 164–174.

Emery, F.E. and E. Trist (1965), "The causal texture of organizational environments", *Human Relations*, 18: 21–31.

Faria, A. and Wensley, R. (2002), In search of 'interfirm management' in supply chains: recognizing contradictions of language and power by listening, *Journal of Business Research*, 55(7): 603–610.

Feldman, Martha, S. and Brian T. Pentland, (2003), Reconceptualizing Organizational Routines as a Source of Flexibility and Change, *Administrative Science Quarterly*, 48(1), March: 94–118.

Feynman, Richard, P. (1985), *Surely You're Joking, Mr. Feynman*, London: W. W. Norton & Co.

Finch, J. (2012), *The Report: Accessibility, sustainability, excellence: how to expand access to research publications*, (available at www.researchinfonet.org/wp-content/uploads/2012/06/Finch-Group-report-FINAL-VERSION.pdf).

Fincham, Robin and Timothy Clark (2009), Introduction: Can We Bridge the Rigour–Relevance Gap?, *Journal of Management Studies*, 46(3), May: 510–515.

Finney, D. J. (2006), Calibration Guidelines Challenge Outlier Practices, *The American Statistician*, 60: 309–314.

Forman, Ernest, H. and Saul I. Gass, (2001), The Analytic Hierarchy Process: An Exposition, *Operations Research*, 49(4), July – August: 469–486.

Frank, R. (1988), *Passions within Reason*. New York: Norton.

Forster, Edward Morgan (1927), *Aspects of a Novel*, New York NY: Harcourt, Brace & Company.

Fulford, Robert (1999), Eugen Weber: An eye for detail, a passion for France, *Globe and Mail*, 13 March (available at www.robertfulford.com/EugenWeber.html).

Gabbay, John and Andrée le May (2004), Evidence Based Guidelines Or Collectively Constructed "Mindlines?" Ethnographic Study Of Knowledge Management In Primary Care, *British Medical Journal*, 329(7473), October 30: 1013–1016.

Gale, John, Kenneth G. Binmore and Larry Samuelson (1995), *Learning to Be Imperfect: The Ultimatum Game, Games And Economic Behavior*, 8, 56–90.

Geertz, Clifford (1973), *Interpretation of Cultures: Selected Essays*. New York: Basic Books.

Geertz, Clifford (1974) From the Native's Point of View: On the Nature of Anthropological Understanding, *Bulletin of the American Academy of Arts and Sciences*, 28(1), October: 26–45.

Gentry, James W. (1990), What is Experiential Learning? In James W. Gentry (Ed.) *Guide to Business Gaming and Experiential Learning*. London: Nichols/GP, pp. 9–20. (Available at: http://sbaweb.wayne.edu/~absel/bkl/BG/BGa2.pdf)

Gilbert, T. F. (1982), Human Incompetence: The Autobiography of an Educational Revolutionist, in Phillip K. Duncan (Ed.) *Current Topics In Organizational Behavior Management*, New York: The Haworth Press.

Gladwell, Malcolm (2006), *Blink: The Power of Thinking Without Thinking*, London: Penguin Books.

Gladwell, Malcolm (2008), *Outliers: The Story of Success*, New York: Little, Brown and Company.

Goddard, Jules and Tony Eccles (2012), *Uncommon Sense, Common Nonsense: Why some organisations consistently outperform others*. London: Profile Books.

Goold, M (1996), *Learning, planning and strategy: extra time*, California Management Review, 38(4): 100–102.

Gordon, R.A. and J.E. Howell, (1959), *Higher Education for Business*, New York: Columbia University Press.

Goure, L., A. J. Russo and D. Scott (1985), *Some Findings Of The Viet Cong Motivation And Morale Study: June-December 1965*. (Available at: www.rand.org/pubs/research_memoranda/2006/RM4911-2.pdf).

Greiffenhagen, Christian and Wes Sharrock (2008), School mathematics and its everyday other? Revisiting Lave's 'Cognition in Practice', *Educational Studies in Mathematics*, 69:1–21.

Grieves, J. (2008), Why We Should Abandon the Idea of the Learning Organization, *The Learning Organization*, 15(6): 463–473.

Grint, K. (2010), *Leadership: a Very Short Introduction*, Oxford: Oxford University Press.

Grint, K. (2011), Leadership – A Very Short Introduction, Warwick Book Club (available at www2.warwick.ac.uk/knowledge/projects/bookclub/10/).

Grol, Richard and Jeremy Grimshaw (2003), From Best Evidence to Best Practice: Effective Implementation of Change in Patients' Care, *Lancet*, 362: 1225–1230.

Grubbs, F. E. (1969), Procedures for Detecting Outlying Observations in Samples, *Technometrics*, 11: 1–21.

Guth, W., R. Schmittberger and B. Schwarze (1982), An Experimental Analysis of Ultimatum Bargaining, *Journal of Economic Behavior & Organization*, 3: 367–388.

Hahn, U. and N. Chater, (1998), Similarity and Rules: Distinct? Exhaustive? Empirically Distinguishable?, *Cognition*, 65: 197–230.

Hansard, 11 December 1912 (http://hansard.millbanksystems.com/commons/1912/dec/11/sir-francis-bridgemean-retirement).

Hay, A. and M. Hodgkinson (2008), More Success than Meets the Eye – A Challenge to Critiques of the MBA. Possibilities for Critical Management Education?, *Management Learning*, 39(1), February: 21–40.

Hegel, G.W.F (1975), *Lectures on the Philosophy of World History: Introduction* (1830, translated by H. B. Nisbet, 1975).

Helsey, Melvyn and Fintan Codd (2012), Aviation: Proposals for an Airport in the Thames Estuary, 1945–2012, Standard Note: SN/BT/4920, House of Commons Library, Business and Transport Section (available at www.parliament.uk/briefing-papers/sn04920.pdf).

Henley, Amy B., Christopher L. Shook and Mark Peterson (2006), The Presence of Equivalent Models in Strategic Management Research Using Structural Equation Modeling: Assessing and Addressing the Problem, *Organizational Research Methods*, 9: 516–535.

Hensmans, Manuel, Gerry Johnson and George S. Yip (2013), *Strategic Transformation: Changing while Winning*, London: Palgrave Macmillan.

Hinterhuber, Hans H. and Popp, Wolfgang (1992), Are You a Strategist or Just a Manager?, *Harvard Business Review*, 70(1), January–February: 105–113.

Hodgkinson, G.P., Langan-Fox, J. and Sadler-Smith, E. (2008), Intuition: A Fundamental Bridging Construct in the Behavioural Sciences, *British Journal of Psychology*, 99: 1–27.

Hodgkinson, Gerard P. and Denise M. Rousseau (2009), Bridging the Rigour–Relevance Gap in Management Research: It's Already Happening!, *Journal of Management Studies*, 46(3), May: 534–546.

Hoover, Kevin D. (2009), Review of Nancy Cartwright, Hunting Causes and Using Them: Approaches in Philosophy and Economics, 18 January (available at http://public.econ.duke.edu/~kdh9/Source/Materials/Research/Cartwright/Hunting/Causes/19/January/2009.pdf).

Hróbjartsson, Asbjørn and Peter C. Gøtzsche (2006), Follow-up Commentary, *Journal of Clinical Epidemiology*, 59: 340–341.

Huberman, Michael (1990), Linkage between Researchers and Practitioners: A Qualitative Study, *American Educational Research Journal*, 27(2), Summer: 363–391.

Ishibuchi, Hisao, Ryoji Sakamoto and Tomoharu Nakashima (2001), Evolution of Unplanned Coordination in a Market Selection Game, *IEEE Transactions on Evolutionary Computation*, 5(5): 524–534.

Iszatt-White, M. and C. Saunders, (2013, forthcoming), Leadership Theory and Practice – A Critical Text, Chapter 11, Oxford: Oxford University Press.

Johnson Craig and David Philip Spicer (2006), A Case Study of Action Learning in an MBA Program, *Education + Training*, 48(1): 39–54.

Johnson, Gerry, George S. Yip and Manuel Hensmans (2012), Achieving Successful Strategic Transformation, *MIT Sloan Management Review*, 53(3), 20 March.

Juarrero, Alicia (2002), *Dynamics in Action: Intentional Behavior as a Complex System*. Cambridge MA: MIT Press, pp. 222–223.

Kadane, Joseph, B. and Patrick D. Larkey (1982), Subjective Probability and the Theory of Games, *Management Science*, 28(2): 113–120, February.

Kahneman, Daniel (2011), Thinking, Fast and Slow, London: Allen Lane: London.

Kaplan, Steven N. (2006), Mergers and Acquisitions: A Financial Economics Perspective, February 2006 (available at http://govinfo.library.unt.edu/amc/commission_hearings/pdf/kaplan_statement.pdf).

Kay, John (2012a), London's new airport held to ransom by folly, *Financial Times*, 7 November (available at www.johnkay.com/2012/11/07/london's-new-airport-held-to-ransom-by-folly).

Kay, John (2012b), Equity Markets and Long-Term Decision Making, Final Report, July (available at www.bis.gov.uk/assets/biscore/business-law/docs/k/12-917-kay-review-of-equity-markets-final-report.pdf).

Kay, John (2012c), BBC Today broadcast, Friday 29 June (available at http://news.bbc.co.uk/today/hi/today/newsid_9733000/9733291.stm).

Keating, Malcolm (2009), Born to Run: How sporting seasons determine success, *Guardian*, 21 October Sport, p. 10. (available at www.guardian.co.uk/sport/blog/2009/oct/21/sporting-success-season-birthday).

Keynes, John Maynard (1923), *A Tract on Monetary Reform*, London: MacMillan and Co.

Keynes, J.M. (1936), *The General Theory of Employment, Interest and Money*, first published by Macmillan Cambridge University Press, for Royal Economic Society.

Khurana, Rakesh (2007), *From Higher Aims to Hired Hands: The Social Transformation of American Business Schools and the Unfulfilled Promise of Management as a Profession*, Princeton, NJ: Princeton University Press.

Kienle, G.S. and H. Kiene, (1997), The Powerful Placebo Effect: Fact or Fiction?, *Journal of Clinical Epidemiology*, 50: 1311–1318.

Kierstead, B.S. (1972), Decision Taking and the Theory of Games, in C.F. Carter and J.L. Ford (eds), *Uncertainty and Expectation in Economics: Essays in Honour of G.L. Shackle*, Oxford: Blackwell.

Kieser, Alfred and Lars Leiner (2009), Why the Rigour–Relevance Gap in Management Research Is Unbridgeable, *Journal of Management Studies*, 46(3), May: 516–533.

Knight, Frank (1921), *Risk, Uncertainty and Profit*, Boston, MA: Hart, Schaffner & Marx.

Kolb, D.A. (1984), *Experiential Learning*, Englewood Cliffs, NJ: Prentice Hall.

Korzybski, Alfred (1958), *Science and Sanity: An Introduction to Non-Aristotelian Systems and General Semantics*, International Non-Aristotelian Library, Laxeville, CT.

Kotter, John P. (1982), British Steel: Interview with Sir Monty Finniston (Abridged), Video, Harvard Business School Video Supplement, 882–521, March.

Kotter, John P. and John M. Stengrevics (1985), British Steel Corporation: The Korf Contract, Harvard Business School Case, 9-481-110.

Krantz, James and Thomas N. Gilmore (1990), The Splitting of Leadership and Management as a Social Defense, *Human Relations*, 43(2), February: 183–204.

Lave, Jean (1988), *Cognition in Practice: Mind, Mathematics and Culture in Everyday Life*, Cambridge: Cambridge University Press.

Leeflang, Peter S.H. and Dick R. Wittink (1996), Competitive Reaction Versus Consumer Response: Do Managers Overreact?, *International Journal of Research in Marketing*, 13: 103–119.

Levin, Daniel Z. and Rob Cross (2004), Mediating Role of Trust in Effective Knowledge Transfer, *Management Science*, 50(11): 1477–1490.

Lindblom, C.E. (1959), The Science of "Muddling Through", *Public Administration Review*, 19(2): 79–88, Spring.

Lindblom, C.E. (1979), Still Muddling, Not Yet Through, *Public Administration Review*, 39(6): 517–526, November–December.

Lippman, S.A. and R.P. Rumelt, (1982), Uncertain imitability: An analysis of inter-firm differences in efficiency under competition, *The Bell Journal of Economics*, pp. 418–438.

Loasby, Brian J. (1971), Hypothesis and Paradigm in the Theory of the Firm, *Economic Journal*, 81(324), December: 863–885.

Loasby, Brian J. (2001), Industrial Dynamics: Why Connections Matter, DRUID ACADEMY Winter Conference, Klarskovgaard, 18–20 January (download at www.druid.dk/conferences/winter2001/paper-winter/Paper/loasby.pdf).

Mair, A. (1999), Learning from Honda, *Journal of Management Studies*, 36(1), January: 25–44.

Malle, B.F. (2004), *How the Mind Explains Behavior: Folk Explanations, Meaning, and Social Interaction*, Cambridge, MA: MIT Press.

Management Lab Briefing (2009), Innovation: Scenario Planning (available at http://managementlab.org/files/u2/pdf/classic%20innovations/Innovation_Scenario_Planning.pdf).

March, James G. (1991), Exploration and Exploitation in Organizational Learning, *Organization Science*, 2(1): 71–87.

March, James G. and Robert I. Sutton (1997), Crossroads—Organizational Performance as a Dependent Variable, *Organization Science*, 8, November/December: 698–706.

Marsh, P., P. Barwise, K. Thomas and R. Wensley (1988), *Managing strategic investment decisions in large diversified companies*, Centre for Business Strategy, London Business School.

Martin, Joanne, Martha Feldman and Mary Jo Hatch (1983), The Uniqueness Paradox in Organizational Stories, *Administrative Science Quarterly*, 28: 438–453.

Marx, Karl, (1869), *The Eighteenth Brumaire of Louis Bonaparte* (1852, English translation, 1869).

Mason, Richard O. (1969), A Dialectical Approach to Strategic Planning, *Management Science*, 15(8): B403–B414.

Mason, R. O. and Miroff, I. (1981), *Challenging strategic planning assumptions: Theory, cases, and techniques*, New York: Wiley.

McCloskey, D. (1986), *The Rhetoric of Economics*, Madison, WI: University of Wisconsin Press.

McCloskey, D. (1994), *Knowledge and Persuasion in Economics*, Cambridge: Cambridge University Press.

McCloskey, Deirdre (2002), *The Secret Sins of Economics*, Chicago: Prickly Paradigm Press (available at www.deirdremccloskey.com/docs/paradigm.pdf).

McEvoy, Phil and David Richards (2006), A Critical Realist Rationale for Using a Combination of Quantitative and Qualitative Methods, *Journal of Research in Nursing*, 11: 66–78.

McKenna, Christopher D. (2006), *The World's Newest Profession: Management Consulting in the Twentieth Century*, Cambridge: Cambridge University Press.

McMaster, H.R. (1997), *Dereliction of Duty: Johnson, McNamara, the Joint Chiefs of Staff, and the Lies that Led to Vietnam*, New York: HarperCollins.

Mezirow, J. (1991), *Transformative Dimensions of Adult Learning*. San Francisco: Jossey Bass.

Miles, Raymond E. and Charles C. Snow, (1978), *Organizational Strategy, Structure, and Process*, New York: McGraw-Hill Book Co.

Miller, E. and Gwynne, G. (1972), *A Life Apart*, London: Tavistock.

Miller, Franklin G. and Donald L. Rosenstein (2006), The Nature and Power of the Placebo Effect, *Journal of Clinical Epidemiology*, 59, 331–335.

Miller, G.A. (1956), The Magical Number Seven, Plus or Minus Two: Some Limits on Our Capacity for Processing Information, *Psychological Review*, 63(2): 81–97.

Mingers, J. (2000), What Is It To Be Critical? Teaching a Critical Approach to Management Undergraduates, *Management Learning*, 31(2): 219–237.

Mintzberg, Henry (1973), *The Nature of Managerial Work*, New York: Harper & Row.

Mintzberg, H. (1996), Reply to Michael Goold, *California Management Review*, 38(4), 96–99.

Mintzberg, H. and J. Waters (1990), Does Decision Get in the Way?, *Organization Studies*, 11(1): 1–5.

Mintzberg, Henry and Frances, Westley (2001), Decision Making: It's Not What You Think, *Sloan Management Review*, Spring, 42(3): 89–93.

Mohr, L. (1982), *Explaining Organizational Behavior*, San Francisco: Jossey-Bass.

Moitra, Deependra and Jai Ganesh (2005), Web services and flexible business processes: towards the adaptive enterprise, *Information & Management*, 42(7): 921–933, October.

Montrose, L. (2002), International Study and Experiential Learning: The Academic Context, *Frontiers*, VIII (available at www.frontiersjournal.com/issues/vol8/vol8-08_montrose.htm).

Moore, James, (2013), Worse than Fred Goodwin! *Independent*, 5 April.

Moore, Mark (1995), *Creating Public Value: Strategic Management in Government*, Boston, MA: Harvard University Press.

Moroney, M.J. (1964), *Facts from Figures*, Harmondsworth, Middlesex: Pelican Books.

Morrell, K. (2008), The Narrative of 'Evidence Based' Management: A Polemic, *Journal of Management Studies*, 45(3), May: 613–635.

Morrison, A. and R. Wensley (1991), Boxing Up or Boxed In? A Short History of the Boston Consulting Group Share/Growth Matrix, *Journal of Marketing Management*, 7: 105–129.

Navarro, Peter (2008), The MBA Core Curricula of Top-Ranked U.S. Business Schools: A Study in Failure?, *Academy of Management Learning & Education*, 7(1): 108–123.

Nelson, Richard (1974), Intellectualizing about the moon-ghetto metaphor: A study of the current malaise of rational analysis of social problems, *Policy Sciences*, December, 5(4): 375–414.

Newsinger, John (1997), *Dangerous Men: The SAS and Popular Culture*, London: Pluto Press.

Nicol, Alexandra (2001), *The Social Sciences Arrive*, Swindon: ESRC.

Nicolaides, N.J. (1960), Policy-decision and Organization Theory, doctoral dissertation, University of Southern California.

Nordgren, Loran F., Maarten W. Bos and Ap Dijksterhuis (2011), The best of both worlds: Integrating conscious and unconscious thought best solves complex decisions, *Journal of Experimental Social Psychology*, 47(2): 509–511.

Nunes, Terezinha, Analucia Dias Schliemann and David William Carraher (1993), *Street Mathematics and School Mathematics,* Cambridge University Press: Cambridge.

Oaksford, Mike and Nick Chater (1998), *Rationality in an Uncertain World,* Hove: Psychology Press.

Oaksford, M. and N. Chater, (2002), Commonsense Reasoning, Logic and Human Rationality, in R. Elio (ed.), *Commonsense Reasoning and Rationality,* Oxford: Oxford University Press.

OECD/Eurostat (2005), Oslo Manual, Guidelines for Collecting and Interpreting Innovation Data, third edition. Available at: http://dx.doi.org/10.1787/fmt-2011-5kg55qw0qsbv (accessed on 25 April 2013).

(http://epp.eurostat.ec.europa.eu/cache/ITY_PUBLIC/OSLO/EN/OSLO-EN.PDF).

Orsi, Peter (2012), Cuban Missile Crisis Beliefs Endure After 50 Years, *Salon,* 14 October (available at www.salon.com/2012/10/14/cuban_missile_crisis_beliefs_endure_after_50_years_2/).

Outhwaite, William (1987), *New Philosophies of Social Science: Realism, Hermeneutics and Critical Theory.* London: Macmillan Education.

Partnoy, Frank (2012), *Wait: The Useful Art of Procrastination,* London: Profile Books.

Pascale, R.T., H., Mintzberg, M. Goold, and R.P. Rumelt, (1996), The "Honda Effect" Revisited, *California Management Review,* 38(4): 78–117.

Paulos, J.A. (2010), Stories vs Statistics, *New York Times* (available at http://opinionator.blogs.nytimes.com/2010/10/24/stories-vs-statistics/).

Pearl, Judea (2000), *Causality: Models, Reasoning, and Inference.* Cambridge: Cambridge University Press.

Pentland, Brian T. (1999), Building Process Theory with Narrative: from Description to Explanation, *Academy of Management Review,* 24(4): 711–724.

Pernege, R. and Thomas, V. (2004), Relation between online "hit counts" and subsequent citations: prospective study of research papers in the BMJ, *British Medical Journal,* 329: 546.

Peters, K. (2012), Academics must bridge divide with business, Soapbox column, *Financial Times,* 23 April. Available at: www.ft.com/cms/s/2/7fb18d40-8949-11e1-bed0-00144feab49a.html#axzz2UmAia3qv (accessed on 26 April 2013).

Peters, Tom and Robert Waterman (1982), *In Search of Excellence,* San Francisco: Harper & Row.

Petersen, Harold (1965), The Wizard who Oversimplified: A Fable, *Quarterly Journal of Economics,* 79(2), May: 209–211.

Pidd, Michael (2009), *Tools for Thinking: Modelling in Management Science,* Chichester: John Wiley & Sons.

Pierson, F.C. (ed.) (1959), *The Education of American Businessmen: A Study of University-College Programs in Business Administration,* New York: McGraw-Hill.

Popper, K. (2002), Conjectures and Refutations: The Growth of Scientific Knowledge, first published by Routledge & Kegan Paul, 1963, republished as a Routledge Classic, Abingdon, Oxford.

Powell, Padgett (2009), *The Interrogative Mood: A Novel?,* Profile Books: London.

Rasche, A. and Behnam, M. (2009), As If it Were Relevant: a Social Systems Perspective on the Relation between Theory and Practice, *Journal of Management Inquiry,* 18(3): 243–255.

Raymond, Joad (2010), Protestant Culture: Milton's Angels, *History Today,* 60(12) (available at www.historytoday.com/joad-raymond/protestant-culture-miltons-angels).

Reich, R. (1985), The Executive's New Clothes, *New Republic*, 13 May, 23–28.

Richardson, George B. (1975), Adam Smith on Competition and Increasing Returns, in A.S. Skinner and T.W. Wilson (eds), *Essays on Adam Smith*, Oxford: Oxford University Press.

Rimmon-Kenan, S. (1983), *Narrative Fiction: Contemporary Poetics*. London: Routledge.

Robinson, Colin, (2012), Ten Ways to Save the Publishing Industry, the *Guardian*, Friday 12 October (available at www.guardian.co.uk/books/2012/oct/12/ten-ways-to-save-publishing-industry).

Rumelt, R.P. (1984), Towards a Strategic Theory of the Firm, in Robert Lamb (ed.), *Competitive Strategic Management*, Englewood Cliffs, NJ: Prentice-Hall, p. 568.

Rumelt, Richard (2011), *Good Strategy/Bad Strategy*, London: Profile Books.

Sasser, E. (1986), British Steel Corporation: The Korf Contract: Teaching note, 5-486-124, Cambridge MA: Harvard Business Publishing.

Scandura, Terri A. and Ethlyn A. Williams (2000), Research Methodology in Management: Current Practices, Trends, and Implications for Future Research, *Academy of Management Journal*, 43(6), December: 1248–1264.

Scarborough, H. and G. Burrell, (1996), The Axeman Cometh: the Changing Roles and Knowledges of Middle Managers, in S. Clegg and G. Palmer (eds), *The Politics of Management Knowledge*, London: Sage.

Schiele, Holger, Stefan Krummaker, Rita Kowalski and Petra Hoffmann (2012), Accelerating Scholar-Practitioner Collaborative Research through Speed Consortium Benchmarking: Using the World Café as a Form of Academic Enquiry, paper presented at the Academy of Management annual meeting, Boston MA.

Schön, Donald A. (1983), *The Reflective Practitioner: How Professionals Think in Action*, New York: Basic Books.

Scriven, Michael and Richard, Paul (1987), Critical Thinking as Defined by the National Council for Excellence in Critical Thinking, 8th Annual International Conference on Critical Thinking and Education Reform, Summer. (available at www.criticalthinking.org/pages/defining-critical-thinking/766).

Selznick, P. (1984 [1957]), *Leadership in Administration: a Sociological Interpretation*, Berkeley: University of California Press.

Senge, Peter M. (1993), *The Fifth Discipline: The Art and Practice of the Learning Organization*, New York: Doubleday Currency.

Seth, V. (1986), *The Golden Gate*, London: Faber and Faber.

Shugan, Steven M. (2002), Editorial: Marketing Science, Models, Monopoly Models, and Why We Need Them, *Marketing Science*, 21(3), Summer: 223–228.

Simon, Herbert A. (1969b), The Architecture of Complexity, in *The Sciences of the Artificial*, Cambridge, MA: MIT Press, pp. 192–229.

Simon, Herbert A. (1969a), *The Sciences of the Artificial*, first edition, Cambridge MA: MIT Press.

Simon, Herbert A. (1972), Theories of Bounded Rationality, in C.B. McGuire and Roy Radner (eds), *Decision and Organization*, New York: North-Holland Publishing Company.

Simon, H.A. (1991), Bounded Rationality and Organizational Learning, *Organizational Science*, 2(1): 125–134.

Sims, D., C. Huxham, and N. Beech, (2006), On Telling Stories But Hearing Snippets: Sense-taking from Presentations of Practice, *Organization*, 16, 3, May: 371–388.

Smart, T. (1996), Jack Welch's Encore, *Business Week*, 44, 23 October (available at www.businessweek.com/1996/44/b34991.htm).

Spencer, L., J., Ritchie, J., Lewis and L. Dillon, (2003), *Quality in Qualitative Evaluation: a Framework for Assessing Research Evidence*, London: Government Chief Social Researcher's Office.

ESRC (2005), SSRC/ESRC – the First Forty Years, Swindon: ESRC.

Stanford Encyclopaedia of Philosophy (2001), Aristotle's *Ethics* (available at http://plato.stanford.edu/entries/aristotle-ethics/).

Starbuck, William H. (2006), *The Production of Knowledge: The Challenge of Social Science Research*, Oxford: Oxford University Press.

Starbuck, William H. and Mezias, John M. (1996), Opening Pandora's Box: Studying the Accuracy of Managers' Perceptions, Information Systems Working Papers Series, NYU Working Paper No. 2451/14187 (available at http://ssrn.com/abstract=1284293).

Stark, David (2009), *The Sense of Dissonance, Accounts of Worth in Economic Life*, Princeton, NJ: Princeton University Press.

Starkey, Ken and Paula Madan (2001), Bridging the Relevance Gap: Aligning Stakeholders in the Future of Management Research, *British Journal of Management*, 12, Special Issue, S3–S26.

Starkey, Ken, Armand Hatchuel and Sue Tempest (2009), Management Research and the New Logics of Discovery and Engagement, *Journal of Management Studies*, 46(3), May: 547–558.

Stimpert, J.L. and I.M. Duhaime, (1997), Seeing the Big Picture: The Influence of Industry, Diversification, and Business Strategy on Performance, *Academy of Management Journal*, 40: 560–583.

Streiner, D.L. and G.R. Norman, (1989), *Health Measurement Scales: a Practical Guide to Their Development and Use*. New York: Oxford University Press.

Strick, Madelijn, Ap Dijksterhuis, Maarten W. Bos, Aukje Sjoerdsma, Rick B. van Baaren, and Loran F. Nordgren (2011), A Meta-Analysis on Unconscious Thought Effects, *Social Cognition*, 29: 738–762.

Sullivan, Chatham, Thomas N. Gilmore and Rebecca Plum (2010), The Power of Small Leadership, in David L. Dotlich, Peter C. Cairo, Stephen H. Rhinesmith and Ron Meeks (eds), *The 2010 Pfeiffer Annual: Leadership Development*, Chichester: John Wiley & Sons, pp. 220–231.

Surowiecki, James (2004), *The Wisdom of Crowds: Why the Many Are Smarter than the Few*, New York: Little, Brown.

Surowiecki, James (2008), The Financial Page: Greasing the Slide, *New Yorker*, 3 November.

Taleb, N. (2001), *Fooled by Randomness: The Hidden Role of Chance in Life and in the Markets*, New York: Random House.

Taleb, N. (2007), *The Black Swan: The Impact of the Highly Improbable*, London: Allen Lane.

Taylor, A.J.P. (1969), *War by Timetable*, London: Macdonald & Company.

Tesfatsion, L. (2001), Guest Editorial: Agent-Based Modelling of Evolutionary Economic Systems, *IEEE Transactions on Evolutionary Computation*, 5(5): 437–441.

Thompson, Silvanus Phillips (1976), *The Life of Lord Kelvin*, 1, reprint. London: Chelsea Publishing Company.

Thompson, William (1883), Lecture to the Institution of Civil Engineers in London on "Electrical Units of Measurement", published in *Popular Lectures and Addresses*, I, 3 May: 80–81 (http://en.wikiquote.org/wiki/William_Thomson,_1st_Baron_Kelvin).

Tonkin, Boyd (2008), Review of Outliers, by Malcolm Gladwell: Book of the Week, *Independent*, 21 November (available at www.independent.co.uk/arts-entertainment/books/reviews/book-of-the-week-outliers-by-malcolm-gladwell-1027343.html).

Tosey, Paul (2005), The Hunting of the Learning Organization: a Paradoxical Journey, *Management Learning*, 36(3), September: 335–352.

Tranfield, David, David Denyer and Palminder Smart (2003), Towards a Methodology for Developing Evidence-Informed Management Knowledge by Means of Systematic Review, *British Journal of Management*, 14(3), 207–222.

Tukey, John W. (1977), *Exploratory Data Analysis*, Boston MA: Addison-Wesley.

Turner, Aidar, (2010), What Do Banks Do, What Should They Do and What Public Policies are Needed to Ensure Best Results for the Real Economy? CASS Business School 17 March (available at www.fsa.gov.uk/pubs/speeches/at_17mar10.pdf).

Vaara, Eero (2002), On the Discursive Construction of Success/Failure in Narratives of Postmerger Integration, *Organization Studies*, 23(2): 211–248.

Van Aken, Joan Ernst (2005), Management Research as a Design Science: Articulating the Research Products of Mode 2 Knowledge Production in Management, *British Journal of Management*, 19: 19–36.

Van de Ven, Andrew H. (2007), *Engaged Scholarship: A Guide for Organizational and Social Research*, Oxford: Oxford University Press.

Van de Ven, A.H. and M.S. Poole, (1995), Explaining Development and Change in Organizations, *Academy of Management Review*, 20: 510–540.

Vedral, Vlatko (2012), The Surprise Theory of Everything, *New Scientist*, 15 October.

Volberda H.W. and A.Y. Lewin, (2003), Co-evolutionary Dynamics Within and Between Firms: from Evolution to Co-evolution, *Journal of Management Studies*, 40 (8), December: 2111–2136.

Waddington, C.H. (1977), *Tools for Thought*, St Albans: Paladin.

Walton, Douglas (2003), The interrogation as a type of dialogue, *Journal of Pragmatics*, 35: 1771–1802.

Watson, T.J. (1994), *In Search of Management: Culture, Chaos and Control in Managerial Work*, London: Routledge.

Weick, Karl (1976), Educational Organizations as Loosely Coupled Systems, *Administrative Science Quarterly*, 21: 1–9.

Weick, K.E. (1990), Introduction: Cartographic Myths in Organizations, in A. Huff (ed.), *Mapping Strategic Thought*, Chichester and New York: John Wiley & Sons, pp. 1–10.

Weick, K.E. (1991), The Nontraditional Quality of Organizational Learning, *Organization Science*, 2(1): 116–124.

Weick, K.E. and F. Westley, (1996), Organizational Learning: Affirming an Oxymoron, in S.R. Clegg, C. Hardy and W.R. Nord (eds), *Handbook of Organizational Studies*, London: Sage.

Weil, Debbie (2004), Top Tips to Write a Persuasive Case Study, WordBiz Report (available at www.wordbiz.com/archive/writecasestudy.shtml).

Weiner, Tim (2008), *Legacy of Ashes: The History of the CIA*. London: Penguin Books.

Wildavsky, Aaron and Jack Knott (1980), If Dissemination Is the Solution, What Is the Problem? *Science Communication*, 6(1): 537–578.

Winch, Graham M. (2010), *Managing Construction Projects*, Chichester: John Wiley & Sons.

Woodward, S.N. (1982), The Myth of Turbulence, *Futures*, 14(4), August: 266–279.

Zhong, Chen-Bo, Ap Dijksterhuis and Adam D. Galinsky (2008), The Merits of Unconscious Thought in Creativity, *Psychological Science*, 19(9): 912–918.

Index

NOTE: page numbers in *italic type* refer to figures and tables.

3M Post-it story, 197–9
10 per cent rule, 119–21

Abbot, Andrew, 128–9
Abbott, Edwin, 138
abduction, 210–11
Abolafia, Mitchel Y., 147
academe-practice relationship, 2, 65–6, 70–1, 170–1
academic journals, 189–90
accountability, 203, 204
acquisitions, 149–51
action
   choices, decisions and, 32–3
   and practical wisdom, 132–3
   representing, 31–3
action bias, 100
action learning, 175
administration, 194, 196
adversaries, 150
Agarwal, Rajshree, 87
agent-based modelling, 139
AHP (analytical hierarchy process), 25, 78–9
airport capacity, 82
alternative hypothesis, 116
Alvesson, Mats, 37, 208
analysis
   by experts and novices, 169–70
   combined with synthesis, 17–20
   extended analysis, 21–2
   and intuition, 34–5, 178–9, 208–9
   legacy of 1960s, 15–16
   and practical wisdom, 132
   relationship with process, 21–3
   representing *see* representation
   role in practice, 164
   stress testing, 196–7
   see also statistical analysis
analytical approach, 208–9
   in management education, 193–4
   as two-stage process, 20–1
analytical hierarchy process (AHP), 25, 78–9
'angels on a pinhead', 207
Argyris, Chris, 38–9, 40
Aristotle, 131–3

Art of Action, The (Bungay), 204–5
Aspen Institute, 7
Asplund, Johan, 208
assumptions, in representations, 142
Atkinson, Paul, 86
attribution bias, 42–3
audience issues, 1–3
autonomy, 77
averages, 105–7

Bach, George Leland, 34
balance of probabilities, 3, 156–7
Bar Eli, Michael, 100–3
Bargh, John A., 181
Barnett-Page, E., 18, *19*
Bartram, Söhnke, 87
Barwise, Paddy, 23, 33, 157, 172
Bayus, Barry L., 87
BCG *see* Boston Consulting Group
Behnam, M., 66
Beck, Richard, 117–18
Berlin, Isaiah, 153–4
Bettman, James R., 42–3
bias *see* action bias; attribution bias; confirmatory bias
Binmore, K., 99
Birkinshaw, Julian, 167
Blink (Gladwell), 178–80
Blundell-Wignall, Adrian, 86
Boal, Kimberly B., 200–1
Bortkiewicz, Ladislaus, 4
Boston Consulting Group (BCG), 151, 152
Boston Consulting Group (BCG) matrix, 136–7
boundaries, 40
bounded cognition, 140
bounded rationality, 33, 34
box plots, 109–11
boxes, 40, 138
   see also 'thinking outside the box'
Bradshaw, Della, 3
Brennan, Alan, 183
British Medical Journal, 121
Brunsson, Nils, 33–4
Bungay, Stephen, 204–5, *206*
bureaucracy, 133

Bush, George W., 6–7
business schools *see* Foundation Reports;
    Harvard Business School
Buzzell, Bob, 120
Butler, Richard, 158
Byrne, David, 159

Caldwell, Raymond, 48
Californian Management Review, 151, 152
Carroll, Lewis, 31
Cartwright, Nancy, 128
case examples, 160, 166–7
case studies, 160–2
    Decision series, 171–3
    Honda, 151–3
    learning from, 165–7
    purpose of, 167–9
case study learners, 169–70
causal history of reason (CHR) approach, 43
causality, 72–3, 125–6, 127–9, 207
centralisation, 88
Chancellorsville, battle of, 180
Chang, Myong-Hun, 139
chaos, 74
Chater, Nick, 63–4
chess, 94
Chia, R., 61
Chintagunta, Pradeep K., 134
choices, decisions and action, 32–3
CHR (causal history of reason) approach, 43
citation of scholarly work, 6
closed systems, 84
cluster analysis, 25, 77–8
co-evolutionary perspective, 138–9
Cochrane Collaboration, 66–7
Codd, Fintan, 82
Cohen, Jacob, 114
Cohen, Yoav, 143
collaborative interrogation, 190–2
collaborative research, 4–5
columns, 24–5
common sense, 64–5, 77,
        131, 142–4
competition, and imitation, 57, 58
competitive behaviour, 92–3
competitive strategy, 139–40
competitors, wisdom of, 55–6
complexity, 72–3, 74–5
concentration of variables, 105
confirmatory bias, 37, 42
conjecture testing, 123
conjectures, 37–8
conjunction fallacy, 161
consensus
    nature of, 59–60
    role of dialectic, 58

consultancies, 71, 156, 204
Contardo, Ianna, 168
contestation, 186
context dependency, 53, 61, 62–3
contrarian strategies, 57
correlation
    and causality, 127
    and orthogonality, 135
Covey, Stephen, 98–9
Cowan, Nelson, 25
creative insight, 145–6
credibility of narratives, 161
critical realism, 8, 18, 19–20, 210–11
critical thinking, 8
Cronbach alpha, 135–6
Cross, Rob, 49
crowds, wisdom of, 55–6
Cuban Missile Crisis, 7–8

Dappled World, The (Cartwright), 128
datasets, 105
Davis, Philip, 38
de Holan, Pablo Martin, 46
debate, 58, 187–8
decentralisation, 88
Decision documentaries, 83, 171–3
decision processes, 157–9
    conscious and unconscious, 178–82
    fast and slow thinking, 183–5
    and rationality, 33–4
    slow thinking, 182–3
decision trees, 79–83
decisions, choices and action, 32–3
deductive approach, 167, 211
derivatives markets, 85–6, 87
deutero-learning, 39
devil's advocate approach, 59
dialectics, 58–9, 187, 188
Dijksterhuis, Ap, 180
Dilbert (cartoon), 154
DiMaggio, Paul, 56
dimensionality, 134
diseconomies of scale, 88
dispersion of variables, 105, 106–7
disruptive innovation, 189–90, 199
dissent, 60–1, 186
dissonance, 185–6, 187, 188
distribution
    box plots, 109–11
    normal and fat-tail, 107–9
    outliers, 111–13
DNA, 163–4
documentaries, *Decision* series, 83, 171–3
'doing first' perspective, 178
double blind experiment, 67
double-loop learning, 38–9

Dubois, Anna, 211
Duhaime, I.M., 123–5
Dunning, Brian, 118, 119
Dylan, Bob, 145–6
dynamic systems, 89–90
dynamics, representing, 138–40
Dynamics in Action (Juarrero), 89

Easterby-Smith, Mark, 4, 46
Easton, Geoff, 165–6, 169–70
Eccles, T., 144
economic science, 115
economies of scale, 88, 137
Eijkman, 47
Einstein, Albert, 131, 144
Emery, F.E., 189
entrepreneurship, 199–200
epistemology, 18
equifinality, 142
equivalence models, 122–5
error (statistical), 116–19
ESRC (Economic and Social Research
     Council), 15–16
EU Community Innovation survey, 49–50
evidence-based management (EBM), 9,
     52–3, 66
evidence-based movement, 68–9
evidence-based policy, 52
evidence-based practice, in medicine, 66–7
expected value of perfect information (EVPI),
     182–3
experiential learning exercises, 174–6
expert approach to planning, 59
expert learners, 169–70
extended analysis, 21–2

factor analysis, 134, 135
fads and fashions, 154–6
failure, narratives of, 149–51
Faria, Alex, 159
fat-tail distribution, 107–9
feedback, 87–8, 91
Feldman, M.S., 45
Feynman, Richard, 115–16
financial crises, 54–6
Finniston, Sir 'Monty', 172, 173
'five whys' strategy, 17, 23, 40
folk wisdom, 62–4
followers, 202–3
football penalty game, 100–3
Ford, Henry, 147–8
formalisation
   of dialectic approach, 59
   of management knowledge, 62–3
Foundation Reports, 15, 34, 167, 193
frequency plots, 107–9

Freud, Sigmund, 179
Fulford, Robert, 148

Gabbay, John, 48–9
Gadde, Lars-Erik, 211
Gale, Brad, 99–100, 120
game theory, 92–3
   multi-period and multi-player games, 94
   normal form games, 93–4
   penalty game, 100–3
   prisoner's dilemma, 97–8
   simulation and scenario planning, 94–6
   ultimatum game, 99–100
   win-win outcomes, 98–9
GDP growth forecasts, 81, 91
Geertz, Clifford, 89, 90
Gentry, J.W., 174
Getty Museum, 179
Geus, Arie de, 95, 149
Gilmore, Thomas N., 194–5
Gladwell, Malcolm, 111–13, 178–80, 183–4
Goddard, J., 144
Good Strategy/Bad Strategy (Rumelt), 166
Goodhart's Law, 36
'goodness of fit', 122
goods, growth in, 85
Goold, Michael, 152, 153
Gordon, R.A., 35
Goure, 196
Graef, Roger, 83, 171
Greiffenhagen, C., 63
Grieves, Jim, 47–8
Grint, Keith, 202–3
growth, 85–7, 136–7
Grubbs, F.E., 111
Guth, W., 99

habit/reflex, 178
Hahn, U., 64
Harrington, Joseph E. (Jr.), 139
Harvard Business Review, 120, 121
Harvard Business School (HBS), 160, 165, 166,
     167–8, 172
Harvard Law School, 168
Hay, A., 176
Heisenberg uncertainty principle, 37, 53
Helsey, Melvyn, 82
Henley, Amy B., 123–5
hermeneutics, 89, 90, 210
heroic leadership, 201–2
Heyworth Committee, 16
hidden variables, 135
hierarchy, 74–5
   analytical hierarchy process, 25, 78–9
   and military strategy, 75–7
Hinterhuber, Hans, 77

history, 147–8, 153–4
Hodgkinson, Gerard P., 176
Hodgkinson, M., 65
Holt, R., 61
Honda, 151–3
Hooijberg, Robert, 200–1
Hoover, Kevin D., 128
House of Commons, questions in, 23–4, 187–8
Howell, J.E., 35
human genome, 163–4
Human Resources approach, 79
Hunting Causes and Using Them
    (Cartwright), 128
hypothesis testing, 123
hypothetical variables, 135

idealism, 18–20
Imagine (Lehrer), 145–7
incommensurability of theories, 19
incremental innovation, 189, 199
inductive approach, 167, 211
influence diagrams, 83–4
informants, 50, 127–8
innovation, 188–90
    and entrepreneurship, 199–200
    stories of, 197–9
    see also creative insight
intentionality, 43, 138
internal data, 48–50
interpretation, 89–90
Interpretation of Cultures (Geertz), 89, 90
interquartile range (IQR), 107
interrogative approach, 6–8, 23–4, 190–2, 208
    see also questions and questioning
interviews, 173
intuition, 34–5, 178–9, 184–5, 194, 208–9
Iraq invasion, 6–7
isolating mechanisms, 57–8, 200
isomorphism, 56
Iszatt-White, M., 201

Johnson, Craig, 175
Johnson, Gerry, 60–1, 186
Joule, James, 22–3, 130
journals, 189–90
J,Paul Getty Museum, 179
Juarrero, Alicia, 89, 128
judgement, 179–80

Kadane, Joseph B., 93
Kahneman, Daniel, 184–5
Kaplan, Steven N., 150–1
Kärreman, Dan, 37, 208
Kay, John, 82
Keating, Malcolm, 111–12
Kennedy, John F., 7–8

Keynes, J.M., 148
Khurana, Rakesh, 204
Kieser, Alfred, 66
Knight, Frank, 53, 54
Knott, Jack, 68
knowledge
    folk theories and science, 63–4
    management knowledge, 61, 62–3
Kolb Learning Cycle, 41
Korzybski, Alfred, 29–30
kouros statue, 179
Krantz, James, 194–5

lag structures, 126
Larkey, Patrick D., 93
latent variables, 135
leaders, accountability of, 203
leadership
    and followers, 202–3
    image of heroic leadership, 201–2
    and management, 194–6
    study of, 200–1
learners, novices and experts, 169–70
learning
    double-loop learning, 38–9
    from case studies, 165–7
    from others, 41–4
    from practice, 170–6
    from questioning, 176–7
    organisational learning, 44–50
    reflective practice, 40–4
    simulations and projects, 174–5
    value of surprises, 36–7
    video material, 171–3
Learning from Case Studies (Easton), 165–6
learning organisation (LO), 46–8
Leeflang, Peter S.H., 100
legal case studies, 168
Lehman Brothers, 54–5
Lehrer, Jonah, 145–6
Leiner, Lars, 66
lemmings, 56–7
Levin, Daniel Z., 49
Levitt, Ted, 89
Lindblom, Ed, 34
linearity, 129, 141
lists, 24–5
Loasby, Brian J., 140, 141
'loose-tight' linkages, 88
Lowell, Lawrence, 165
LTCM (Long-Term Capital Management), 54–5
Luhmann, Niklas, 2

McCloskey, Deirdre, 69, 115, 156
McEvoy, Phil, 210–11
McKenna, Christopher D., 204

Macmillan, Harold, 37
McNamara, Robert, 196
Madan, Paula, 69
Mair, A., 153
Malle, B.F., 39, 42, 43
management, and leadership, 194–6
management consultancies, 71, 156, 204
management education and development,
     193–4
  innovation, 197–200
  interrogative approach, 207–8
  leadership, 194–6, 200–4
  management and leadership, 194–6
  management research, 205–7
  military strategy, 204–5
  see also academe-practice relationship
management knowledge, 61, 62–3
management trends, 154–6
maps, 30–1
  mental maps, 39
March, James G., 9, 44–5
market evolution, 139
market share/market growth matrix, 136–7
Marks & Spencer, 188
Marsh, Paul, 23, 33, 157
Mason, Richard, 59, 185–6
materialism, and realism, 19
matrices see two-by-two box
May, Andrée le, 48–9
mean, 106
measurement, tyranny of, 22
median, 106
mediators, in statistical analysis, 121–6
medicine, evidence-based practice in, 66–7
mental maps, 39
mergers, 149–51
meta-analysis, 17–20
military practice, 8–9, 75–7, 94–5, 138, 158,
     180, 204–5
Miller, George A., 25
mindlines, 48–9
Mintzberg, Henry, 152–3, 157, 178, 193–4
Mitroff, Ion, 185–6
mixed methods approach, 103
mobilisation timetables, 32
mode, 106
moderators, in statistical analysis, 121–6
modularity/modularisation, 33, 40, 88
Moltke, Helmuth von, 75, 204–5, 206
Moon Ghetto Paradox, 16
Moroney, M.J., 105
Morrell, K., 68–9
movement, representation of, 29–33
Moynihan, Michael, 146
multi-period games, 94
multi-player games, 94

naive realism, 18, 19, 20
narrative approach, 162–4
narratives/stories
  3M Post-it story, 197–9
  and case studies, 151–3, 160–2, 168–9
  Honda case study, 151–3
  insights from, 159–60
  merger narratives, 149–51
  plausible narratives, 147
  power of, 145–6
  statistical, 160–1
Navarro, Peter, 174, 175
negative feedback, 87–8, 91
networks, 90–2
new markets, and growth, 87
NICE (National Institute of Clinical
     Excellence), 67
Nicol, Alexandra, 16
Nicolaides, N.J., 157
'no-brainer' choices, 187
normal distribution, 107–9
normal form games, 93–4
Norman, G.R., 135–6
novice learners, 169–70
null hypothesis, 116–17, 122
Null Hypothesis Statistical Test (NHST), 114
Nunes, Terezinha, 62

Oaksford, Mike, 63–4
objective idealism, 18, 19–20
oil prices, 95–6
onus of proof, 156–7
open access journals, 189–90
open systems, 84
optimizing paradigm, 100
O'Reilly, Tony, 106
organisational learning, 44–50
organisational performance, 9
organisational routines, 45
Ormerod, T., 169–70
Orsi, Peter, 7–8
orthogonality, 25–9, 135–6
Oslo Protocol, 50
'other', construction of, 150
Outhwaite, William, 210
outliers, 110, 111–13
over-reaction, 100

parliamentary questions, 23–4, 187–8
partial equilibrium, 126, 140
Partnoy, Frank, 103, 182, 183, 184, 197–9
Pascale, Richard, 151–2
Paul, Richard, 8
Paulos, J.A., 161
Pearl, Judea, 125–6
penalty game, 100–3

Pentland, Brian T., 45, 162–3
Peters, K., 52
Peters, Tom, 88–9
Phillips, Nelson, 46
Pidd, Mike, 72–3
plagiarism, 31
Plank's constant, 53
plausible narratives, 147
Poisson distribution, 4
policy, evidence-based, 52
Popp, Wolfgang, 77
Popper, Karl, 37
positive feedback, 87–8, 91
Post-it story, 197–9
Powell, Colin, 7
Powell, Padgett, 23
Powell, Walter, 56
practical wisdom, 131–3
   and common sense, 142–4
practice
   impact of research on, 3–5, 66
   learning from, 170–6
practice-academe relationship, 2, 65–6, 70–1,
      170–1
   see also case studies
practice-research time cycles, 69–70
prisoner's dilemma, 97–8
problem-driven research, 4–5
procedural rationality, 33, 64, 88–9
process, relationship with analysis, 21–3
procrastination, 182–3
projects, learning from, 175
proof, 156–7
public goods problems, 97
Pym, Dennis, 171

qualitative data meta-analysis, 17–18
quantitative data meta-analysis, 17
questions and questioning, 6–8
   learning through, 176–7
   limit to, 23–4
   regarding data, 49–50
   see also interrogative approach

Rand Corporation, 196
Rand, David, 74
range, 106
Rasche, A., 66
rationalistic discourse, 150
rationality
   complex notion of, 35
   in decision processes, 33–4
   and game theory, 92–3
realism
   and analysis, 18–20
   critical realism, 8, 18, 19–20, 210–11

reflection, in management development, 193
reflective practice, 40–4
reflective practitioner, 40, 50–1
refutations, 37–8
Reich, Robert, 195
relevance, 66, 68–9
representation
   assumptions in, 142
   box plots, 109–11
   of dimensions, 134
   of dynamics, 138–40
   frequency plots, 107–9
   lists and columns, 24–5
   and orthogonality, 25–9, 135–6
   simplification, 33–5, 68, 77, 133–4
   time and movement, 29–33, 79–83, 141–2
   two-by-two box, 25–9, 136–8
research
   impact on practice, 3–5, 66
   insights from, 9, 205–7
research case studies, 160
research-practice relationship, 2, 65–6, 70–1,
      170–1
research-practice time cycles, 69–70
resource partitioning approach, 139
retail services, 85
retroduction, 210–11
Revans action learning, 175
rhetoric, 59
Richards, David, 210–11
risk, 54–5, 87
Risk, Uncertainty and Profit (Knight), 53
Roskill Commission, 82
Rousseau, Denise M., 65
routine, and change, 45
rule of 10 per cent, 119–21
Rumelt, Richard, 57–8, 166
Ryle, Gilbert, 113

Saaty, Thomas, 78
Sapienza, Alice, 173
Saunders, C., 201
scenario planning, 95–6
Schön, Donald, 38–9, 40, 50–1, 180
Schwartz, Peter, 95–6
science
   economic science, 115
   and folk wisdom, 63–4
scientific history, 153–4
scientific management, 22
scientific method, 116
scientific realism, 18
Scriven, Michael, 8
securitisation, 85
'seeing first' perspective, 178–9
Senge, Peter, 46–7

Sense of Dissonance, The (Stark), 185
Seth, V., 52
Sharrock, W., 63
Shell, 95–6, 149
SIGMA I and SIGMA II war games, 95
significance (statistical), 113–16, 207
Simon, Herbert, 33, 40, 44, 64, 74–5
simplification, 33–5, 68, 77, 133–4
Sims, D., 42
simulations, 94–6, 139, 174
single-loop learning, 38
slow thinking, 182–5
Smith & Nephew, 61
Smith, Adam, 132
Snow, Charles, 22
social science, and common sense, 64–5
Social Science Research Council (SSRC), 15–16
Spicer, David Philip, 175
sports game analogy, 139–40
standard deviation, 107
Starbuck, William H., 114–15
Stark, David, 185, 186
Starkey, Ken, 69
statistical analysis
    averages, 105–7
    box plots, 109–11
    causality, 125–6, 127–9
    frequency plots, 107–9
    mediators and moderators, 121–6
    outliers, 111–13
    rule of 10 per cent, 119–21
    significance, 113–16
    time series datasets, 126–7
    type I and II errors, 116–18
    type III error, 118
    type IV error, 119
statistical case studies, 160–1
statistical error, 116–19
statistical inference, 68
statistical significance, 113–16, 207
Stimpert, J.L., 123–5
stories *see* narratives/stories
strategic form games, 93–4
strategic leadership, 200–1, 203–4
strategic planning, 59
strategic position, *58*
strategy
    and decisions, 158
    see also military practice
street mathematics, 62–3
Streiner, D.L., 135–6
stress testing of analysis, 196–7
structural equation modelling (SEM),
    122–6, 161
structural isomorphism, 56
subjective idealism, 18, 19

substantive rationality, 64
success, narratives of, 149–53
Sullivan, Chatham, 201–2
Sultan, Ralph, 120
supervisory leadership, 200–1
Surowiecki, James, 55–6
surprise, value of, 36–7
survival of companies, 149
sustainability, 58, 199–200
sustainable transformation, 60–1
Sutton, Robert I., 9
synthesis, combined with analysis, 17–20
systematic review, 17–20
systems
    dynamic, 89–90
    open and closed, 84

Taleb, Nassim, 108–9
Taylor, A.J.P., 32
Taylor, F.W., 22
teaching case studies, 160
teaching notes, 166, 168, 172, 173
tension, encouraging, 61
Tesco, 61
theory *see* academe-practice relationship
theory driven research, 4–5
think tanks, 71
thinking *see* decision processes
Thinking, Fast and Slow (Kahneman), 184–5
'thinking first' perspective, 178
'thinking outside the box', 39, 40, 189, 190
Thomas, A., 18, *19*
Thomas, Kathryn, 23, 33, 157, 159
Thompson, Silvanus Phillips, 131
Thompson, Sir William, 22
time cycles, of research and practice, 69–70
time dimension, 140–2
    of decisions, 157–8
    representation of, 29–33, 79–83, 141–2
time series datasets, 126–7
timetables, and war, 32
Tonkin, Boyd, 112–13
Tools for Thinking (Pidd), 72–3
Tools for Thought (Waddington), 72, 73–4
Toyota Production System (TPS), 17, 23, 40
translation issues, 1–3, 127, 143, 208
tree diagrams, 75, *76*
    analytical hierarchy process, 78–9
    cluster analysis, 77–8
    decision trees, 79–83
trends, 154–6
Trist, E., 189
trust, 49
truths, 3
Tukey, John, 109
turbulence, 189

Turner, Aidar, 85
two-by-two box, 25–9, 136–7
type I and II errors, 116–18
type III error, 118
type IV error, 119

ultimatum game, 99–100
unanimity, 60
uncertainty, 54–5, 179
unconscious thought effects (UTE), 179–81
unconscious thought theory (UTT), 181–2
Unilever, 61
uniqueness paradox, 162
untruths, 3

Vaara, Eero, 149–50
valuation models, 54–5
value, and derivatives, 87
Van de Ven, Andrew, 115
variance, 107
Vedral, Vlatko, 130
vernacular knowledge, 62–3
video material, 171–3
Vietnam war, 95, 196–7
Vinland map, 179

Wack, Pierre, 95
Waddington, C.H., 72, 73–4, 84
Wait (Partnoy), 103, 182
Walton, Douglas, 191–2
war, and mobilisation, 32
War by Timetable (Taylor), 32
war games, 94–5
Waterman, Robert, 88–9
Waters, J., 157
Watson, T.J., 63
Weber, Eugen, 148
Weick, Karl, 30–1, 45, 88
Weitz, Barton A., 42–3
Wensley, Robin, 23, 33, 74, 157
Westley, Frances, 178
Wildavsky, Aaron, 68, 154
win-win outcomes, 98–9
Winch, Graham M., 37–8
wisdom
    of crowds, 55–6
    practical wisdom, 131–3, 142–4
Wisdom of Crowds, The (Surowiecki),
    55–6
Wittink, Dick R., 100
Woodward, Nick, 189